tony sanchez i was
keith richards'
drug dealer

BLAKE

Grateful acknowledgement is made for the use of *Mick Jagger: Everybody's Lucifer* by Tony Scaduto. Copyright@ 1974 by Anthony Scaduto. Used by permission of Anthony Scaduto and David McKay Company, Inc.

All photos by Tony Sanchez except for the following: on page 144 and page 194 photographs by Michael Cooper; on page 202, photograph by Bernard Primmf

Published by Blake Publishing Ltd., 3 Bramber Court, 2 Bramber Road, London, W14 9PB

First published in Great Britain under the title *Up and Down With the Rolling Stones*

This hardback edition published in 2003

ISBN 1 85782 526 8

Typeset by Maron Graphics, Wembley, Middlesex

Jacket and additional design by ENVY

Printed in the UK by CPD, Wales

1

I was still just a little in awe of the Rolling Stones in the midsixties. The Beatles were richer and sold more records. But they had compromised their integrity with neat hair and command performances. In London the Stones were the new potentates. Their hairstyles, their attitudes, their clothes were aped by every young man with aspirations to style — from elegant, leisured aristocrats to schoolboys barely out of short trousers. It is hard to remember now just how vast, if transient, an influence they were. No other musicians in history had wielded such power for social revolution.

At the centre of it was Brian Jones. He was the musically gifted Stone, the one who could pick up any instrument — from a saxophone to a sitar — and learn to play it in less than half an hour. The one who was playing pure, soaring rhythm and blues for a living when Mick Jagger was a mediocre student at the London School of Economics and Keith Richard was just another grubby, delinquent art student who thought he was Chuck Berry because he could pluck three chords on his out-of-tune guitar.

Brian epitomized the arrogantly hedonistic attitude that was the mainstay of the Rolling Stones' special appeal. He had left six illegitimate children — all boys and all by different girls — in his wake. He was the one who grew his hair longest. He was the first to wear outrageously androgynous clothes — chiffon blouses and Ascot hats — with make-up and yet carry such an aura of street guerrilla aggressiveness that no one would dare suggest to his face that he looked anything less than totally masculine. Where Brian led the other Stones limped along behind.

Lately things had changed. The word among those who worked with the Stones was that Mick and Keith were inadvertently grinding Brian down, breaking him, destroying him. Egocentric, obsessed with

5

becoming stars themselves, they couldn't forgive Brian Jones for having bent them to his will musically and visually in their early days. Such rumours are common in the tough, bitchy world of rock music, and I hadn't taken them seriously — until now.

I was sipping a scotch on the rocks in a dark London nightclub called the Speakeasy, waiting for my girl friend, a nightclub dancer, to show up. It was two in the morning, and the club was crowded with the young and beautiful men and women who had turned London, momentarily, into the hip capital of the Western world. "Swinging London" may be a dusty cliché now. But then it was a reality we all were working hard to perpetuate.

At clubs like the Speakeasy everyone tries to appear supercool but spends most of the evening looking around for famous faces. You can tell when a star arrives because everyone — even the dancers — starts gaping. When it happened this time, I glanced up, and there, lurching towards me, was Brian Jones.

This wasn't the Brian I knew from twelve months before. Then his golden hair had glowed like the sun, and he had been tanned and lithe and beautiful. Now his hair hung lank and greasy around his deathly pale face, his eyes were bloodshot and the shadows across his face were those of a man who hadn't slept for a long time. "Hi, Tony — how's it going, man?" He smiled, and I ordered him a scotch and felt flattered that the lead guitarist with the Rolling Stones had not only remembered my name but had singled me out among all the other people he knew in a fashionable club like the Speakeasy.

We talked for a while about records and new films; then he casually dropped the question I'd been expecting: "Any drugs about, Tony?"

I'm not a pusher, but as a boy I'd worked in Soho, first as a nightclub bouncer, then as a croupier, so I knew exactly where to go for anything from a bag of grass to a Thompson submachine gun. Conse-

Brian Jones

quently people in the rock world had come to use me as a reluctant go-between in their flirtations with the London underworld. Though I was frightened that my role might lead to big trouble, I was young enough and star struck enough to figure that the risks were worth taking if they were the price I had to pay for friendship with people like Brian Jones.

"What are you looking for?", I asked Brian, though what I really longed to do was change the subject.

He clutched my arm and almost shouted, "Anything, get me anything. I don't care what it fucking well is, just get me something."

I remember his lost, sad eyes. Brian Jones, the most famous, outrageous, flamboyant superstar of them all was now pathetic. I pulled my arm away and walked over to a black guy I knew who sometimes pushed drugs for a little pocket money.

"What do you want?", he whispered. "I've got anything you want, man: coke, acid, smoke."

"Hang on." I went back to Brian to see which goodies took his fancy.

Brian didn't even think for half a second. "Get me everything, Tony," he urged, "the whole thing. I don't care what it costs."

The price was £250. I promised the black guy the money would be in his hands the next day, and since he knew and trusted me, he handed the whole stash over in a small brown paper bag. By the time I got back to our table in the middle of the room, next to the dance floor, Brian was behaving so strangely that I was frightened he would gobble the drugs right in front of everyone. Before I handed over the bag, I warned him that he would have to go to the toilet if he were going to use anything at all while he was at the Speakeasy.

Before I could finish what I was saying, he snatched the bag, like a kid grabbing a lollipop, and sprinted off to the loo. When he returned, he appeared relaxed, and he was smiling as he handed me the bag and asked me to look after it in case he was searched by the police. I had started to use a certain amount of cocaine and when Brian invited me to help myself to whatever I wanted from his bag of tricks, I accepted gratefully. I could hardly believe my eyes when I locked myself into the toilet and opened the bag. Not only had Brian taken an entire bottle of coke, but he had also apparently swallowed a whole handful of mixed uppers and downers. I returned to the table, steeling myself to find Brian unconscious on the dance floor, but instead, he was smiling and joking with a girl friend while he sipped his fifth scotch of the evening.

We stayed for another hour, and even after a couple more scotches, Brian seemed to be only mildly stoned. It took me some weeks before I realised that Brian was like the variety of alcoholic who walks around in a permanent twilight world — never really drunk, but never really sober either.

I drove him back to his flat in Courtfield Road, Earls Court, in my white Alfa Romeo. It was a warm night with a huge full moon, so we drove fast, very fast, with the top down. Brian seemed to enjoy the speed and the feel of the wind blowing his hair into his eyes because I could hear him mumbling to himself, "Go baby, go — faster, baby, faster."

He invited me into the second storey flat in the big red brick building for a smoke — Brian's name for a joint — and I accepted. As he fumbled with his door key, I asked conversationally, "What's all this I hear about Anita going off with Keith, man?"

It was common knowledge that Anita Pallenberg, whom I knew fairly well, had left Brian for Keith Richard. Brian jerked back as if he'd been knifed. "Don't ever mention that chick's name to me again," he said. But his words couldn't hide the pain that was eating him up inside, destroying him. When Keith lured Anita away, he had pulled out the last prop that was holding Brian up and had condemned him to a life where the only reality Brian wanted was oblivion.

This became even more obvious when we walked into the flat to be greeted by Nikki and Tina, two beautiful lesbian girls who had been living with Brian for some weeks. Brian made it perfectly clear that the three of them all shared his outsize bed. It was almost equally obvious that they all loathed one another.

As I rolled a joint from Brian's paper bag, he dipped in and scooped out a scrap of blotting paper that had been impregnated with LSD. After all the booze and the cocaine and the uppers and downers he had taken I was worried about the effect this was going to have on him, but he seemed to know what he was doing, so I kept my mouth shut.

Amazingly Brian still seemed reasonably *compos mentis*, though by that time I wasn't exactly stone-cold sober myself, so I wasn't really fit to pass judgment. He suddenly got it into his head that he was going to play some tape recordings of music he'd written. His mind must have been turning somersaults inside his skull. As he tried to put the tape on the player, it spiralled everywhere, and the harder Brian tried to sort out the mess, the worse it got. Eventually he was sitting on the floor, crying, with hundreds of feet of tape tangled all around him. Then, until I managed to

Brian on a trip

stop him, he started hacking at the tape — which represented weeks of work — with scissors. Once he cut off a couple of yards so that I could listen to a meaningless chunk of something which sounded as though it might just have been a really good song. Whether it was or not, no one will ever know.

Then he started trying to tie the tape together in knots because, in his confusion, he believed that was the only way it could be repaired. Later he started playing a chunk of the tape backward, and he kept repeating, "Terrific, terrific, terrific." I had tried acid myself, and I understood: it made everything sound great.

As the night wore on, Brian's condition worsened. Every twenty minutes he would roll another huge joint or swallow a few more pills and pass out on the floor. Once he peered at me maliciously and snarled, "I'm going to kill you, Mick," but then he realized it was me and said, "I'm sorry, Tony. It is Tony, isn't it?"

And all the time the two girls puffed on the joints, completely unperturbed. "He's always like this," was all they said, giggling, when I asked them if we should lock him in the bedroom.

Then Brian started crying, sitting there with his head in his hands like a wounded animal. To see this stunningly handsome and talented man, who was envied and worshipped by millions of people, so eaten up by a grief deep inside hurt me more than anything I had ever seen. . . .

The sun was shining through the windows as I blinked and rubbed myself and wondered where on earth I was. My leg had turned numb, my neck was stiff and my head felt as though a football team had been using it for practice. Brian lay with his head pillowed on the tape recorder. The two girls — who appeared considerably less exotic in the harsh morning light — were cradled in each other's arms on one of Brian's priceless Persian rugs.

I fumbled around in the kitchen and managed somehow to make four cups of strong black coffee to wake everyone up.

We sipped it slowly; then Brian crushed a little cocaine on a small scrap of glass, and we snorted through a rolled bill. I know most people swear by bacon and eggs, but there are an awful lot of rock people who would find it hard to start the day without the adrenalin — provoking, rocket fuel burst of a quick snort of coke.

Once the cocaine was bubbling through his system Brian felt as happy as a little boy on the first day of a summer holiday. He informed us that he was taking us out for a real breakfast at the Antique Market in Kings

Road, Chelsea. We piled into his car, a flawless metallic silver Rolls Royce Silver Cloud with black windows, and we were off with a lurch — Brian and I in the front and the girls in the back.

I suspected from the start that Brian wasn't really in any condition to walk, let alone drive a Rolls, and within three hundred yards my fear was justified. Brian swerved around a corner on to Fulham Road and straight into the back of a parked car. As he fumbled for reverse gear, it was obvious he planned to beat it. The impact had made a tremendous noise however, and I was sure that a number of people had seen what had happened. I quickly jumped out and scrawled an apologetic note which I tucked under the windscreen wiper of the damaged car.

"What the hell did you do that for?", I asked when I had climbed back into the Rolls.

"It was in my way," was all he would reply.

I tried to persuade him to let me drive us the rest of the way to Kings Road, but he was insistent that he was perfectly able to handle the car. We zigzagged our way in the direction of Chelsea like a pack of Keystone Cops.

Again and again during the journey I was forced to put my foot across to Brian's side and stamp on the brake to prevent another crash. And all the way people were staring at us — a bunch of rock stars going bananas in a runaway Rolls. Astonishingly we managed to arrive at the Antique Market without hitting anything else, but there were a lot of cars parked outside, so l suggested he go into the market with the girls while I parked for him.

"What do you think I am," he exploded, "an imbecile or an idiot or something? I can park my own car, thank you very much."

So, with a twist of the steering wheel, he turned the big car across to the other side of the road, straight across the pavement and into a brick wall. The whole crash seemed as though it was happening in slow motion or in a scene from a film. There was absolutely no possible excuse or explanation Brian could have offered if the police had suddenly arrived on the scene.

The next thing I knew Brian was climbing out of the Rolls with the girls, smiling broadly and calmly asking me to park the car. So I climbed into the driver's seat as dozens of people stared at this huge black windowed Rolls which had been driven into a brick wall for no apparent reason. But I managed to back up and park around the corner, and that was the end of that little incident. From that day on I have been a huge Rolls fan, because although the wall was completely demolished, the car

11

got only a slightly dented grille.

After we had our coffee and croissants, Brian asked me to drive him and the girls around Chelsea for the rest of the day. He got a kick out of lowering the back window a fraction and peeping out so that a few fans would recognise him and rush toward the car for autographs. When he tired of this game, we smoked a few joints, and then Brian persuaded the girls to kiss each another passionately. The next thing I knew he was making love to one of them on the back seat while I was sitting in a traffic jam in Kings Road, trying to pretend I didn't know what was going on.

Brian was earning a legendary reputation as a lover, and as I grew to know him intimately, I realised that to a certain extent it was deserved. When he wasn't too badly drugged, he thought little of making love to two or even three different girls in the space of a single night. But the other thing I realised was that sex had nothing whatsoever to do with love for Brian. He used sex as a weapon to degrade and humiliate the women who were drawn to him. Sometimes he would satisfy himself with mere verbal sadism, like denigrating to me a particular woman's performance in bed in a voice so loud that it was impossible for her to avoid hearing.

On other occasions his cruelty was manifested in even more dangerous ways. He seemed to gain enormous pleasure from beating women. Again and again I would see girls at the flat with black eyes and puffy lips. But no one ever went to the police or caused trouble, and many of the girls came back for more. I surmised that though they might not have actually enjoyed being slapped around, they were prepared to tolerate it if it was the price they had to pay for sharing a Rolling Stone's bed.

But hurting women didn't seem to be something Brian did simply to give himself physical pleasure. It was as though he had a terrible, searing pain somewhere deep inside and the only way he could get momentary relief was to pass that pain on to somebody else.

Sometimes, when there were no women around, we would smoke a joint and talk into the early hours, and I gradually began to understand the trauma that was tearing him apart. He had been brought up in Cheltenham a pretentious, seedy old lady of a town. His parents had fitted in well to the place, with his mother giving piano lessons and his father working in a grey, Cheltenham kind of job. Brian escaped from this claustrophobic world by throwing himself into three things — playing the clarinet, listening to jazz records and seducing every young woman who came near him.

Jazz became a religion to him, and he told me he would spend hours in his bedroom trying to imitate the music of the great Charlie Parker. He

12

had few friends, and all his adolescent anger and frustrations were channelled into music. Though he was bright, he lost interest in school-work and came close to being expelled from Cheltenham Grammar School.

He had joined a local traditional jazz band — trad was the big craze then — but his elation at playing with other musicians had rapidly worn off, and he had tired of playing the kind of commercial rubbish the nightclub crowds wanted to hear, so he had quit. He had drifted into a job in a local architect's office, but then, inevitably, a girl friend had become pregnant, and Brian had decided to flee from Britain to escape the wrath of her parents, his parents and his employers. Taking his two most prized possessions, his saxophone and his guitar, he had hitch-hiked to Scandinavia because he had heard a lot of stories about all the free-loving blondes who were supposed to live up there. He had survived by busking and he often told me that those few months had been the most free and happy of his life. And, yes, those blonde ladies were apparently all they were cracked up to be.

Eventually he ran out of money and drifted quietly back to his parents. He took a succession of Cheltenham-type office jobs and played with a few local jazz groups, but life seemed to have no meaning. "Then," Brian told me one night, "I discovered Elmore James, and the earth seemed to shudder on its axis."

James was a slide guitarist with an uniquely emotive way of playing the blues. Even in his native United States hardly anyone had heard of him. Brian told me he was so moved by James's ability to lay his soul bare through his music that he went straight out and spent every penny he had on a slide guitar. Then he stopped going to work and spent hour after hour, day after day learning to play the blues like Elmore. He became obsessed with the blues and spent every spare second playing or listening to the music of bluesmen like the legendary Muddy Waters, Robert Johnson, Sonny Boy Williamson and Howlin' Wolf. When he was eighteen, Brian started to play bar slide guitar with Britain's first real blues band, Alexis Korner's Blues Incorporated, and he had his first taste of stardom. He wasn't famous, but whenever Blues Incorporated played their regular gig at a little club in Ealing, it was Brian's solos that drew the applause and it was Brian's angelic good looks that attracted ever increasing crowds of little girls to hang around for him after he had finished playing.

One night two kids his own age came to one of the gigs at Ealing. They talked to him afterwards and told him their names were Mick Jagger and Keith Richard. They were very much in awe of him. It wasn't just that his musical knowledge and ability dwarfed theirs. It was their thinly concealed envy for the fact that he lived dangerously and walked firmly on the wild side of life, while they combined rebellion with a cosy life at home with their mums and dads. Keith, particularly, talked about fights he'd been in and things he'd shoplifted but even he couldn't hide his shock when Brian casually mentioned his worry over his two illegitimate children.

Things happened rapidly after that. Jagger joined Blues Incorporated as an occasional guest vocalist, and Keith turned Brian on to the raunchy, more commercial rhythm and blues of people like Chuck Berry and Bo Diddley. Though Brian was still playing occasional gigs with a dreary trad jazz band to earn a little money, he started taking more and more nights off to play guitar with Keith.

Jagger and Richard had their own amateurish band then called Little Boy Blue and the Blue Boys. But Brian and Keith got such a high from playing with each other that they decided to form a completely new band. From the start it was obvious that Brian was to be the band's leader, and he it was, therefore, who chose to call the group the Rolling Stones after the title of a Muddy Waters song. With Brian, Mick and Keith in that first group were Ian Stewart, who was one of the finest boogie pianists in Britain until his untimely death in 1985, Dick Taylor on bass and Tony Chapman on drums. The Stones weren't really conceived with any kind of commercial aim in mind, Brian always insisted; they were just a bunch of like minded musicians who got a buzz from playing together. At first, indeed, the Stones were essentially a part-time group, and Jagger was also continuing to work with Blues Incorporated while Brian continued to play with several other jazz bands.

Gradually Taylor and Chapman drifted away and were replaced by Charlie Watts on drums and Bill Wyman on bass. The line-up was complete. At that time Ian Stewart still played piano with the band. By then Mick, Brian and Keith were sharing a distinctly un-savoury flat in Edith Grove, Chelsea, and they were living on the few pounds a week they managed to earn as a warm-up band in clubs like the Marquee, in Soho. Years later I asked Brian why he would never eat potatoes, and he told me that he, Keith and Mick had virtually lived on potatoes — mashed, boiled or fried — for a while at Edith Grove because that was all they could afford. "I promised myself then I'd never eat potatoes again once I could afford not to," he said.

Brian also told stories of how they would supplement the spuds by stealing food from their neighbours. In another flat in the house, two school teachers held what they considered to be wild beer and jazz parties. Since they had no lock, Mick, Brian and Keith would wait for the revelers to collapse in a drunken stupor and then sneak upstairs to help themselves to any left over beer and sandwiches. "We were so good at it they never once suspected us," Brian boasted to me.

In the early sixties Brian was king. Mick and Keith vied for his friendship as he tried to teach them both all he knew about music. For weeks Jagger had been attempting to learn to play blues harmonica without any spectacular success. Brian picked up the discarded instrument, and with his extraordinary talent for mastering anything musical, he was playing impressively in the space of a single day. Far from being humiliated, Jagger was apparently grateful when Brian offered to show him how it was done.

Sometimes, Brian said, they would all become depressed — particularly when they found it impossible to keep up the hire purchase payments on their instruments. But the three of them would sit around and talk and tell a few jokes, and it didn't seem to matter much anymore.

Mick was tortured by self doubt. He had bitterly upset his parents by dropping out of the London School of Economics. And then he had thrown away his big break as singer with Blues Incorporated. For what? To sing an obscure American form of folk music that no one seemed to want to hear. On top of that, he worried that his voice wasn't right. Try as he might, he couldn't manage to sound remotely like a black blues singer. He also sounded flat on many of the tape recordings made by the band.

Brian and Keith had no such doubts. They knew that what they were doing was right. They had made no real sacrifices for the Rolling Stones, and they felt such a buzz of magic every time they played together on stage that money and food and recognition all became peripheral to making the music they believed in.

"We knew all along, you see," said Brian. "The blues were real. We only had to persuade people to listen to the music, and they couldn't help but be turned on to all those great old blues cats. I'd been through the jazz scene, and I knew that it had to die because it was so full of crap and phoney musicians who could hardly play their instruments. And Keith knew a bit about the ordinary pop scene, so he knew what a lot of rubbish that was. We didn't like being hard up, but we put up with it because it was the price we had to pay to play decent music. Plus, we were beginning to sense that more and more people were getting sick of traditional jazz, and they were looking around for something different — and we all knew that something was us."

He was right, of course, and it wasn't long before word began to spread on the music business grapevine about this very young, very strange, very arrogant new band. But most people were sceptical — weirdo teenagers like this bunch would never get anywhere.

Several times Brian arranged for the Stones to cut demo discs, but they were always rejected as perfunctorily as first efforts from most great newcomers (including Elvis Presley and the Beatles) have always been. It remains to this day a truism that record companies discourage anyone attempting to push musical boundaries; they seem convinced that anything unfamiliar can never be commercially successful.

Meanwhile, Brian had developed a friendship that was to give the Stones the break they needed, and deserved, so badly.

Giorgio Gomelski was one of London's most extraordinary characters. Born of a Russian father and a French mother, he had hitch-hiked his way around the world, later setting up Italy's first jazz festival. After a spell in Chicago, he developed a passion for the blues that bordered on obsession and he moved to London where he promoted a vast, open air jazz and blues festival. And now he had opened the hippest club in the capital. It was called the Crawdaddy and the Rolling Stones were drawn to Richmond to see some of the young rhythm and blues bands Giorgio was putting on stage there.

Brian genuinely liked Giorgio, and he would often drop down to Richmond to talk about jazz and the blues. But he did have an ulterior motive: More than anything in the world the Stones wanted a gig at the Crawdaddy. And, though Giorgio was forever giving them advice about how to improve their performances, he seemed immune to any hints about an engagement. In reality he was biding his time, waiting for the Stones to learn enough songs and get their act together sufficiently to play the Crawdaddy without blowing it. Eventually he did have a spare evening to fill, the Stones were ready and he 'phoned Brian.

On the first date sixty-six people turned up, and the Rolling Stones received the huge wage packet of £2 per man. Within weeks the audience had doubled, tripled and quadrupled until there were long queues along Kew Road every Sunday afternoon.

The young and hip and beautiful travelled from all over London to dance to and meet and cheer this aggressive, rebellious new music that

16

perfectly mirrored the attitudes of a generation of people throughout the world. Ronnie Wood, who was then just another out-of-work teenager, met his wife, Chrissie, as they both marvelled at the wickedness and skill of Brian Jones at the Crawdaddy. They could have had no inkling that thirteen years later Ronnie would be taking over Brian's role in the band. And all the rest of the people who were to become Swinging London — David Bailey, Jean Shrimpton, Mary Quant and the others — were skipping Sunday lunch and hopping on trains to Richmond to see the new sensation for themselves.

If it had happened now, of course, the Stones would have been on television and written about in magazines and newspapers throughout the country. But then the media were middle-aged in outlook, and pop groups hardly merited serious comment.

Eventually the local paper was forced to sit up and take notice. A reporter from the *Richmond and Twickenham Times* arrived to write a story about all these strange young men with long hair and girls with zany clothes who almost rioted when the Stones finished a show. It was an exciting and well written story that caused some apoplexy among the retired majors of Richmond. But the writer did not omit to mention that the Rolling Stones were a band who played music more exciting than any other in the country, that they were alive and passionate and young, while all the established trad jazz bands were torpid and dull and old. And that they might, just might, be a force that was going to shake the world.

For Brian the article was everything he had strived for. Years later he still carried it around with him as a good luck talisman. To him it was proof that his group, the Rolling Stones he had created and led, were on their way to the big time at last.

Even the Beatles, who were then glowing with the success of their first hit, "Love Me Do," deigned to take notice, and one afternoon George Harrison came to see them after a gig to tell them they were the best new group he had ever seen. They took him back to the flat in Edith Grove, where they met up with the other three Beatles and talked heady talk long into the night about music and revolution and Chuck Berry and how they were all going to change the world.

Then Norman Jopling, one of the *Record Mirror's* most respected journalists, came away from the Crawdaddy in April 1963 and wrote:

"As the trad scene gradually subsides, promoters of all kinds of teenbeat entertainments heave a sigh of relief that they have found something to take its place. It's rhythm and blues, of course – the number of R and B clubs that have suddenly sprung up is nothing short of fantastic.

... [At] the Station Hotel, Kew Road [the building which housed the Crawdaddy], the hip kids throw themselves about to the new "jungle music" like they never did in the more restrained days of trad.

And the combo they writhe and twist to is called the Rolling Stones. Maybe you've never heard of them – if you live far from London the odds are you haven't.

But by gad you will! The Stones are destined to be the biggest group in the R and B scene — if that scene continues to flourish. Three months ago only fifty people turned up to see the group. Now Gomelski has to close the doors at an early hour — with over 400 fans crowding the hall.

The fans quickly lose their inhibitions and contort themselves to truly exciting music. Fact is that, unlike all other R and B groups worthy of the name, the Rolling Stones have a definite visual appeal. They aren't like the jazzmen who were doing trad a few months ago and who had converted their act to keep up with the times. They are genuine R and B fanatics themselves and they sing and play in a way that one would have expected more from a coloured U.S. group than a bunch of wild, exciting white boys who have the fans screaming and listening to them.

... [They] can also get the sound that Bo Diddley gets – no mean achievement. The group themselves are all red-hot when it comes to U.S. beat discs. They know their R and B numbers inside out and have a repertoire of about 80 songs, most of them ones which the real R and B fans know and love.

But despite the fact that their R and B has a superficial resemblance to rock 'n' roll, fans of the hit parade music would not find any familiar material performed by the Rolling Stones. And the boys do not use original material — only American stuff. "After all," they say, can you imagine, a British-composed R and B number — it just wouldn't make it."

Within days of the article the Stones had been signed to a record deal by two men — a fast talking, brilliant young hustler named Andrew Oldham, who had once worked as publicist for the Beatles, and his partner, show–business agent Eric Easton.

The deal meant screwing up their friendship with Gomelski — they had a verbal management deal — and with lan Stewart, who, Oldham confided, looked all wrong with his short hair and jutting Neanderthal jaw. It was agreed, however, that Stewart would continue to play piano on the Stones' records but that he would no longer appear on stage with them.

But to Brian and Mick, who wanted — needed — so very badly to make it, walking over a couple of old friends was a small price to pay for the break that Oldham and Easton were offering them.

Nine days later the Stones went to the Olympic recording studio, in Barnes, to cut their first real record. None of them had the slightest idea how a record should be mixed or of how to make a song exciting without the adrenalin producing presence of an audience. Hardly surprising, therefore, that their recording of the Chuck Berry classic "Come On" was not merely inferior to their powerhouse stage version — it was awful.

Decca, which had been talked into paying the Stones a sizeable advance by Oldham, was displeased. But the group went into the studio again and again until, at the fifth try, they managed to produce a tolerable recording. On the day it came out the Stones also made their TV debut — on a particularly vapid show called *Thank Your Lucky Stars*.

Though all five of them wore suits for the programme, they were stunned at the hostility their brief appearance provoked among middle-aged TV viewers. The station and the newspapers were deluged with complaints from people who objected to the Stones' long hair and the menacing, unsubtle sexuality of Mick and Brian.

A typical letter read: "It is disgraceful that long-haired louts such as these should be allowed to appear on television. Their appearance was absolutely disgusting . . . ."

Brian and the rest of the Stones were surprised and slightly hurt by the reaction. But Andrew Oldham was delighted.

"We're going to make you exactly the opposite to those nice, clean, tidy Beatles," he exclaimed. "And the more the parents hate you, the more the kids will love you. Just you wait and see."

The Stones found it hard to believe that Andrew was right on target. Surely getting everyone uptight couldn't be the best way to turn people on to rhythm and blues, they reasoned. But they played along and

20

became nastier and more threatening every day. Brian even ordered Charlie Watts to grow his hair because he looked too respectable. And suddenly it worked. It was all coming true, just the way Andrew had said it would. For Brian every dream he had ever had was becoming reality. But he couldn't understand why he felt the strangest, tiniest twinge of fear deep inside.

Anita Pallenberg

2

THE PAST COUPLE OF YEARS HAD BEEN A BLUR: "I WANNA BE YOUR MAN," "Not Fade Away," "It's All Over Now," "Little Red Rooster," "The Last Time," television, tours of Britain and America and always controversy, rows, anger and ever-rising pressure. Sometimes Jagger would vie with Brian for leadership, but when that happened, Keith would always side with Brian, and it would be the two real punks — Brian and Keith — against Jagger; the fraud, the suburban middle-class kid with an amorality as fake as his cockney accent.

Brian was still loving it all then, in 1965. He was the beautiful Stone, the one the fans screamed over while they told jokes about 'old rubber lips' Jagger. Brian was living with Linda, the loving mother of one of his many children. He seemed to have become almost settled, almost content.

Until the sexiest blonde I had ever seen arrived in London.

Her name was Anita Pallenberg, and no one ever seemed to know quite where she came from or who she was. When pressed, she would reveal that she was half Italian and half German and that she had worked as an actress with the Living Theatre. She had only to walk along the street to cause a string of traffic accidents. She had tumbling, shining blonde hair, a long lithe body and wickedly beautiful cat's eyes. She was no dumb blonde, either, and the combination of witty conversation and devastating looks rapidly turned her into the darling of aristocratic London. Before long she was being invited to society events by people like Lord Harlech and Guinness heir Tara Browne.

Inevitably she met the Rolling Stones and she could, of course, have taken her pick of any of them; Jagger's romance with Chrissie Shrimpton had become a scratching, brawling travesty of love. Richard, as usual, had no serious woman in his life, and Brian, well, Brian never refused a beautiful woman. The other two Stones — Bill and Charlie —

didn't count, of course. Even then they weren't proper Rolling Stones; they were content to do their jobs well, live their lives as quietly as possible and stay out of trouble.

Mick, Keith and Brian all wanted Anita, but once she had met Brian, there seemed to be no contest. The two of them spent every spare second together, cuddling and giggling at private jokes, and within a few weeks Brian had abandoned Linda and their baby to move Anita into his flat.

As a couple Brian and Anita exuded an almost surrealistic aura; they began to look, dress and think so much alike that they became one — a single presence in silk and satin. They were, at that moment, the reigning Beautiful Couple of Europe and they took full advantage of the power they possessed over the young dukes, lords and other high born friends and admirers who flocked to pay homage. In a way, their arrogance was justified. Brian's band had fought the short-haired, nine-to-five establishment ideal and won. To cap it all, rhythm and blues had taken over from jazz as the dominant influence in British music.

Sometimes of Brian and Anita's arrogance was frightening. Those who displeased them would be banished from the flat and shunned immediately by any friends who wished to avoid offence to their highnesses. Brian and Anita were similar in more than just hairstyles: They each carried a cruel streak in their nature, the seed of self-destruction.

Marianne Faithfull tells the story of how Linda, Brian's ex, showed up outside the flat with her baby and tried to make Brian feel guilty about not paying her any maintenance. Inside the house Anita and Brian, giggling, refused even to talk to her.

Another time Anita persuaded Brian to be photographed in a full Nazi SS uniform, with his jackboot grinding a doll into the dirt. Brian thought the uniform made him look exotic, and Anita told him that he should send the picture out to newspapers and tell them it was an anti-Nazi protest.

When the picture was misconstrued by almost everyone, Brian and Anita were genuinely astonished that the world couldn't see the point of their little joke. The incident was symptomatic of the fact that Anita and the courtiers were cocooning Brian from the real world. Together they went ever further for their kicks. Their sexual activities were extraordinary, and they took up astrology and magic. Eventually they were given some acid by one of their sycophants, and Brian and Anita tripped together for the first time. That moment marked the peak of Brian's brief life and the start of his personality disintegration.

On LSD, the door to the vault of his mind swung open, he told me, and he was able to write songs and play guitar the way he had always dreamed.

If he had doubts, he had only to read the words of Timothy Leary, the Harvard University acid prophet, for reassurance.

"It's as though there are all sorts of amazing songs floating around in my head that I can't get out," Brian told me once. "Acid lets it all out. I hardly even know I'm writing when I'm on a trip, yet the next day I find I've written pages of the most amazing numbers."

At that time Brian was turning all the beautiful people around him on to the drug, and there was something enormously alluring about the exotic, faraway, stoned world they seemed to inhabit.

I was at the flat one day with some friends, and he asked me if I'd like to take a trip. I jumped at the chance and quickly gulped down the sugar lump he proffered me, expecting the kind of instantaneous buzz I'd had in the past from cocaine.

After half-an-hour I felt nothing, so I concluded that an awful lot of people were deluding themselves about the mind-blowing powers of LSD. Either that or I was immune in some strange way. But then I gradually felt that things were beginning to look just a little odd, though only when I looked at them out of the corners of my eyes. If I glared at them, they immediately became normal again.

I scratched my nose, and that was definitely extremely odd. There was a far off noise like a penny being scraped over the paintwork of a car, and my hand was suddenly huge. It was almost as if my arm were disjointed from me, as if it were scratching my nose without my having any power to control it.

Then the trip really began to take over. A red Persian rug hanging on the wall began to glow like neon signs in Piccadilly Circus; the wooden floor sparkled like rock crystal sugar. I had to shield my eyes from these dazzling sights, but when I raised my hand, the ticking of my watch was loud as a bass drum.

The strange effects seemed to wear off. I heaved a sigh of relief and thought, "Thank God it's all coming to an end." Suddenly I felt it starting again. This time I could hear Brian breathing, and since each breath was a roar, I had the sensation that there was a lion in the room. Next, it was my heart I could hear beating. I could make it beat faster or slower simply by concentrating my mind on it. Someone was talking to me then. I could only

25

see him mouthing the words, and the speaker seemed to be dressed as a court jester, and I felt very lost and afraid.

The worst thing about the trip was that it was impossible to stop. There were periods of quiet, and I thought it was almost over; but then it would gain momentum again, and I found myself in a world of strange fantasies. I felt like a small child trapped on a fast-spinning fun-fair ride that has been going on too long. You know that if you stay in your seat, you will be sick, but you have no control. There's no way you can stop the ride or scream for help. Then, every time the ride seems to be slowing down and you start almost sobbing with relief, it picks up again and whirls you around faster and faster until you think you will die if you have to put up with it any longer.

But strangely, when it was over, I felt I had benefitted from it. And using the drug in the mid-sixties meant you were part of an exclusive camaraderie: the fellowship of acid heads. Consequently, much as I had hated that first trip, I was persuaded to try acid again. The second experience was also hideous, and to this day, I rarely touch acid.

Like me, Keith was young and impressionable, and he had always been content to follow where Brian led. He turned Keith on to acid, and they were drawn together, jamming better and writing songs. Suddenly the most fantastic things seemed possible. Like millions of ordinary kids who were about to follow their deluded example, the two of them believed that swallowing an hallucinogenic drug had in some way expanded their consciousness and made the realisation of every fantasy a real possibility. Brian and Keith and Anita grew so close on acid that Keith started spending more and more nights there — until, eventually, it seemed only sensible that he should move in permanently.

Mick was odd man out. Brian, especially, treated him with thinly veiled contempt, laughed at him because he was afraid of acid. For Mick was guilty of the worst transgression of all: being a straight. To annoy him, Brian and Keith started referring to him as Jagger, rather than by his first name, and a rift began that looked as though it might break up the band.

Keith and Brian's closest friend during the LSD phase was a charming, lovable young heir, Tara Browne. Tara had often stayed at the flat with Brian, Keith and Anita, and they'd talk long into the night about mysticism and music and all the revolutionary things acid was doing for them.

It was also at this point that it dawned on Brian that Keith Richard was falling in love with Anita Pallenberg.

26

He didn't worry unduly. He knew that Mick, too, fancied Anita, but she was faithful to Brian, always telling him she loved him. It was the beginning, though, of a time of change. Keith moved out of the flat because Brian was making it obvious he regarded him as a potential threat. Brian's deep-seated insecurity made him fear that the only woman he had ever loved would be snatched away from him.

Keith dropped acid with Mick Jagger, and the trip marked the beginning of an alliance between them. This time it was Brian who was to be ostracized. He knew that Mick and Keith both wanted Anita very badly and they were shunning him because she was his woman.

Brian began, then, to resent the power that his love for Anita gave her. He felt he was losing control of his life, losing Mick and Keith, losing his music because of a mere woman. Brian Jones, father of six illegitimate children, the man who had always been able to discard girls like cigarette ends, was being held in thrall by a chick.

I was married by then, and my wife, Gloria, and I lived with our baby son in a little flat in North London. Soon Brian was 'phoning every couple of days asking me to come and visit — but I knew what he really wanted was dope, more and more of it.

Then Tara Browne died when his Lotus Elan crashed into a lamp-post, and the death of his best friend left Brian stunned and confused. Afterwards, he would talk to me for hours about how meaningless life had begun to seem to him. At first I understood his grief and shared it, but gradually it began to turn to something else. Brian seemed unbalanced, paranoid, eaten up by misery and loneliness.

He talked about the false hope that acid had given him, and then he'd swallow great handfuls of barbiturates, Mandrax and Tuinal, to blot out the misery of life. One day I arrived at his place in Chelsea to find Anita with bruises all over her face, and it was obvious he had beaten her savagely. When I asked her what had happened, she said, "It's none of your business." Another time I dropped by to find Brian almost hysterical. "Anita's dead! I can't rouse her!" Anita was lying in their antique bed. I shook her, then slapped her face, but got no reaction; she'd taken too much of something. Brian and I carried her downstairs to the Alfa and drove her to the hospital. They stomach-pumped her, and when she came to, Brian was crying. Then she started sobbing silently, with a terrible wounded look in her beautiful eyes.

Meanwhile, Keith and Mick were writing together with a brilliance and confidence they had never felt before. I started to see Keith fre-

27

quently, and one day I said, "Seems like you and Mick hardly ever speak to Brian anymore."

"Well, he's burned out, isn't he?" Keith whispered.

He turned away so I couldn't see his face. "The only problem now is what to do about him."

3

IF ANITA WAS AS ALLURING AND MYSTERIOUS AS NIGHT, THIS WOMAN WAS AS blithe and pure as a midsummer's day. She was perhaps even more beautiful than Anita. Her body was slender, frail as a blade of grass. But it was the woman's face that was singular — it was the face of an angel, with its big, blue, innocent eyes, soft, pouting lips and a frame of blonde hair that glowed like the sun with youth and health. It was a face that stopped all talk whenever she entered any gathering of people — a face that subjugated all men to her will. Marianne Faithfull was her name.

She was the daughter of a penniless Austrian baroness and a brilliant, slightly eccentric English professor of art and philology. Though she felt most relaxed and at ease among academics and aristocrats, Marianne gained a vicarious thrill from mixing with the coarse, clever, energetic young men who played the new no-compromise, high-energy music that was clearly changing the world.

Marianne was seventeen years old then, and she clung to the security of a boyfriend who came from her world. His name was John Dunbar, he was a student of art at Cambridge and he was one of the architects of London's exciting underground art and literary scene.

Through John Dunbar Marianne met Paul McCartney, and she was impressed by his charm, his openness, the way he appeared unspoiled by sudden wealth and adulation. He seemed fond of her too, and early in 1964 he invited her and John to a party in London for singer Adrienne Posta. The other Beatles were there, and so were several Rolling Stones and a lot of other people whom Marianne recognized but did not know. Several of the men talked to her, but she sensed that they appeared to feel almost intimidated by her beauty and her husky, aristocratic voice. She enjoyed her new found power and wondered what her school friends would say if they could see all the rich, famous young men who chased after her now.

Marianne Faithful

Marianne had suffered from tuberculosis as a child, and she was still not strong. These men were common, and they were becoming boring with their predictable lines. So she sat on the stairs, feeling weary and talking idly to another pretty girl. She glanced up, and there, looming over her, was Mick Jagger. He wore no tie, which was unusual at a party in 1964, and his hair was like a girl's — longer than any man's hair she had ever seen. She had never listened to a Rolling Stones record (Mozart and Bach were more to her taste), but she knew that Jagger was the new idol of hip London. Even Paul McCartney had raved about the authenticity of Jagger's phrasing, and he was not a man to praise his rivals lightly.

So she was intrigued that he left his beautiful girl friend sitting alone to come and talk to her.

" 'ello, luvly, 'ow's it goin' then?" he said, his voice a grotesque parody of a cockney accent. At close range, she noticed with disgust, his face was greasy and pimply.

Clumsily he spilled a few drops of his drink over the new blouse she had bought specially for the party. She scowled then marched away without a word. The man was an oaf, a boorish, working-class, ignorant oaf. Marianne was much more charmed by a strange man, wearing make-up, who introduced himself as Andrew Oldham and said he was the Rolling Stones' manager.

"I am going to make you a star," he told her intensely. But Marianne only giggled and told him she was quite happy the way she was, thank you very much. Good God, couldn't the man dream up anything more imaginative than a line from a Busby Berkeley musical?

But Oldham was serious, and at the time his finger was very firmly on the pulse of the new generation. He knew that this perfect, uniquely beautiful child-woman had charisma enough for the whole country to fall in love with her.

Marianne, meanwhile, had no urge to be any kind of star — least of all the kind that a freak like Oldham would be likely to create. She was studying for her A-levels at St. Joseph's Convent School, in Reading, Berkshire, and the over-riding ambition of her life was to get into a good University, get her degree and live up to the standards set by her parents.

All her life she had been a lost, lonely, sickly child. Her parents' marriage had broken up when Marianne was eight years old, and she had promptly been enrolled as a boarder at St. Joseph's. The confusion of this little girl, whose life seemed to be falling apart, was made worse because the school was run by devout Roman Catholic nuns — and Marianne was not a Roman Catholic. Her parents had arranged for her to go there as a charity boarder because other, more suitable schools would have been too expensive. The other girls and even, sometimes, the nuns had resented her, until eventually the pressure drove her to change to the Roman Catholic faith. In the midst of all this anguish she had suffered from recurring attacks of tuberculosis which had left her skinny, nervous and unattractive.

Gradually she recovered until she had bloomed into adolescence like a rose and become exquisitely beautiful. Then boys had chased her and whistled at her in the street, while the girls who had once snubbed her feted her and realized that her beauty set her apart from them. By then hardship had tempered Marianne, so she was careful not to abuse her new found power.

Now she knew what she wanted from life; a home, security and the love of a brilliant, handsome young man like John Dunbar. Freaky teenage idols and managers with eye shadow were intriguing, but they were far from the life she wanted.

Andrew Oldham, though, had no intention of letting a solid gold superstar slip through his fingers. He telephoned and wrote and lobbied John Dunbar until Marianne was persuaded, during the school holidays, to travel to London to see Andrew and sign a recording contract. She met Mick Jagger again, and he gave her a song called "As Tears Go By", that he said she had inspired. Marianne was flattered but suspected the song was a Stones reject.

At the recording session at Olympic, Mick Jagger, Keith Richard and Brian Jones all made plays for her and tried to talk her into their beds. She liked Brian best. He looked a little like her, and he seemed to be the leader of the band. Keith and Mick both were attractive but their spots were awful, and she didn't think she could ever bring herself to kiss a man with spots. Besides, Mick was living with Chrissie Shrimpton, and the newspapers were always going on about how in love they were and how they were planning to marry.

"As Tears Go By" was a huge hit, and Marianne's wistful television appearances to promote the song triggered a strange mixture of lust and a desire to protect among all the men who saw her. Once again Andrew Oldham's words had proved prophetic — the whole country was falling in love with her.

The adoration of so many was a heady potion for a girl who had known strong feelings of isolation and rejection for much of her life. Succumbing to temptation, she dropped out of school and made another record, "Come And Stay With Me," which was almost as big a hit as her first disc. But she was beginning to feel lost and confused as the superstar machine whirled her around and around.

Marianne was pregnant. She married John in May 1965, and she was back on the straight and narrow. She didn't know just how badly Jagger wanted her, wasn't aware that his relationship with Chrissie Shrimpton had been totally crushed by the pressures of stardom. It would have made no difference, however. Marianne knew by now that Mick Jagger was not the lout he pretended to be, but he was still a pop singer without a fraction of John's taste or intellect.

Her pregnancy wasn't allowed to intrude on her career; those in charge knew there was a limit to how long a singer like Marianne could stay this hot. There were more hit records — "This Little Bird" and "Summer Nights" — more gigs in clubs and a tour supporting the Rolling

Stones. The birth of her son, Nicholas, was little more than a momentary interruption. She felt she loved John, but somewhere deep inside she seemed to need the mass adulation she was attracting still more. John grew jealous, there were arguments and somehow she drifted into casual affairs with first Brian Jones, then Keith Richard and finally Mick Jagger. But there was never any time to develop a real relationship with any of them. She always knew that the madness would be over soon, and then she would be able to return to the sanity of her life with John and Nicholas.

Ever so vaguely she was aware of a rivalry that seemed to have developed in some inexplicable way between her and Anita Pallenberg. But it was not a rivalry she wanted. Anita seemed to crave power; she needed to bend men to her will. But Marianne, well, all Marianne wanted was to be loved.

Mick Jagger loved her very much — he made that obvious every time they met. Quite apart from her beauty Marianne had the class and style that Mick craved. His new found wealth and influence had made him popular among the young aristocracy, but he knew he lacked their sophistication. Marianne delighted in educating him, teaching him literature and art and manners. Gradually she realized that he was sensitive and that he was hurt when Brian and Keith seemed to gang up against him. She realized, too, that she loved him.

Almost imperceptibly, over a period of months, she slipped further and further from John while Jagger severed the ties with Chrissie, until Mick and Marianne were living together. Sometimes they would meet with Brian and Anita, but Brian, paranoid and hostile, made friendship impossible. Keith seemed reserved too, especially when someone teased him that he was the only Rolling Stone without a beautiful woman.

4

ROBERT FRASER HAD LONG BEEN A CLOSE FRIEND OF THE ROLLING STONES.
He was an art dealer, a dark, brilliant, handsome man who was as intent
on breaking down the power of the pretentious, unadventurous galleries as
Brian, Keith and Mick had been on tearing away the stranglehold of trad
jazz. At the same time the Stones were drawing crowds of young, thinking
people to the Crawdaddy, Fraser was pulling them to his small gallery in
Duke Street, Mayfair. His daring, yet honest taste in the avant-garde art of
the sixties kept him consistently ahead of imitators and earned him
grudging respect from the art establishment — even as they watched him
hacking away at their roots.

He was also a charming man, and he began to build a large circle of
friends among the rock stars, who were fast becoming a kind of aristocracy. They trusted his advice when he talked about fine art investments
for their new wealth, and they found his combination of culture and hip
vitality enormously stimulating. Unlike most grasping middle-aged gallery
owners, this man used dope and spoke their language, so they trusted him
not to rip them off.

As a teenager, my great passions were rock music and big-time
villainy — roughly in that order. I had a cousin who had gone way, way off
the rails and who had become deeply immersed in organized crime. While
my parents complained about the shame he was bringing on our family, I
could only look at his big car and beautiful women and pray to God he
would show me how it was done. Crime seemed glamorous and romantic.
He told me stories about being chased by police cars and about the twins
who were ruling East End London with a panache Capone himself would
have envied. He always carried huge rolls of money. At a time when a
man was successful if he earned £30 a week, my cousin would often carry
£1,500 or more in his pocket.

35

Keith Richards and John Dunbar

He tried to dissuade me from following his example and even arranged for me to train as a croupier at a little Mayfair club he had an interest in, called Le Chat Noire. The work was interesting, but by far the most exciting part of it, for me, was the extraordinary opportunity it afforded me to meet the corps d'elite of London's criminal fraternity. Albert Dimes, the steely-eyed Italian Godfather whose territory covered all of the West End, had a nightclub in Soho, and he became a firm friend. I have since heard that he was once one of the most feared men in England, but I found him a man of charm and erudition. Though I was nineteen then, I looked very much younger, and Albert took it into his head to look after me. Once, when he was slightly the worse for large brandies, he called me over and, putting his arm around my shoulder, told me, "Soho is a hard place, Tony, but if you ever have any trouble whatsoever, remember I am right behind you."

Another powerful underworld character then was a huge, barrel-chested Liverpudlian woman known (behind her back) to one and all as Shaggy Sheila. Sheila controlled the Gerrard Street area before it became Chinatown, and she was tougher and more ruthless than any man.

There were rumours that Sheila had once used her bare hands to strangle a man who had tried to muscle into Gerrard Street. I believed them implicitly. She had also managed to scare off the psychopathic Kray twins when they made moves to open a gambling club in her area. No one knew quite how Sheila had forced them to back down, but there were many knowing smiles in Soho when the underworld heard that the Krays had decided there were richer pickings to be had in the netherland of Knightsbridge, so they were opening their club, the Barn, there.

Into this world of intrigue, sudden violence and bitter feuds dropped Robert Fraser. We met as I sipped a solitary espresso at the Bar Italian in Soho's Frith Street. It was afternoon, and I was killing time before going to work at the club.

Robert sat next to me, and we fell into a conversation. Robert mentioned that he had gone to college in Spain. Both my parents are Spanish, and I speak the language as fluently as I speak English. This excited Robert, and he jumped at the chance to talk with me in his very erudite Spanish. I remember that we discussed the politics of Spain and the civil war for an hour, and then Robert had to go to an appointment. I left him my 'phone number, and we arranged to meet again. Robert would drive to Soho frequently in his souped-up car to pick me up, and we would drive around to score some hash.

Once or twice he talked vaguely about "problems" that were worrying him. Then, late one night as we drank in a little bar off Berwick Street, he dramatically slammed down his scotch and told me, "I'm being destroyed, Tony."

His tale of woe was an all too common one at that time. Like hundreds of other rich young men, he had been so overwhelmed by the advent of legalized gambling that he had over-reached himself.

"I owe the Barn Club more than twenty thousand pounds," he confessed. "They are 'phoning me every day, and now they have started sending thugs to the gallery. They're threatening me if I don't pay up — but I just don't have that kind of money."

I couldn't help smiling wryly; we used exactly the same extortion techniques at Le Chat Noire, and, nine times out of ten, they worked. But I thought better of mentioning that to Robert. Instead, I just told him I had friends at the Barn and I would see what I could do.

I spoke to Albert Dimes when I ran into him in the street a couple of days later, but he didn't want to get involved. "If the sucker owes money, that's his problem," was all he would say. "If you want to tangle with the twins, that's up to you." I sensed that tough old Albert Dimes — the man who ruled Soho with a rod of iron — was afraid. For some reason he didn't have the courage to tangle with these flashy, youthful East End hoodlums. I was young and reckless, sorting out Robert's problems became a macho affair to me, a thing of honour.

The Barn was tastelessly opulent, but it was, nevertheless, intimidating, and I felt the slightest tremor of fear as I stalked in through the front door. I was relieved to find Curly King, a small-time hood who had defected from Soho to the Krays, standing by the reception desk in a black suit with a bow tie.

"Tell Reggie and Ronnie I want to see them, Curly," I said, trying to sound braver than I felt. There was something about the bulge inside his jacket that was distinctly intimidating.

"I'm sorry, Tony, they are very busy men," he began, in his lugubrious way. "I've got orders they don't want to see anybody. And they especially don't want to see punks like you."

"Look, Curly, you tell them that either they can see me here or I'll come to their house tomorrow — but I'm going to see them."

He glowered at me and stomped off. But he returned a few minutes later and ushered me into a surprisingly small office where Reggie sat behind a desk, looking every inch a respectable businessman.

"All right, Tony, what can I do for you?" he said with a friendly smile. "Any friend of Albert's is a friend of mine."

He offered me a ludicrously huge Havana cigar from a cedarwood box on his desk while I poured out Robert's tale of woe. When I finished, he nodded his head sympathetically and went to fetch the relevant file.

"It's a bad business," he said moodily, "when a gentleman like him has no honour — look at all these." He spread the returned cheques on the desk in front of me. "The man's given me bouncing cheques for more than five grand. But I'll tell you what I'll do. Because Albert is a friend of mine, I'll cut my losses on this guy if he pays me three grand by this time tomorrow. I can't say fairer than that."

I almost danced down the road as I looked for a 'phone box to ring Robert. The Krays, the big boys, the killers even Albert Dimes was wary of, had backed down to me. What a story to tell my cousin! When I finally managed to speak to Robert, he was stunned for several minutes by the news. "Christ, Tony," he kept repeating, "you've saved my life."

We grew closer after that. I helped him win his money by rigging a game of *chemin de fer* at Le Chat Noire. I didn't feel particularly guilty about that because as a croupier I knew that most of the games were subtly rigged against the customers.

Robert started inviting me back to his splendidly tasteful, luxurious flat in Mount Street, Mayfair, where he would introduce me to his fashionable friends as "Spanish Tony." Once several members of an unknown Midlands pop group called the Moody Blues were there, and Robert asked me if I wanted to turn on with them. Though I often talked casually about drugs, I had, in fact, never smoked pot, and I was excited to watch Robert mysteriously unwrap the drug from its silver foil package and roll it into a joint.

We ritually passed the bulging cigarette around as we sat in a circle on the floor listening to the hi-fi gently moaning out the music of John Lee Hooker. My turn came, and I drew deeply to find a pleasant, herbal taste that seemed to burn slightly as I inhaled it into my lungs. Graham Edge, the drummer, was the first to succumb, and he just lay back giggling inanely while I watched in mild surprise. Pretty soon his giggles had infected us all, and we all were rolling around the floor with tears of laughter streaming from our eyes. Cannabis, I decided, was okay.

I started to buy some of my own from a friend in Soho who was nicknamed the Candy Man because he could sell you any kind of drug you wanted. A bag of grass cost about £5 then, which seemed reasonable.

The Moodies became good friends, and they would often drop into my little flat in Palmerston Road in Kilburn, for a smoke.

Meanwhile Robert was trying, paternally, to wean me away from the villainous world I was inhabiting because he was convinced I would end up serving a long stretch in prison. I had always been a keen amateur photographer, so Robert encouraged me to develop my talent. He introduced me to a brilliant fashion photographer named Michael Cooper who taught me about light and camera angles and explained the sort of equipment I should buy. Every day, before I started work at the club, I would practice with my newly purchased Pentax camera, using different lenses,

The Moody Blues

until I was confident that my pictures were as good as any I had seen in glossy magazines. The Moodies were impressed by my work, too, and asked me to photograph them for the cover of their soon to be released debut album.

We went to Hampstead for the session, a beautiful North London suburb of cobbled alleyways, trees and centuries old pubs. The photographs were dark, moody and far and away the best I had ever taken. The group's manager was so pleased he gave me a big bonus, and I remember thinking that at last I had discovered my destiny. I knew then what I was going to do with my life.

40

Tony Sanchez

Though I was still young, I had known many beautiful women intimately. In the West End the exotic show girls and hostesses seemed to get a strange kick out of taking a relatively inexperienced boy like me to their beds and teaching him all they knew. They were warm, loving women, and to this day I number several of them among my closest friends.

But I had never in my life seen, far less spoken to, a woman of such perfection as Robert was sharing a joint with when I dropped by his flat that night. He had introduced her as Marianne Faithfull, and the name had meant nothing. She wore just ragged old Levi's and a shirt so tight that her full, firm breasts were clearly visible through the thin material. She was the first woman I had met who didn't wear a bra. Yet she somehow still looked virginal, with her cornflower blue eyes and ready smile.

Though she looked very young she spoke authoritatively with Robert about contemporary artists and sculptors while I just listened to the sound of her deep, sensuously husky voice. Robert knew that art bored me, so he skilfully twisted the topic to drugs and told Marianne about my friend the Candy Man and how he could provide anything at any time.

"That's fantastic," she said. "Everyone I know has so much trouble getting hold of grass."

Robert, too, was having trouble finding enough grass to satisfy his ever widening circle of hip young friends. So, more and more often, he would ask me to go to Soho in my Alfa Romeo to buy some stuff so he could turn everyone on.

Marianne was often at Robert's flat with her husband, John Dunbar, but more often with Brian or Keith or Mick. Once she asked me if I could get hold of half an ounce of grass for her. Then, when she came to my flat in Kilburn to score, we turned on together. I noticed that tears were running down her perfect face.

"I'm so alone, Tony," she said. "I can feel myself slipping away from John. We seem to drift apart all the time. I don't know where I'm going anymore."

I put my arm around her tiny shoulders; she put her head on my chest. And we made love.

Robert was becoming bored with marijuana. He smoked half-a-dozen joints or more a day, but they didn't seem to have much effect anymore. He started to eat hash cakes, to put hash into his coffee, but no matter what he did, the buzz didn't seem to be there anymore. When an

American friend called Bill Willis told him about the wonders of cocaine, he was intrigued. Willis managed to get hold of a little coke which Robert sniffed into his nose through a rolled pound note. Afterward he would talk for hours to anyone who would listen about the sensational uplift the drug had given him.

"It was like filling my body with liquid fire," he said. No one dared tell him what they were all thinking: Cocaine was a killer, and Robert was beginning to allow drugs to play too dominant a part in his life.

Bill Willis moved away then, and Robert wanted to buy some more coke, wanted to turn his friends on to this sensational new wonder drug. I was extremely curious, so when he asked me if I could pick up some from the Candy Man, I drove quickly to Soho to buy some. It cost as much as five bottles of Vodka which seemed to me an awful lot of money for a little medicine bottle containing a few white crystals.

In those far-off days the government had not woken up to the fact that cocaine was – unlike heroin – non-addictive, so many regular users were actually being prescribed coke by "junkie doctors". The Candy Man simply offered their patients a reasonable price for their dope, then resold it for three, four or five times as much.

I watched fascinated as Robert carefully made two thin lines of coke on a pocket mirror, rolled up a new five-pound note and vacuumed the powder into his nostrils. He breathed deeply, and I noticed his eyes were watering. "Phewee!" he exclaimed. "It almost blasted my head from my shoulders. Would you care to indulge?"

Snorting coke wasn't quite as simple as Robert made it look, and I found myself blowing the precious white dust across the table at my first attempt. But I tried again, and it was as though someone had squirted ice inside my face. A cold, vague numbness spread across my cheek, and that was all. Somehow I had expected more. Robert had led me to believe that the drug would set me ablaze, would alter my perception of the cosmos, and here I was, with a numb cheek, watering eyes and nothing more. But we talked then and I was aware of an extraordinary sharpness and lucidity in my thoughts and conversation. The confusion I had felt in my mind about the direction of my life was gone, and suddenly all the intricate tangles unravelled in bright, shining sentences that I could hardly believe I was capable of uttering. Essentially that, for me, was the huge appeal – and danger – of coke. It sharpens the mind, clarifies everything quite unlike any other drug. Alcohol and, to a lesser extent, grass tend to befuddle the mind. Amphetamines – speed – create nervousness and paranoia. But cocaine is like an instantaneous course of regular meals and early nights.

I was so overwhelmed that I read everything I could about this extraordinary drug. Sigmund Freud was, I discovered, one of the first people to champion coke as a 'stimulating euphoriant.' As a young neurologist he found that it not only focused his mind but also fanned his already raging libido. In 1884 he was moved to write to his fiancée: "Woe to you, my Princess, when I come. I will kiss you quite red and feed you until you are plump. And if you willfully resist, you shall see who is the stronger, a gentle little girl who doesn't eat enough or a big, wild man with cocaine in his veins."

A worldwide cocaine craze followed soon after, and in the Naughty Nineties the whole world seemed to have been snorting coke. Many people believe Coca-Cola contained a large shot (hence its name and its reputation as a powerful refresher). There were coke bonbons, coke cigarettes and even coke ointment. But a growing public feeling that the drug was responsible for many crimes led to it being outlawed in 1906.

In decadent, pre-war Nazi Germany, cocaine became popular among the rich. The most prominent user was Hermann Goring, head of the Luftwaffe, who used it in conjunction with morphine. Some historians have claimed that excessive abuse of cocaine was one of the major factors contributing to the delusions of strength and paranoia rampant among Nazi leaders. It has even been suggested that Hitler was doing coke when he said, 'Russia? Why not?'

Though the drug fascinated me, I still believed it to be addictive, so I tried not to use it more than once a week. Brian and Keith had discovered the heady effects of cocaine from Robert, and they came to his flat weekly to get high with him. They asked me if I could buy some for them, but I always refused because I was genuinely worried that I would become labelled as a dangerous drug dealer — a crime which carried a certain jail sentence.

I was mesmerized by the Rolling Stones then. I played their music constantly at my place in Palmerston Road, and friends would ask me what they were really like, whether they were as wicked as all the newspapers said they were. Sometimes I would invite Brian or Keith to the flat, and we would smoke or snort a little coke together. Of Marianne I saw little. She was deeply immersed in work, motherhood, Mick Jagger and her marriage; she had little time for either me or Robert. But at four o'clock one morning, the doorbell rang, and I staggered out bleary eyed to find Marianne with Brian, Anita, Keith and some people I'd never seen before.

"Hi, Tony, how are you?" said Brian.

"What the hell do you want? It's four in the morning," I replied irritably.

"Have you got anything then, Tony?" he asked, grinning.

"What do you mean have I got anything?"

"You know, man — something to snort."

I poured the tiny quantity of cocaine I had on a plate and made lines for each of them to snort. I felt like a nurse ladling out spoonfuls of oatmeal to deprived infants as they lined up for their rations.

Despite speculation that the Rolling Stones smoked pot, none of the fans had the slightest inkling yet of how essential drugs were to Brian and Keith. What was apparent to everyone, however, was that the Stones were an increasingly powerful political force. With their long hair and their refusal to compromise they were the heroes of a generation that questioned every rule, every taboo that had been foisted upon it. There is no question that many people of influence were worried by the stance of these five street guerrillas.

The first squall of the gathering storm had come when the group's van had drawn into a service station late at night with Mick, Brian and Bill all bursting to use a loo. When the contentious garage attendant had bloody-mindedly refused them permission, they had discreetly urinated against his wall. The attendant called the police, and the three were modestly fined in the subsequent, much publicised court case. The Stones, far from being chastised, capitalised on the incident. They talked about it at every opportunity, and it became a symbolic gesture. No one told these boys what to do.

The message was rammed home with "Satisfaction," the band's biggest hit so far. It was a powerful anthem that told all the politicians, the clerics, the businessmen and the journalists that what they called a free world was no such thing. It was a world where freedom of sexuality and life style was not possible. The song mirrored perfectly the emotions of millions of aware young people around the world, and it became the Stones' theme song.

In Berlin Mick decided to fill the song's awkward instrumental break by goose-stepping around the stage. The audience was already screaming and rioting when he started his parody, and he could feel this sending them completely over the top. The enormous power he felt seemed to sway his judgment; he took the whole act way too far, throwing the crowd Nazi salutes and scowling at them. For the angry young of a repressed, divided city, the show was an explosive catalyst. They ran riot inside the hall, then fought police in the streets, looted shops and wrecked trains.

Jagger had shown no remorse over the incident, only an intoxicated pride at the re-doubled power his theatricals were bringing to the Rolling Stones.

"I get a strange feeling on stage," he told a journalist. "I feel all this energy coming from an audience. They need something from life and are trying to get it from us. I often want to smash the microphone up because I don't feel the same person on stage as I am normally.... I entice the audience, of course I do. I do it every way I can think of.... What I'm doing is a sexual thing. I dance, and all dancing is a replacement for sex. What really upsets people is that I'm a man and not a woman. I don't do anything more than a lot of girl dancers, but they're accepted because it's a man's world. What I do is very much the same as a girl's striptease dance. I take my jacket off, and sometimes I loosen my shirt, but I don't stand in front of a mirror practicing how to be sexy, you know."

In 1967 the Stones delivered what was intended as a coup de grâce to the old values with their flagrantly provocative record "Let's Spend the Night Together." Despite the furor engendered by the song's alleged immorality, they were invited to sing it before nine million viewers on the most popular variety show of the day, *Sunday Night at the London Palladium.* Though merely seeing this notorious group singing that wicked song on television was enough to cause mass apoplexy, the Stones, characteristically, decided to go one better. A much cherished, schmaltzy tradition of the Palladium show was that everyone who had appeared on it should, for the finale, stand on a revolving stage and wave good bye to the cameras. The Stones decided that this was a piece of foolishness they were not prepared to tolerate, and despite furious attempts at persuasion by Andrew Oldham and the show's producers, they stuck to their guns. It is hard, now, to understand the fury that was unleashed by that trite protest. But to many people it was as though these arrogant street kids were striking for the first time into their homes. They were deriding a favourite programme, mocking something that was a cherished and important part of many people's lives. "They are insulting me and everyone else," howled the show's director. Then comedian Terry Scott and singer Susan Maughan made a savage attack on the Stones during a top-rated television talk show.

Jagger fanned the flames as he unrepentantly told reporters, "The only reason we did the show was because it was a good national plug — anyone who thought we were changing our image to suit a family audience was mistaken".

"It was a mediocre show, and it made us the same. It was all terrible. I'm not saying we were any better than the other acts — it was just too depressing . . . we will never do a programme there again."

This was too much for the millions of ordinary, short-haired, hard-working folk who regarded the programme as their own. But all they could do was seethe with impotent fury and complain in factories and offices that something ought to be done about that bunch. One could imagine in the Fleet Street office of the biggest circulation newspaper on earth, *News of the World*, something was being done. "People have had a gutful of those flash little bastards. It's about time they got their come-uppance," was the message a senior editorial executive was giving a couple of his reporters. "Let's see what we can rake up on them."

5

GRADUALLY MICK WAS TAKING OVER FROM BRIAN AS SPOKESMAN FOR THE
Stones. After the Palladium row it was Mick who had talked to reporters,
appeared on television, got his photograph in the papers. No one seemed
particularly interested in Brian's opinion anymore. Piqued, he had ordered the Stones' publicist to arrange interviews for him so he could
postulate about the way the Stones, his Stones, were changing society.
Unbeknown to Brian all the interviewers were carefully selected in advance and warned of a whole list of taboo subjects — like drugs and illegitimate children — so the resulting articles were, not surprisingly, highly
favourable. One music paper writer had described him as, "the most intelligent Stone." And in *New Musical Express* he was allowed to talk lucidly
of the barriers *his* band was demolishing:

> "Our generation is growing up with us and they believe
> in the same things we do. Our real followers have moved with
> us — some of those we like most are the hippies in New York,
> but nearly all of them think like us and are questioning some of
> the basic immoralities which are tolerated in present day
> society — the war in Vietnam, persecution of homosexuals,
> illegality of abortion, drug-taking.
>
> All these things are immoral. We are making our own
> statement — others are making more intellectual ones. Our
> friends are questioning the wisdom of an almost blind accept-
> ance of religion compared with total disregard for reports
> related to things like unidentified flying objects which seem
> more real to me. Conversely I don't underestimate the power
> or influence of those, unlike me, who do believe in God. We
> believe there can be no evolution without revolution. I realise

there are other inequalities — the ratio between affluence and reward for work done is all wrong. I know I earn too much but I'm still young and there's something spiteful inside me which makes me want to hold on to what I've got. I believe we are moving on to a new age in ideas and events."

Reading his words in print, feeling that he was being taken seriously, that it was he — not Jagger — who was the architect of the changes society was going through gave Brian's self-esteem a desperately needed boost. He grew more confident, started to feel dominant and important again.

Brian craved reassurance more than drugs, more than music, more than anything. Anita had again left him for Keith, and this time it looked as though there was to be no reconciliation. Anita hadn't wanted to go with Keith; his ears stuck out, his top lip protruded and he had none of Brian's charisma or beauty. But when Brian threw her love back in her face, wounded her with his fists and his savage words, Keith had always been there. He loved her, he had talked to her about Brian and he had always been strong, always dependable. When too many bad trips had led to Brian being secretly admitted to a nursing home in Switzerland, she had wept as Brian screamed at her to "get the fuck out of it."

Keith had been there, and they went away together to smoke grass, talk, make love, and life had been normal again, the way it was before the bile had started to bubble out of Brian's soul.

She went back to Brian when he regained his sanity. But though they never spoke of it, he knew she had been with Keith. He tried to blot out the realisation with more drugs, but they served only to make him more vicious toward her, forcing Anita ever closer to Keith.

Marianne, too, for reasons of her own, helped lure her away. Marianne and Mick were going to stay with friends at a castle in Ireland. She covertly asked Anita, then Keith, to come with them carefully excluding Brian.

Later they all decided to go to Morocco together; Brian, Keith, Mick, Anita, Marianne and half-a-dozen other friends took a crazy, acid-dropping holiday together. Brian, as always, overdid it and became so paralytically stoned that he was unable to get out of bed for a week. Anita left him then, told him they were through, said she was flying back to England with Keith. Brian mumbled that he was relieved to get rid of her, but deep inside it was as though his heart had been torn out. Everyone he loved — Tara, Anita, Keith — had deserted him. He was quite alone now, and perhaps he was, as they all said, no good to anyone, not even himself.

The newspapers were still his allies. They treated his words as gospel. He was amicable, therefore, when a couple of friendly, if slightly straight, young men introduced themselves to him as journalists as he sat, sipping vodka and swallowing bennies to keep himself awake, in the gloom of Blases Club, in Kensington, late one evening. They chatted about mysticism, and then the conversation turned to the speed Brian was taking and the growing use of drugs in the pop world.

Outside the club the two young men grinned at one another meaningfully. "That Mick Jagger" said one — mistakenly referring to Brian — "has just talked his way into a whole lot of trouble."

The *News of the World* published extracts from the interview on February 5 as the first part of a series luridly headed 'POP STARS AND DRUGS'

Beneath a photograph of Jagger was a caption which said that he had been a visitor to a house in Roehampton that had been leased by the Moody Blues and used for wild drug paries and that Jagger had admitted to investigators that he had 'sampled LSD.' The article added:

> "He told us: "I don't go much on it (LSD) now the cats (fans) have taken it up. It'll just get a dirty name. I remember the first time I took it. It was on our tour with two American rock 'n' roll stars."
>
> During the time we were at the Blases Club, in Kensington, London, Jagger took about six benzedrine tablets. "I just wouldn't keep awake in places like this if I didn't have them," he said.... Later at Blases, Jagger showed a companion and two girls a small piece of hash (marijuana) and invited them to his flat for "a smoke."

Jagger was stunned and infuriated by the article. He had always been scrupulously careful not to take so much as an indigestion tablet publicly, and he was well aware of the dangers of talking about drugs with people he didn't know. He was certain the entire story was no more than a malicious piece of fiction. The same evening he was appearing on the hugely popular Eamonn Andrews talk show, and he took the opportunity to announce that he would be suing the *News of the World* for substantial libel damages.

The pressure on Mick became intense after that, and he became ability to control individuals, audiences, even societies — and he knew Satan wasn't to thank for his strength in that direction.

"Of course, I do occasionally arouse primaeval instincts," Mick told a reporter. "But I mean, most men can do that. They can't do it to so many. I just happen to be able to do it to several thousand people. It's fun to do that. It's really just a game, isn't it? I mean these girls do it to themselves. They're all charged up. It's a dialogue of energy. They give you a lot of energy and take a lot away. Maybe they want something from life, from me. Maybe they think I can give it to them. I don't know.

"I get a strange feeling on stage. I feel all the energy coming from the audience. I feel quite violent sometimes. I quite often want to smash up the microphone or something. I don't feel the same person on stage as I am normally."

Mick's fascination with power, coupled with his conventional middle class upbringing, led him inevitably to conventional politics, and for many years, he harboured a deep and secret ambition to become a Member of Parliament for the Labour Party.

He was actively encouraged by Tom Driberg, the MP for Barking, in Essex, who later became Lord Bradwell. Like many homosexuals, Driberg found Jagger attractive, but he also recognised in him the charisma necessary for success in politics. After all, argued Driberg, if show-biz personalities like Ronald Reagan could achieve prominence in American Government, how much more so could an educated, thoughtful man like Jagger.

The two were introduced by the American poet Allen Ginsberg, who was a mutual friend. "He's a terrific guy, really hip." Ginsberg had said.

"Yeah, I've heard of him," said Mick. "He's the guy who complained in the Commons about the way Robert and I were handcuffed together at Chichester. And he's keen on legalisation of dope, too, isn't he?"

They met first at Mick's flat in Marylebone Road and hit it off immediately. Mick didn't guess for a moment that Driberg was gay. Later, when Jagger did find out, it only increased his liking for the MP. Many of Mick's closest friends are men who, he knows, long to go to bed with him. The feminine side of his complex personality seems to delight in the flattery and admiration they heap flirtatiously upon him. Yet paradoxically, he is extremely masculine, and any advances are rebuffed.

When Mick and Marianne moved to their big house in Cheyne

"Are you the owner and occupier of these premises?" the man, Chief Inspector Gordon Dineley, asked.

Before Keith could understand what the officer was talking about, a search warrant issued under the Dangerous Drugs Act of 1965 was thrust into his hands, and he was ordered to read it.

"How do you mean? What do you want?" asked Keith, still too dazed to understand what was happening.

"That, sir, is a search warrant," explained the policeman.

Realisation began to dawn on Keith, and he ambled his way back into the living room, followed by the squad of police who had been surrounding the house in case anyone attempted to leap from the windows.

"Look, there's a lot of little ladies and gentlemen outside," he shouted over the hi-fi. "They're coming in. They have this funny piece of paper... all sorts of legal rubbish...."

As all the policemen with their short hair and huge boots barged into the room, everyone started to giggle. This was just too silly... it couldn't be real.

Marianne grinned at Michael Cooper, then opened the rug a little so that the policeman would realise she was naked beneath it. She smiled seductively at one of the younger constables and was delighted when he flushed crimson.

"It's like a trip," she thought, "play it trippy . . . ."

Someone put a Dylan album on the stereo, and he screamed his anti-authoritarian pro-dope songs through the huge speakers. The irony of being searched to a musical backdrop of Dylan suddenly struck Keith as hysterically funny, and he collapsed, giggling, on one of his huge Oriental floor cushions.

A policewoman told Marianne she was to be searched, and she called to Mick in her haughtiest accent, "Mick, Mick, help — this dykey woman wants to search me. What does this bloody lesbian want from me? Where is she going to search me? I have no clothes on . . . ."

With that she flashed the rug open to show her breasts, the soft blonde shadow of her pubic hair to everyone in the room. Every head turned, with the country policemen peering over one another's shoulders for a closer look. As the policewoman hustled her upstairs, Marianne turned mischievously and yelled, "Help! I'm going to be raped by this lady copper."

Robert Fraser watched bemused as the clumsy policemen started to slip joss sticks and pipes into little polythene bags. Then a senior officer came across to his chair and, apologetically, asked him if he would object to being searched. Robert, unthinkingly, told the policeman to go right ahead. In his pockets there were two boxes of pills; one containing eight amphetamine tablets, and one containing six tiny pharmaceutical heroin jacks, no bigger than saccharin tablets, for Robert had recently moved on to snorting heroin for his kicks.

"What are these?" the officer asked him.

Robert — speaking as though to a child — said the tablets were medicine for his diabetes. "I do have a prescription," he added.

The policeman apologized and handed the tablets back. But then he thought better of his action and told Robert, "I'm very sorry, sir, but I will have to send a sample of your medicine away for tests. It is, of course, purely a formality, sir."

So he took a few of Robert's pills and slipped them into an envelope. In a bedroom another policeman had found a green jacket which he brought out into the drawing room. "Who does this belong to?", he asked distastefully. Jagger said it was his.

Mick watched, horrified, as the officer pulled a small chunk of hash from a pocket. But he put it back again, wiping his fingers fastidiously. "Christ," thought Mick, "the moron thinks it's a piece of dirt."

Next, he pulled out a small phial containing four tablets. "Are these yours?", he asked.

"Sure," agreed Mick, "they were given to me by my doctor — Dr. Firth — to stay awake and work."

Then the police moved to search King. His small attaché case was lying beside him, and they asked him if it was his.

"Yes, it is," he replied. And everyone knew that the case was crammed full with White Lightning, cocaine, cannabis and just about every other drug known to mankind.

The constable who casually opened the case appeared unexcited by the small packages, wrapped in aluminum foil, he found inside.

"That's film," said King. "I'm a filmmaker, and that's un-processed film. Please don't open it; you'll expose it, and my movie will be lost. A year's work."

"Certainly, sir," he replied, and moved on to search King's jacket, where he found, with barely concealed glee, a small tin containing a few scraps of cannabis.

The police appeared satisfied by their haul; drugs they had come for and drugs they had found. Keith was relieved, too. They had missed so much, and not one scrap of dope had been found that could be linked with him or Mick; they had miraculously escaped.

Keith politely showed his uniformed visitors out, keen that it should not occur to them to take a closer look around. But the last officer to leave looked disdainfully at Keith and warned him, "Should laboratory tests prove that dangerous drugs have been used on these premises, and not related to any individual, you will be held responsible."

"I see," said Keith. "They pin it all on me."

Robert had invited me to go to the Redlands party with him, but by then the thought of taking any kind of hallucinogenic drug frightened me. Besides, barring Marianne, there were to be no women at the house, so that seemed another good reason for staying at home. Robert had asked me, however, if I could get hold of a few jacks of heroin for him on the Thursday before, so I had contacted a dealer in Soho. The tablets cost only 25p each, and I had realised, as Robert had greedily snatched them from me, that he was becoming desperate to sniff more and more of them up his nose. In the end Robert had taken his elegant South

American man-servant, Guatamalan George, to the party with him and I had spent a quiet weekend at home with my wife and our baby son, Jason.

It was after midnight on Sunday when I was awakened by the persistent ring of the telephone. Robert was at the other end, and he sounded distraught.

"We got raided, Tony," he said. "And what do you think they found on me?"

My heart sank because in those days possession of heroin meant a virtually certain sentence of imprisonment.

"Come over to the flat, Tony," he pleaded. "I've got to talk to you."

He told me the whole story when I arrived. At the end I asked him, "What else did they find down there?"

"I couldn't care less about them," he said bitterly. "It's their bloody fault that I'm in all this trouble. I'd never have been searched if they hadn't been so stupid."

In those days I had friends who claimed to be able to buy off any kind of prosecution. Certainly I knew a couple of policemen myself who were not averse to accepting the occasional discreet present in return for turning a blind eye to some of my more nefarious activities.

I talked to one of my friends about Robert's situation and he told me it was not impossible that the confiscated heroin could be discreetly swapped for harmless glucose, if the price was right.

When I told Robert the good news he wept with relief, "Christ Tony, if you pull this off I'll never, ever be able to repay you," he told me.

I was told by my friends that the cost of perverting the course of justice for Robert, Keith and Mick would be £6,000.

Within hours Robert had made a few 'phone calls and a messenger arrived at his house with a black, leather attaché case. Robert opened the case to show me the money neatly packed away inside.

I could hardly believe my eyes. Though I was used to seeing large sums of money paid over in casinos this was, at that time, sufficient to buy a reasonable family house. However, it would be a small price to pay if the action against Robert and the Stones really could be bought off.

I handed the money over in a pub in Kilburn late on Tuesday night, and it looked as though everything was working out. Not one word of the raid had appeared in any newspaper; no summonses had been issued; it was as though the raid had never happened.

Marianne talked to me about it, though, when we met at Robert's, and she seemed upset that Jagger had taken responsibility for her uppers.

"I bought them at the airport when we were in Italy," she told me. "But Mick insisted on saying they were his when the cops took them away. That took a lot of courage, Tony. He's a lot more chivalrous than most people think."

I basked for a few days in Robert's gratitude until the following Sunday, when he interrupted my revelry with an angry phone call.

"The *News of the World* has got every single detail," he exploded. "They've got my name and the time the raid happened and who was there. It's almost as though they had a reporter sitting in the middle of the room taking notes. They even say that a 'quantity of substances' were taken away."

It seemed extraordinary that the newspaper had first had Mick's libel action against them wrecked by the raid and had then managed to hide their sensational, exclusive information about it from the rest of Fleet Street for a whole week. I worried then because no one was going to risk taking a bribe when the operation was so obviously being carried out hand in hand with a newspaper.

But still, there were no charges, and it began to look as though things could yet be okay.

We all believed by then we knew who had set the whole thing up — it was this guy King or whatever he called himself. Mick's lawyers had discovered that he had vanished after being allowed to slip out of the country. It was King who had let it be known that he had this amazing, legal White Lightning. He who had suggested that they should go to the country and spend a weekend trying it out. It was King who had hospitably turned them all on with the drug as he handed them their morning tea. King seemed to be the man behind the whole business. He was a very sinister character.

We talked then about where he had come from, and we agreed that we had heard vaguely of him as a pusher of acid in California.

"It's obvious, isn't it?", said Keith. "The *News of the World* hired him to set us up, then tipped off the police so they could duck out of Mick's libel action. They knew Mick had an air tight case against them, and the damages would probably have cost them about three quarters of a million pounds. This way there's no chance of Mick going ahead with his case."

Michael Cooper didn't agree. "The guy's much more than an ordinary pusher," he said. "He had a whole collection of different passports in different names and with different nationalities on them. I saw them once when I was looking through his bag for some dope at Redlands."

"And he talked to me about guns and weapons in the same sort of way that most guys talk about chicks. I know it sounds fantastic, but I reckon he was something much more than a creep hired by the *News of the World*. He was like some kind of James Bond character, and someone, someone right at the top, put him in because the Stones are becoming too powerful. They really are worried that you could spark off fighting in the streets if you tried, and now they are going to try to break you. I'm sure the newspaper was in on it somewhere, but it was this guy using them — not the other way around."

"Crap," said Keith succinctly.

But a month later — six weeks after the raid at Redlands — West Sussex police formally announced that Mick was being charged with unauthorized possession of four tablets containing amphetamine sulphate; Keith with allowing his house to be used for smoking cannabis resin and Robert with unauthorized possession of heroin and eight capsules containing methyl amphetamine hydrochloride.

Keith began to wonder if the establishment really was out to smash the Stones.

6

ANITA WAS WITH BRIAN AGAIN. HE HAD COLLAPSED IN BARCELONA, WHERE HE had over-dosed on drink and barbiturates, and this time there had been no one there to look after him, to see that he swallowed a few morsels of food and slept for a few hours each night. By the time he returned to London he was pale and drawn and begging her to come back. They were drawn closer, too, because a film they had worked on together, *A Degree of Murder*, had been chosen as Germany's entry for the Cannes Film Festival. Anita starred in it, and Brian had written and arranged the music plus playing a range of instruments which included sitar, organ, dulcimer, autoharp and harmonica.

With Anita he started to regain his strength and self respect. He still used drugs, but he had stopped dropping acid, stopped trying to obliterate his mind. He was playing well again, too, and looking forward to going on the road for the band's first European tour in more than a year.

Mick and Keith had been reassured by their lawyers; there was an air tight defence for both of them. Mick's doctor confirmed that he had okayed the use of the four uppers. We knew the police would never be able to make the cannabis charge against Keith stick. Robert was probably going to prison because the case hadn't been fixed.

The publicity engendered by the raid had been worldwide, and all the Stones — especially Brian — were taken aback by the hostility they encountered on the European tour because of it.

"It's really getting to him," Anita told me as we talked in Italian a few days after the tour had started.

"Brian 'phoned and told me the customs men even make them take off their clothes as they enter each country. They start off by going through every piece of luggage; then they take all five of them into little rooms and strip search them. They even have to take their underpants off. It's sick."

All Europe was in turmoil. The young took to the barricades in Paris, and around the world, from Warsaw to Washington, the youth were shaking up complacent, repressive, reactionary governments. The Stones hadn't started it; they reflected the anger and frustration of a generation that was educated, critical and brave. The young were demolishing all the obstructions placed in their way by the society that said women couldn't have abortions and consenting adults should go to prison.

And somehow, the Stones' anti-establishment stance had made them the focal point of the revolution. So, at almost every date on that European tour, there were savage, violent clashes between audience and authorities.

At Hälsingborg, in Sweden, exuberant fans were bitten by police dogs and struck with police truncheons during a Stones show. In the ensuing riot, bottles, chairs and fireworks were hurled around the theatre.

In Vienna, police prepared for trouble by installing corrugated iron cells in the city hall on the day the Stones were to play. The audience reacted by throwing smoke bombs and brawling until 154 fans had been battered and incarcerated.

Everywhere the Stones went they were searched, raided and intimidated with a zeal that prompted Keith to comment, "They seem to think we're working for Che Guevara."

Jagger called a press conference to reveal to reporters in Paris that he was on the Customs' International Red List.

"Of course there is a list," he said. "And of course they are after me. In the last two months there have been four occasions when, on landing in London, I have been taken to a private room and searched — obviously for drugs."

The tour reached its climax when the Stones arrived in Warsaw to give their first show behind the Iron Curtain. More than nine thousand angry kids were locked outside the Palace of Culture, where the Stones were appearing, because all the best tickets had gone to the children of high-up Communist Party members. The Stones were so angry that, after a few numbers, they furiously stopped the show. Most of the prosperous people in the front rows fled beneath a tirade from Keith, ordinary kids rushed forward and the show resumed. Outside police fired tear gas grenades and used water cannons and truncheons against two thousand more fans who were trying to smash their way into the hall.

58

"People talk about the riots that happen when we play," Jagger said in an interview. "Of course, there is a certain violent element, and to a certain extent, the kids are conforming to what is expected of them. But there is more to it than that.... I've seen this wild behaviour in so many countries and the pattern is always the same. Because it is the same symptom. Frustration. And these are kids from all kinds of environments ... you can't solve the problem by locking them up... that isn't the answer — you have to find out why it is that the kids are discontented.

The Stones, circa 1967. Jagger had just discovered cocaine.

They are not all morons just spoiling for a fight with the police."

He was eager, too, to knock the police. "Everyone knows that Britain is short of police," he said. "But they send big groups of them raiding clubs and even barns in Lincolnshire. It's madness. The situation is not only becoming ridiculous but frightening. You sit at home, and you think you are safe because you are not in South Africa or some other police state. But when, suddenly, the police move in, it's very disturbing, and you begin to wonder just how much freedom you really have.

59

"There are only about a thousand real addicts in Britain, and nobody is going to make a fortune peddling heroin because the addicts can get it on prescription. But, if you stop this, the Mafia will move in, and we're going to have the same problems as America."

I went with Keith to Mick's flat in Marylebone Road when the Stones returned from the tour, and Mick told me, "They think they can break us, man, but no way. We'll take everything they can throw at us, and we'll still win. We're in a position to tell the kids about all the shit that's going down, and that's just what we are going to do."

He reinforced his point in an interview with the mass circulation *Daily Mirror*:

> "I see a great deal of danger in the air. Teenagers are not screaming over pop music any more, they're screaming for much deeper reasons. We're only serving as a means of giving them an outlet. Pop music is just the superficial issue .... When I'm on that stage I sense that the teenagers are trying to communicate to me, like by telepathy, a message of some urgency. Not about me or our music, but about the world and the way they live. I interpret it as their demonstration against society and its sick attitudes. Teenagers the world over are weary of being pushed around by half-witted politicians who attempt to dominate their way of thinking and set a code for their living .... This is a protest against the system. And I see a lot of trouble coming in the dawn.

Mick wasn't playing at revolution anymore. I realised then that he genuinely wanted to see society overthrown, that he really felt a revolution coming and that he saw the Stones as the vanguard of an historical, bloody period of change. For the first time, I was frightened by what seemed to lie ahead.

Robert Fraser, too, was afraid that the reactionary forces seemed to have singled him out, along with the Stones, for persecution. Only a month before the raid at Redlands he had been brought before a prudish court for 'willfully exposing or causing to be exposed to public view an indecent exhibition of paintings', at his Mayfair gallery. He was beginning to feel crushed by the law. He sensed that Keith and Mick were about to be made examples of, so he arranged for his case to be heard separately. The preliminary hearing into the cases against Mick and Keith was scheduled

60

to be heard on Wednesday, May 10, at Chichester Magistrates Court, and they invited Robert to Redlands with them and other friends so he could see what happened in court. But Robert refused. He said he'd drive down the next day for the case, but he didn't think it was a good idea to stay at Redlands again.

A couple of days before, I had been drinking with Mick, Marianne and Keith, and they seemed nervously excited about the court case. They thought they would almost certainly be discharged and that the police would be crushingly humiliated. Only Marianne had really seemed worried. "It's you they are really after," she told Mick. "And all they have got on you is my pills. Let me go into the witness box and tell them the truth. I'll go to prison for my own pills."

"Nobody's going to prison," Mick laughed. "And the pills were in my jacket anyway, so who would believe you if you said they belonged to you? Anyway, I've told the lawyers I don't want your name mentioned in court. We thrive on publicity like this, but it could kill your career stone dead."

The day of the hearing was one of those perfect early days of summer when England is at its most beautiful. I'd offered Robert a lift to Chichester in my Alfa Romeo, and we lowered the top as the little car roared and squealed along the winding, narrow roads of Surrey. We hit our first traffic jam at a roadside pub just outside Guildford, so I hung my arm over the side of the door and winked at a pretty girl walking by on the pavement. Behind her was an old man selling early editions of the evening newspaper. It took a moment for the words on his board to sink in: 'THIRD ROLLING STONE ON DRUG CHARGE'.

"Oh, my God," said Robert, and dashed across to buy a newspaper.

This time it was Brian. The cops in Chelsea had raided his flat and charged him with possession of cocaine, methedrine and cannabis. The bust seemed to us to have been carefully coordinated to prejudice any chance of Mick and Keith enjoying a fair trial.

"Those wicked, wicked bastards," he muttered.

At Chichester Mick and Keith were each freed on bail but they were seething at Brian's bust. "They know bloody well they haven't got enough evidence to do us," said Mick furiously, "so they have gone out and nicked Brian so that every member of any jury we get will think of drugs and the Stones as being synonymous. It's hard to believe that even cops can be so evil. We are actually in there in court asking for bail, and they are out there tearing Brian's flat apart. All the newspapers tomorrow will be

full of stories making it sound as though the Stones are deliberately defying the drugs laws."

Keith was solemn. "They really want to nail us," he said. "They seem to be trying to lock us all in jail where we can't pose a threat to them anymore."

I worried, though, about Brian. He had been through too much. He was tired and vulnerable. If the police hit him hard enough, they would break him. I knew that much for certain.

Professionally, too, the Stones had problems. They had always been treated by the media as direct rivals of the Beatles — both in image and in music. To some extent the treatment was justified, and the careers of both bands seemed to be evolving along parallel lines. But now, after months of music business rumours, the Beatles had delivered their masterpiece, an album titled *Sergeant Pepper's Lonely Hearts Club Band*. The album was dazzling and innovative and was hailed by critics as the greatest rock album of all time. The cover, by Michael Cooper, set a new standard for album artwork, and the idea of printing Iyrics on the sleeve was one that was to be aped by every band in the world. Musically it was of an originality and imaginative quality that rock music had never seen before.

Mick realised at once that it made all previous records of both the Beatles and the Stones seem curiously old fashioned, outmoded.

"It's psychedelic, man," he argued with Brian. "Pretty soon everything is going to be psychedelic, and if we aren't in there on our next album,

62

we will be left behind. No one is going to want to listen to rhythm and blues anymore." Brian hated the new sound, and he fought bitterly — and vainly — for the Stones to stay true to their roots, to keep on chugging out the high energy rock 'n' roll that had sent audiences berserk in almost every country in the world.

"If he insists on recording that sort of crap, the Stones are dead," Brian told me bitterly.

But Jagger won, and he conceived with Keith the idea of an album called *Their Satanic Majesties Request*, a record that was to be a psycheelic satire on the Queen.

Brian's hurt was compounded because Anita had again drifted back to Keith. And the album became the focus of everything that was going wrong between Mick, Keith and Brian.

I remember driving Brian to Olympic Studios in his Rolls. He babbled on and on about the conspiracy Mick and Keith were hatching to drive him out of the band. It was obvious to me that he was becoming dangerously paranoid and that he desperately needed help and reassurance.

We arrived at the studio to find Keith there with Anita — both making it cruelly obvious that they were enjoying being together. Mick was piqued at Brian's lack of interest in psychedelics and tended to ignore his musical suggestions and any songs Brian had written. I saw them ask Brian to overdub a guitar section on a number they had already worked on, and then, once he was shut in the soundproof studio, they collapsed giggling because they hadn't even turned the recording machine on.

That period marked the low spot of Brian's life. Again he started to sink into the morass of drugs. He would shove anything that would stab or stroke his mind in through his mouth until he was unable to recognize me or even speak.

Sometimes he would arrive in the studio so zonked that he would just collapse on the floor like a wounded animal. And as his confidence went, he seemed unable to play his guitar anymore.

"I don't know what is happening to me," he told me, in a rare moment of lucidity, at the flat. "My mind won't even let me play music anymore."

There seemed to be no conscious malice in the attitudes of Keith and Mick. They were worried about their forthcoming trial, the album wasn't working out, despite the work they were putting into it, and Keith was discovering that he couldn't ignite the fluid, articulate guitar that Brian had made an essential part of every Stone's record.

"He's very tired," I tried to warn Keith once.

"We're all tired, Tony, but if he keeps on getting out of his box like this, we'll have to find a new guitar player," said Keith. "Can't you find some woman to look after him?"

I turned and walked away without speaking. I felt it was Keith's ruthless selfishness that was destroying Brian.

But Keith had other problems. He, Mick and Robert were about to go on trial at West Sussex Quarter Sessions. Significantly the case against Jagger was heard first. To me, in court, it seemed an open-and-shut case. There was no way any reasonable jury could find him guilty of illegally possessing those four silly uppers.

Mick said, as he had said when arrested, that he had bought the pills legally and openly in Italy and that he had telephoned his doctor when he returned to Britain to check that they were all right to use.

Dr. Dixon Firth confirmed that he had told Mick he should use the pills when necessary. Defence Counsel, Michael Havers, argued that the doctor's advice to Mick constituted a prescription, thus making Jagger's possession of the pills legal. It seemed that even the judge saw the logic of this argument when he peered at Dr. Firth and asked, "Had he had none, would you have prescribed something similar?" To which the doctor answered, "Yes."

I gasped with astonishment when the judge proceeded to stand all logic on its head as he directed the jury: "I have ruled in law that these remarks cannot be regarded as a prescription by a duly authorized medical practitioner, and it therefore follows that the defence open to Mr. Jagger is not available.... I therefore direct you that there is no defence to this charge."

It took only a few minutes for the jury to decide on the verdict forced upon them by the judge: "Guilty."

Jagger was shocked. It was all so unjust. It was obvious to everyone in that courtroom that he was innocent, yet somehow a technicality had led to his being found guilty of a crime which, he knew very well, carried a maximum sentence of two years' imprisonment.

The judge ordered him to be remanded in custody until after Keith's trial, which was to be held the following day. Robert had earlier pleaded guilty, so he was shoved with Mick into a grey paddy wagon by hostile policemen and driven to Lewes Prison.

Marianne went with Michael Cooper to visit Mick that night. Michael had hidden a miniature camera inside his jacket, and he planned to take a photograph of Jagger behind bars for a possible album cover. They found Mick, to their surprise, lower than they had ever seen him. "It's just so fucking unfair," he protested. "I was proved innocent, yet the judge turned around and somehow told the jury to ignore all the evidence and find me guilty anyway."

"Don't ever let them get to you, Mick," said Michael. "That's what they want." And he noticed that Jagger looked as though he had been crying.

Michael shot off a terrific roll of photographs of Mick in jail, but inevitably, it was taken away by prison officers on his way out.

The next morning the police took great delight in handcuffing Mick and Robert together for their journey to court, as though they were dangerous criminals who might make a run for freedom. Not surprisingly this ludicrously melodramatic piece of calculated humiliation angered many people and caused a minor outcry in Parliament and the columns of almost every newspaper.

Keith's trial took considerably longer than Mick's because the police were well aware that the case against him was even flimsier than that against Mick.

"It is necessary to prove," said prosecutor Malcolm Morris, "that he willfully and knowingly allowed cannabis resin to be smoked on his premises."

He added: "That there was a strong, sweet, unusual smell...will be clear from the evidence, and you may well come to the conclusion that that smell could not fail to have been noticed by Keith Richard. There was ash — resulting from smoking cannabis resin and Indian hemp — actually found on the table in front of the fireplace in the drawing room where Keith Richard and his friends were."

"The behaviour of one of the guests may suggest that she was under the influence of smoking cannabis resin in a way which Richard could not fail to notice."

Great play was made of this mystery girl's "nude-but-for-a-rug" frolicking so that the jury was firmly under the impression that some kind of wild orgy had been in progress.

In a pub during the lunch break two senior police officers gulped down bottles of beer with crime reporters and sniggered as they told lewd and grossly exaggerated stories about Marianne's behaviour at the time of the raid.

"Oh, yeah," said one, with a wink at his colleague, "she even had a Mars bar in her fanny and Mick Jagger was eating it."

"Disgusting." The reporters grinned. And a totally false and malicious rumour was begun which Marianne has never quite managed to live down.

Back in court Mr. Morris revealed that the only person found in possession of cannabis at the house was a mysterious Mr. X, who was "not before the court and indeed was not now in the country."

When his turn to speak came, Keith's Counsel, Michael Havers, immediately revealed that Mr. X was, in fact, our mysterious friend King, who was "a man virtually unknown to Keith Richard. They had met in New York the previous year, and he was there, with all the trappings and kit of someone interested in drugs. In that party was a man not known to the Rolling Stones as a group, conveniently from across the seas and loaded to the gunwales with cannabis. King was the only man on whom was found any cannabis. He has gone out of England."

That night Keith, Mick and Robert were all in Lewes Prison. The following day Keith took the stand to say that he believed the *News of the World* had arranged to have hash planted at Redlands so that Mick would be convicted of smoking the drug and would thus be forced to drop his libel action against the newspaper.

His fantastic sounding allegation was reinforced somewhat when a police witness revealed that nineteen officers had raided Redlands as the direct result of a tip-off from a newspaper.

But despite the highly suspicious circumstances of the raid, the jury took only one hour to find Keith guilty.

Judge Block turned first to Keith: "The offence of which you have been properly convicted by the jury carries with it a maximum sentence of as much as ten years, which is a view of the seriousness of this offence which is taken by Parliament." In the audience we were stunned, and several girls cried out, "Oh, no!"

He sentenced Keith to a year's imprisonment and ordered him to pay £500 towards the cost of the prosecution. Then Robert was sentenced to six months' imprisonment plus about £200 costs, and finally, he turned to Mick and said, "I sentence you to three months." He also charged Mick £100 costs.

Mick reeled as though he had been hit in the solar plexus, and I thought, for a moment, that he would faint. In the public gallery two young girls were sobbing hysterically as they clasped each other in disbelief. "He's going to prison because they hate his long hair," said one weeping.

Judge Block, meanwhile, wore the smug, bourgeois smile of a man who had done what had to be done, A few months later he was to jest at an agricultural society dinner: "We did our best, your fellow countrymen, I, and my fellow magistrates, to cut those Stones down to size, but alas, it was not to be . . . ."

Robert and Mick were driven off to Brixton Prison for their third night inside, while Keith, for some reason, was locked up in Wormwood Scrubs.

Mick and Keith reacted to prison in very different ways. Keith had always reveled in the romance of being an outlaw, and as a teenager many of his heroes had — like mine — been big-time villains. So his horror at being jailed was mollified by his curiosity about doing time, seeing what it was really like behind bars. Once inside, the guards took away his lace-collared shirt and long, elegantly tailored jacket, replacing them with a baggy uniform. The other prisoners, who all seemed much younger than Keith had expected, made it clear they were on his side as they showered tobacco and cigarette papers into his cell.

Later, when "Satisfaction" came on the radio, the prisoners started to cheer in every cell.

"My people," thought Keith, and smiled ruefully.

Jagger had no romantic illusions about prison. He knew his family would be heartbroken by the sentence, and he felt a bitter sense of grievance at the unfairness of it all. First the *News of the World* had carried that totally untrue story about him, then he was set up for a raid and now he was locked up in jail for some pills that hadn't even fucking well belonged to him in the first place. The feeling was akin to that he had had at school once when he had been caned for a misdemeanour committed by another boy.

He managed to hold everything inside until Marianne came to see him and he had to talk to her through iron bars. He wanted so badly to hold her close, to comfort and be comforted by her that everything seemed to well up inside, and he could feel the tears running down his face. Marianne was upset by what she saw as his self pity and weakness, so she firmly told him that he would just have to pull himself together and make the best of it.

"Besides," she added sincerely, "everyone I have spoken to says you will be out of here by tomorrow. You ought to use the experience; you should write a song about it or something."

Just as Marianne had predicted, the pressure on the judiciary to do something about the obviously ludicrous sentences, which had turned the Stones into martyrs overnight, became so intense that both Mick and Keith were freed by the High Court the very next day on bail of £7,000 each.

Keith and Mick giggled with relief as they settled into the back of Keith's chauffeur driven Bentley. "I've even written a song about it," boasted Mick as they drove to a pub to celebrate their new found freedom with huge scotches.

"Here's to freedom." Keith laughed. "It'll need someone a lot craftier than those wankers to get rid of us."

The young barman refused to accept money for their drinks. "I'm just glad to see you out," he said. His attitude was echoed everywhere. The bungling, blatant attempt to silence the Stones had served only to strengthen them. More than ever before, they epitomised the struggle that was going on between young and old. Even members of Parliament and lawyers were forced by the case to admit for the first time the existence of the struggle and to assess their attitude to it.

Jagger's feelings soared higher still that afternoon when someone shoved a copy of the *Evening Standard* in front of him. "Just look at this advertisement, Keith," he exclaimed. The Who announced that they were releasing two classic Rolling Stones songs, "The Last Time" and "Under My Thumb," as a single, and the ensuing advertisement read:

> "The Who consider Mick Jagger and Keith Richard have been treated as scapegoats for the drug problem and as a protest against the savage sentences imposed on them at Chichester yesterday, The Who are issuing today the first of a series of Jagger/Richard songs to keep their work before the public until they are again free to record themselves."

"What an amazing thing to do," said Keith. "This case is going to unite everyone against those stupid coppers and that bigoted old judge."

The next morning Marianne started to leaf through the *Times*, then stopped, riveted, as the headline over the paper's editorial sprang out at her. 'WHO BREAKS A BUTTERFLY ON A WHEEL?' "Mick, Mick," she called. "You've got to read this — even the *Times* is on your side now."

They read the editorial together with mounting excitement:

"Mr. Jagger has been sentenced to imprisonment for three months. He is appealing against conviction and sentence; and has been granted bail until the hearing of the appeal later in the year. In the meantime, the sentence of imprisonment is bound to be widely discussed by the public. And the circumstances are sufficiently unusual to warrant such discussion in the public interest.

Mr. Jagger was charged with being in possession of four tablets containing amphetamine sulphate and methyl amphetamine hydrochloride; these tablets had been bought, perfectly legally, in Italy, and brought back to this country. They are not a highly dangerous drug, or in proper dosage a dangerous drug at all. They are of the benzedrine type and the Italian manufacturers recommend them both as a stimulant and as a remedy for travel sickness.

In Britain it is an offence to possess these drugs without a doctor's prescription. Mr. Jagger's doctor says that he knew and had authorized their use, but he did not give a prescription for them as indeed they had already been purchased. His evidence was not challenged. This was therefore an offence of a technical character, which before this case drew the point to public attention any honest man might have been liable to commit. If after his visit to the Pope the Archbishop of Canterbury had bought proprietary airsickness pills at Rome airport, and imported the unused tablets into Britain on his return, he would have risked committing precisely the same offence. No one who has ever travelled and bought proprietary drugs abroad can be sure that he has not broken the law.

Judge Block directed the jury that the approval of a doctor was not a defence in law to the charge of possessing drugs without a prescription, and the jury convicted. Mr. Jagger was not charged with complicity in any other drug offence that occurred in the same house. They were separate cases, and no evidence was produced to suggest that he knew that Mr. Fraser had heroin tablets or that the vanishing King had cannabis resin. It is indeed no offence to be in the same building or the same company as people possessing drugs, nor could it reasonably be made an offence. The drugs which Mr. Jagger had in his possession must therefore be treated on their own, as a separate issue from the other drugs that other people may have had in their possession at the same time. It may be difficult for lay opinion to make this distinction clearly, but obviously justice cannot be done if one man is to be punished for a purely contingent association with someone else's offence.

We have, therefore, a conviction against Mr. Jagger purely on the ground that he possessed four Italian pep pills, quite legally bought but not legally imported without a prescription. Four is not a large number. This is not the quantity which a pusher of drugs would have on him, nor even the quantity one would expect in an addict. In any case Mr. Jagger's career is obviously one that does involve great personal strain and exhaustion; his doctor says that he approved the occasional use of these drugs, and it seems likely that similar drugs would have been prescribed if there was a need for them. Millions of similar drugs are prescribed in Britain every year, and for a variety of conditions.

One has to ask, therefore, how it is that this technical offence, divorced as it must be from other people's offences, was thought to deserve the penalty of imprisonment. In the courts at large it is most uncommon for imprisonment to be imposed on first offenders where the drugs are not major drugs of addiction and there is no question of drug traffic. The normal penalty is probation, and the purpose of probation is to encourage the offender to develop his career and to avoid the drug risks in the future. It is surprising therefore that Judge Block should have decided to sentence Mr. Jagger to imprisonment, and particularly surprising as Mr. Jagger's is about as mild a drug case as can ever have been brought before the Courts.

It would be wrong to speculate on the Judge's reasons, which we do not know. It is, however, possible to consider the public reaction. There are many people who take a primitive view of the matter, what one might call a pre-legal view of the matter. They consider that Mr. Jagger has "got what was coming to him." They resent the anarchic quality of the Rolling Stones' performances, dislike their songs, dislike their influence on teenagers and broadly suspect them of decadence, a word used by Miss Monica Furlong in the *Daily Mail.*

As a sociological concern this may be reasonable enough, and at an emotional level it is very understandable, but it has nothing at all to do with the case. One has to ask a different question: has Mr. Jagger received the same treatment as he would have received if he had not been a famous figure, with all the criticism and resentment his celebrity has aroused? If a promising undergraduate had come back from a summer visit to Italy with four pep pills in his pocket would it have been thought right to ruin his career by sending him to prison for three months? Would it also have been thought necessary to display him handcuffed to the public?

There are cases in which a single figure becomes the focus for public concern about some aspect of public morality. The Stephen Ward case, with its dubious evidence and questionable verdict, was one of them, and that verdict killed Stephen Ward. There are elements of the same emotions in the reactions to this case. If we are going to make any case a symbol of the conflict between the sound traditional values of Britain and the new hedonism, then we must be sure that the sound traditional values include those of tolerance and equity. It should be the particular quality of British justice to ensure that Mr. Jagger is treated exactly the same as anyone else, no better and no worse. There must remain a suspicion in this case that Mr. Jagger received a more severe sentence than would have been thought proper for any purely anonymous young man."

Jagger read the editorial, then re-read it. "Christ," he said at last, "this is fantastic. I'm going to 'phone my mother to tell her to go out and buy a copy of the *Times*."

The editorial astonished Fleet Street almost as much. Traditionally newspapers had, until then, refrained from commenting on a case until the last possible appeal had been heard. Many people believed that the *Times's* editor, William Rees-Mogg — who wrote the editorial himself — stood an excellent chance of being sent to prison for contempt of court because of the article. But the following day almost every Sunday newspaper followed the example of the *Times* to protest with words like "monstrous" and "ignorant" against the sentences.

Particularly perceptive was the *Observer*:

> "Taking drugs has become part of a culture of defiance and rejection — which is, of course, why society's attempt to deal with the drug problem also often seems like an attempt to put the rebellious children in their place. In effect, there is resentment on both sides. The parents resent and envy — consciously or not — the freedom and prosperity of their children (both of which are symbolised by the lush living and high rewards of pop stars). The children resent the attempts of the parents to maintain standards which they feel have become meaningless and hypocritical into the bargain."

But the paper Keith read most avidly was the *News of the World*. Under the front page headline, 'A MONSTROUS CHARGE', the paper admitted that it had "passed information to the police," adding defiantly, "It was our plain duty to do so."

But the newspaper vehemently denied other allegations that had been made at the trial.

> "Jagger was not followed by the *News Of The World* or its agents at any time before, during or after the 'Pop Stars And Drugs' series of articles," the newspaper protested.

We didn't believe the *News of the World* then, of course. But much,

much later we discovered that an employee of Keith's had tipped the newspaper off about the party in return for a hefty payment. King appeared to have been no more than a big-time pusher who liked to fantasize that he was James Bond.

The appeals of Mick and Keith went as smoothly as if William Rees-Mogg had been sitting in judgment. Keith's case was heard first, though he was forced to sit by himself in another room because he was suffering from chicken pox. Lord Parker, the Lord Chief Justice, ruled that much of the evidence — particularly about the naked girl — had been inadmissible. He summed up: "It would be unsafe to allow the verdict to stand and accordingly it is quashed."

Jagger was technically guilty, it was ruled, though there were only four pills and the evidence of the doctor was the strongest mitigation there could be. The appropriate sentence was not three months' jail but a conditional discharge; that meant if Mick stayed out of trouble for a full year, his conviction would be struck from the record. Announcing the revised sentence, Lord Parker warned a jubilant Mick:

"I think it right to say that when one is dealing with somebody who has greater responsibilities, as you have — because you are, whether you like it or not, an idol of a large number of young in this country — being in that position you have very grave responsibilities, and if you do come to be punished it is only natural that those responsibilities should carry a higher penalty."

"Rubbish," thought Mick. And he told a television interviewer later, "I simply ask for my private life to be left alone. My responsibility is only to myself."

That night several thousand long-haired young people gave thanks to God for the deliverance of Mick Jagger and Keith Richard at "pray-ins" in Westminster Abbey and Hyde Park. Flower power was just beginning.

73

7

KEITH RICHARD HAD DISCOVERED VERY QUICKLY THAT MONEY REALLY COULD buy just about anything. After he had been fined £15 for driving without a licence, he had had a long, huddled conversation with one of his drivers. I never found out exactly what happened, but Keith bounced up to me one day, showed me his pristine driving licence and announced: "Look Tony, I've passed my test."

"Yeah," I whispered. "You must have hypnotised the examiner or something..."

Even though he had a full licence Keith seemed to have only the most rudimentary idea of how a car should be driven.

He bought a magnificent Bentley S3 automatic soon afterwards, and he asked me to go out for drives with him to give him confidence. Though he had a tendency to hit kerbs, the car was very forgiving, with its power brakes and steering, so that, before long, Keith was able to swing it confidently into bends at 90 mph or more. Anita mocked the car, though; she said it was okay for an old man, but it wasn't as stylish as Brian's Rolls Royce. The taunt smarted. Keith was still uncertain that Anita had really left Brian for good; any kind of unfavourable comparison was unsettling.

He started talking to the Stones' drivers about cars then, and one of them had told him about an extraordinary old Mercedes that had once been a Nazi staff car. The vehicle was rusting away in a garage in East London, the driver said, and he would probably be able to snap it up for Keith for as little as £1,000. Restored, it would be worth three times as much.

Anita had always had a slightly sinister interest in the Nazis, displayed most vividly when she had bought Brian his full SS uniform, and she bubbled with excitement when Keith told her about the car. "Fantastic, fantastic," she said. "That'd be a real man's car. Can you just imagine the looks on peoples' faces when you roll up somewhere in a Nazi staff car?"

The vehicle went away to a specialist in East London for a complete rebuild of the body and mechanics. New leather upholstery was fitted, the car was resprayed khaki and the engine and gearbox had to be rebuilt. The bill came to £2,000 but the car looked stunning. It was nearly eighteen feet long, bigger than a Rolls Royce, and the back had a hood which folded down so the occupants could wave at adulatory crowds. Keith gasped with excitement when I picked it up from the garage for him and delivered it to the flat he was sharing with Mick in Chester Square, Belgravia. "It's got to be the best looking car in the world," he said. "Brian and Mick just won't believe their eyes."

Though Keith had never driven a car with a manual gearbox, he insisted that I teach him immediately how to drive the Mercedes. He picked up the basic idea in a matter of minutes, and the huge power of the car made it possible to speed around Mayfair at 70 or 80 mph. The pubs around here were the only places Keith and I could go for a drink without being hounded.

So, after a few circuits of Chester Square, we set off — like Adolf Hitler and Martin Bormann — to astonish London. I felt as though I was in a carnival procession as people stopped in their tracks to gape, first at

Keith's Bentley

the car, then at the famous Rolling Stone who was driving it. Keith occasionally waved regally when fans called out his name, and in this manner, we proceeded to a chic Bond Street coffee bar called Sands. The car lurched to a halt outside, and we marched through the sightseers to order coffee and sandwiches. "What an amazing motor. It's blowing everyone's mind," he said.

His ecstasy was, sadly, to be short-lived. Climbing into the car again, he threw it into first with a noise like a finger nail scratching a blackboard. It stalled as he let up on the clutch. After two more unsuccessful attempts he asked me to see if I could to do anything. "I thought you'd never ask," I said, sliding across to the driver's seat. I had no more luck; it was obvious the brakes had jammed.

Keith panicked. "Fucking hell, Tony, I've got grass on me, we've got to get out of here. Everyone's looking at me . . . ."

Then before I knew what had happened, he called out, "See what you can do, Tony . . . I'm off." And he had jumped into a cab.

I got a mechanic to fix the brakes, and later Keith drove me from Belgravia to my home in Kilburn. We roared north along the Edgware Road at Keith's customary 60 mph pace. He gave up changing gears, discovering that it was possible to start off in fourth, with a lot of shuddering, and that the car could then be driven in the same way as his automatic Bentley.

Unfortunately the big Mercedes wasn't as easy to stop as the Bentley, and we hurtled through two sets of red lights before the Westway Flyover and then straight into the back of a car standing peacefully at a third set of lights.

I saw the crash coming well in advance, so I managed to brace myself with my feet against the floorboards. Keith, too was unharmed. "Fucking idiot!" he yelled. "What did he stop there for?"

"Keith," I said with all the self-control I could muster, "the guy was standing still. It was entirely your fault."

"You'd better sort it out then, Tony," he said. "I can't hang around."

He hailed a taxi, and I was left standing in the middle of the busy road with a wrecked Nazi staff car and a furious Cortina driver. Somehow I managed to talk my way out of the crisis, and I arranged for the car to be towed back to the renovators in East London again. It was to be a year before the damage was fully repaired. The incident emphasized for me the difference between Keith and Brian. Brian craved people. He needed friends around all the time to reassure himself that he was needed, popular. Keith was an iron man. He used many people but needed none of them. Once I had been with Keith and Brian when we had started to talk about the death of Tara Browne. Keith had said that some people were more vulnerable, seemed fated to die young.

"You'll never make thirty, man," Keith had said to Brian with a grin.

"I know", said Brian glumly, and we had all suddenly felt embarrassed.

When Robert was jailed, many of his famous friends found that they missed their occasional flirtations with drugs at his Mayfair flat. They came to me to ask where they could find dealers in smoke and coke. I told them, and consequently I started to get high regularly with Brian and Keith or John Lennon. John, I feared, seemed to be following Brian into a world where drugs dominated everything. He called almost daily to see if I could help him get hold of dope. I promised myself that I would never become labelled as a dealer. Once he aggressively insisted I supply him with heroin. He sent his chauffeur to my flat to get it. I was so annoyed at the way he was pressuring me that I accepted the £100 proffered by the driver and gave him a jar containing two crushed aspirin.

"That," I thought, "should stop him pestering me once and for all."

The next day John was back on the 'phone asking for more.

"What about the last lot?" I said.

"Oh, I didn't think very much of that," he said. "It hardly gave me a buzz at all."

We remained good friends; John insisted I be photographed with the band for a picture book called *The Beatles Get Back*, but I spent most of my time with Brian and Keith because they were Londoners, like me, and we had a different outlook, different sense of humour to these provincials.

I was deeply concerned about the way Brian seemed to be disintegrating following his drug bust. He hated the music he was being asked to play for the new album, hated Anita for deserting him and hated Keith still more for taking her.

In July he suffered a nervous breakdown and spent two weeks in a nursing home. When he came out, he seemed to have cleared his thoughts a little. "I understand now what Mick and Keith are doing," he said. "They want to prove that they are better than I am, that they don't need me anymore. That's why they won't look at the songs I write, won't consider my ideas anymore. I've got to work on doing more things by myself or they really will finish me off."

His readjustment was to be short-lived. On October 30 at Inner London Sessions he was hugely relieved when the court accepted his plea of not guilty to charges of possessing cocaine and methedrine. Then, as his lawyers had promised the prosecution, he pleaded guilty to the far less onerous charges of possessing Indian hemp and allowing his flat to be used for smoking the drug. The judge, ignoring the lesson that should have been learned from the Jagger-Richard case, promptly jailed him for nine months, and Brian wept unashamedly as he was driven off to Wormwood Scrubs Prison in a police van.

He was freed the next day, of course, on £750 bail, but by then the damage had been done. He had proof now that his paranoia was justified: Everyone really was out to destroy him. When he appeared before the appeals court ten weeks later, three psychiatrists agreed that he was "an extremely frightened young man" ("with suicidal tendencies," one added); his jail sentence was set aside to be replaced by a fine of £1,000 and three years' probation.

He celebrated his release by pouring bottles full of pills into his mouth. He didn't care what the hell they were: acid, coke, speed — anything that would make the world go away. Then, after a day and a night of being totally strung-out, he went to a club in Covent Garden with one of his many women. The people in the club cheered him when he arrived and congratulated him on his success at the appeals court. The resident band invited him to play with them, and he did. He picked up a big double bass and started to play it fluidly, though as he played, he kicked it with his Cuban-heeled boots until it was smashed to matchwood. Brian was so far gone that he carried on playing an invisible instrument, pumping out beautiful music only he could hear.

The crowd cheered, believing that Brian knew what he was doing, that the whole thing was intentional. But then he started to weep uncontrollably, and his girl was forced to shove him into a cab and take him home. Once there he couldn't speak, and the tears were running down his face, pouring out the misery within. The girl, frightened, dialled 999 and asked for an ambulance. At St. George's Hospital he came to and told the doctor he had been under a great deal of pressure. Within an hour he was allowed to go home.

Jagger was too busy with his own life to worry about Brian. Mick's

case had made him a martyr, a hero, a spokesman for his generation, and he reveled in this new found power.

The most extraordinary event related to Mick's trial was a bizarre television confrontation between Jagger (for the young) and a team which included former Home Secretary Lord Stow Hill, the Bishop of Woolwich and William Rees-Mogg, the editor of the *Times*. Jagger was flown at great expense to a special fresh-air studio set up in the country estate of Sir John Ruggles-Brise, the Lord Lieutenant of Essex. The American Air Force even agreed to stop all flights from their nearby base so that the event should not be interrupted.

Unfortunately Mick overdid the Valiums he used to calm himself before interviews and appeared to have serious trouble staying in his seat — and his speech was so garbled that the debate was universally dismissed as a farce.

Jagger was angry with himself when he talked about the show in the Ad Lib the next night. "It was all of them against me, and I just blew it," he said.

But his humiliation seemed to have made him more rebellious than ever: "We ought to stock acid in their reservoirs, turn the whole country on," he said. He seemed serious when he told a journalist:

> "We have got them on the run now and we have to finish what we have started. The way things are run in Britain and the States is rotten and it is up to the young to change everything. The time is right now, revolution is valid. The kids are ready to burn down the high-rise blocks and those stinking factories where they are forced to sweat their lives away. I'm going to do anything, anything that has to be done, to be a part of what is about to go down."

His brave words were contradicted by his life style. Jagger lived among the politicians and leisured aristocrats in a vast, elegant Georgian mansion beside the Thames on Cheyne Walk, Chelsea. His car, a cream-coloured two-door Bentley, was exactly the type of vehicle his neighbours drove. In life style his aspirations seemed no different from those of any other pretentious, self-made young man whose roots were among the suburban middle classes.

He hired the trendy designer Christopher Gibbs, a close friend, to organize the decor, and Gibbs came up with a scheme that resembled nothing so much as an Indian bazaar, one with a very nice line in Oriental rugs and tapestries. But it was Marianne who chose the furniture and explained to Mick the wisdom of buying good antiques. She went to Mayfair and bought an antique chandelier of cut crystal for their

80

drawing room at a cost of £8,000 (then the price of a fair-sized house).

Mick had exploded when she told him how much she had spent. But secretly he had felt rather proud to be living amid such opulence; besides, he was shrewd enough to realise that seventeenth-century chandeliers made excellent investments.

Mick and Marianne seemed to be deeply in love. Many nights they would stay at home with Marianne's son, Nicholas, playing a little music, smoking a little grass. Other times they would drop into the Speakeasy or the Ad Lib. He often asked her to divorce John and marry him, but Marianne knew the time was wrong.

"I love you," she said. "But I'm not ready to go through marriage again — not after last time."

Everywhere Mick and Marianne went they were feted, photographed and treated as gurus of the new hedonism. Caroline Coon was inspired by the trial of Mick and Keith to put together Release, an organization dedicated to helping victims of the increasingly frequent London drug busts.

A horde of influential and celebrated people signed a full-page advertisement in the *Times* calling for legalization of cannabis and quoting as their ally Spinoza:

> "All laws which can be violated without doing anyone any injury are laughed at. Nay, so far are they from doing anything to control the desires and passions of man that, on the contrary, they direct and incode men's thoughts towards those very objects; for we always strive towards what is forbidden and desire the things we are not allowed to have. And men of leisure are never deficient in the ingenuity needed to enable them to outwit laws framed to regulate things which cannot be entirely forbidden . . . . He who tries to determine everything by law will foment crime rather than lessen it."

"Couldn't have put it better myself," Mick grinned when he read it.

In August, Mick and Marianne donned caftans and went with the Beatles to seek divine guidance from one of 1967's most bizarre figures, the transcendental mystic Maharishi Mahesh Yogi, at the Teachers' Training College, in Bangor, North Wales.

"Bloody old con man," Mick spluttered to Keith later. "I can understand George falling for all that peace, love and pay-the-bill crap, but not

John. I'd always thought John was a bright lad."

But though Jagger was becoming increasingly influential, the Stones were far removed from the universal popularity of the Beatles. "We Love You," the song Jagger had written in prison, was released as a single a few days before Mick and Marianne set off to see the Maharishi. Everyone had expected a jubilant public to rocket the record straight to the top of the charts; instead, it reached only to number eight. A National Opinion Poll purported to show that 56 percent of the public aged between twenty-one and thirty-four thought Jagger deserved a longer sentence than a mere three months in prison for possessing pep pills.

"All that shows," said Mick, riled, "is that there are a lot of people around who aren't very good at thinking." And he added later in an interview with the London *Evening Standard*: "In the year 2000, no one will be arrested for drugs and those sort of things. It will be laughable, just like it would be laughable if people were still hanged for stealing sheep. These things have to be changed, but it takes maniacs obsessed with individual microcosmic issues to bring it about. I could get ever so obsessed about the drugs thing, and if I really worked hard at it, I might speed up the process of reform by perhaps ten years or five years or perhaps only six months. But I don't feel that it's important enough."

The *Satanic Majesties* record wasn't going well; what with the drug busts and Brian's disintegration, it had already taken almost a year, and it was costing a fortune. At heart Mick and Keith both knew that Brian was right: This wasn't Stones music; this was pretentious crap. But they tried to hide the weakness of the music by exotic packaging; a three-dimensional camera was even imported from Japan so that Michael Cooper could take an unusual cover photograph.

They started to take their musical frustrations out on Andrew Oldham, the man who had taken them from the Crawdaddy to international superstardom in just four years. To force a confrontation, the Stones spent two consecutive days at Olympic Studios playing the blues so badly that Oldham was wasting his time in trying to produce them. He took the hint and walked out, never to return, leaving them to be exclusively managed by the New York lawyer Allen Klein. For the first time in their lives, the Stones had to produce an album without assistance.

Eventually it was finished. *Their Satanic Majesties Request* was finally released to the waiting world. The record was received as badly as Brian had predicted it would be, almost all the critics realized that it was a feeble attempt to imitate the success of *Sergeant Pepper*, and it was generally put down as a pot-pourri of half-cocked electronic doodlings.

"Thank Christ for that," said Brian. "Now perhaps we can get back to playing music again."

Jagger wasn't about to let Brian use this disaster to climb back to power. He called a press conference in the office of Les Perrin, the Stones' publicist, ostensibly to talk about the new record. But again and again he used the occasion to intimate subtly: "Brian's a junkie; he's burned out; we're going to have to tour without him."

"There's a tour coming up," he began. "There are obvious difficulties, one of them is with Brian, who can't leave the country."

Later he talked about how the Stones were going to rip Japan apart: "Except Brian, again, he can't get into Tokyo because he's a druggie . . . ."

I wondered when I read the resulting articles at Jagger's cruelty. Brian wasn't a threat to him anymore; Keith had seen to that when he stole Anita away and left Brian psychologically castrated. The guy was so weak, so dissipated now that he couldn't even play guitar, but still, Jagger seemed to see him as a threat. It could be only because he knew what no one outside the Stones' immediate circle knew — that Brian really was what Jagger pretended to be. Brian was genuinely out of his skull on drugs most of the time, while Jagger used only minuscule quantities of dope because he was worried that his appearance would be affected. Brian was into orgies, lesbians and sadomasochism, while Jagger lived his prim, prissy, bourgeois life with his baroness's daughter and worried in case someone spilled coffee on his Persian carpets. I knew then that there could be no future for Brian with the Stones. Keith felt guilty every time he saw him because he had stolen Anita and in doing so had pushed Brian over the edge; and Jagger, well, Jagger knew he could never really be the most beautiful, most glamorous Rolling Stone while Brian was around.

Suddenly Keith asked me if I would work for him full time for £150 a week. He had, he said, someone working for him he wanted to get rid of, and I could take his place.

"Thanks all the same, Keith," I said. "We are good friends, but I have my own plans . . . big plans."

8

MICK AND KEITH AND I DREAMED UP THE IDEA OF THE VESUVIO CLUB AFTER we received a huge bill at the Speakeasy. Keith was furious at the way nightclubs consistently overcharged him and Mick because they knew they wouldn't want to be seen arguing over money.

He grudgingly slammed a dozen five-pound notes on top of the bill, turned to me and said, "It's about time we had our own club, man, instead of being ripped off everywhere we go." It had long been a dream of mine to have a place of my own because I was well aware that fortunes can be made more quickly in the nightclub business than in any other; besides, I now had so many rich, famous friends that I felt the club couldn't fail to be a huge success. Within a month I'd arranged a partnership with an old friend, and we found the perfect place on Tottenham Court Road. It was a basement in an appalling condition, with paper peeling from the walls and bare wires hanging from the ceiling. We set out to modernize it ourselves.

Keith and Mick came down a couple of times to tell me how they wanted it to look and to ask me if I could score any dope for them, but I'd just give them a paint brush or scraper, and that ensured they didn't come back too often. Once I asked them to paint an old honky-tonk piano I'd found, and they sat down at it and started bashing out a new song they had dreamed up. It was an amazing, thundering great number — even though it didn't have any words at that time. Much later the tune became "Honky Tonk Woman," which is probably the best record the Stones have ever made.

It took only two months to transform that dingy cellar into one of the best clubs London has ever seen. The Vesuvio was designed to look like an exotic Arab tent. There were a dozen cubicles, each shielded by huge Moroccan tapestries. Inside each there were heaps of big cushions

84

together with a small, ornate table and a hubble-bubble opium pipe. I gave a brilliant young artist friend of Robert's all the grass he could smoke to decorate the walls with Inca sunbursts and beautiful designs that went wild under black lights. These were interspersed with blow-ups of the Stones, which Michael Cooper had taken in Morocco. There was a silver-foil airship filled with helium that floated around at body level.

While I was busy with my paintbrush, the Stones put out a hum-dinger of a single called "Jumpin' Jack Flash" that more than made up for the *Satanic Majesties* debacle. Now they flew to Los Angeles for the final mix of their follow-up album *Beggars Banquet*. They were all due to return on Mick's twenty-fifth birthday, July 26, 1968, so I 'phoned all of the Stones' friends and arranged to combine Mick's party with the opening night of the Vesuvio. Mick flew in dramatically at the last minute, with the first advance pressing of *Beggars Banquet*, the album the whole world was waiting to hear, for this was a record on which the band's entire future hung. If they can't make a good album by now, the music business was saying, they never will.

Everything was perfect for the party. The club looked beautiful with huge silver bowls of Mescaline spiked punch, plus plates full of hash cakes, which had become a craze, and little dishes with hash for people to smoke beside every hubble-bubble pipe.

My only fear was our proximity to Tottenham Court Road police station. It was only three hundred yards away, — and a couple of inquisitive cops would have been able to arrest just about every superstar in Britain if they had decided on a raid that night. I kept my fears to myself and put three huge Spanish boys on the door with instructions that no one was to be allowed through the locked entrance until I had vetted him. (At least then, I thought, I could flush most of the drugs down a toilet before the police could break the door down.) Among the first to arrive was Paul Getty II with his stunning young wife, Talitha, who wore a dress as sheer as gossamer, without a stitch underneath. The couple lived in Cheyne Walk, a few doors away from Mick, and they had become firm friends. Mick arrived, then Charlie Watts and John Lennon drifted in, and last of all came Paul McCartney.

As Paul walked in, everyone was leaping around to *Beggars Banquet*, which — with tracks like "Sympathy for the Devil" and "Street Fighting Man" — was far and away the best album of the Stones' career.

Paul discreetly handed me a record and told me, "See what you think of it, Tony. It's our new one." I stuck the record on the sound

85

system, and the slow thundering build up of "Hey, Jude" shook the club. I turned the record over, and we all heard John Lennon's nasal voice pumping out "Revolution." When it was over, I noticed that Mick looked peeved. The Beatles had upstaged him.

Eventually John Lennon staggered across to me, looking as though his eyes were going to pop out of his head, and asked me if I could arrange a taxi to take him and Yoko home. I had warned all the people working for me not to drink the punch or eat the cakes, but they had been so excited by the sight of all these rock stars that they had started munching away at the extremely potent hash cakes and knocking back glasses of the punch. I asked the doorman, who looked the least mind-blown, to dash out for a cab. He just said, "Yes," and wandered off into the night. Half-an-hour later he hadn't returned, and John came back to ask me where his taxi was. I explained that my man had gone half-an-hour before to find one, and John muttered, "What kind of doorman takes half-an-hour to find a taxi in Tottenham Court Road ?"

I dashed up to the reception area to send another of my boys out for a cab. Twenty minutes later he hadn't come back either. I ran back up and sent the only man I had left, warning him, "Look, those other two idiots have vanished and John is freaking out. For Christ's sake, get a cab within five minutes — it can't be that difficult."

Of course, he didn't come back either, and John and Yoko were becoming angry by then. "What do you mean they've all vanished?" John was yelling. "What kind of a club is this?" I was getting scared by then; were the cops hauling everyone off to Scotland Yard as soon as they walked out of the door? Later I discovered that they all had gone completely gaga when the fresh air combined with the mescaline and hash they had taken. One of the fellows didn't come down for twelve hours, and then he had found himself lying in the middle of a rose bed in St. James's Park.

Mick asked why John was shouting. When he heard the disappearing waiter saga, he laughed and handed me the keys to his car — a beautiful midnight blue, black windowed Aston Martin DB6. I went to my cousin, who was a guest at the party, and asked him to drive John and Yoko home in the car. An ardent Beatles fan, he leapt at the opportunity. John and Yoko got in the back of the car while he climbed into the driving seat. Then his problems really began. The 160 mph Aston Martin was such a sophisticated, advanced piece of machinery that my cousin couldn't even locate the ignition keyhole, much less the interior light switch. To make matters worse, the car was parked on a yellow line, which was against the law.

86

Suddenly there was a tap on the window, and a huge policeman peered in. John was doing a lot of cocaine at that time, and he was convinced he was about to be busted, so he discreetly dropped a little bottle of the stuff on the floor of the car. All three of them were totally stoned anyway, so they just stared at the policeman in terror.

The cop smiled helpfully and said, "Good evening, sir, good evening, madam. What seems to be the trouble, young man ?"

My cousin spluttered out his story of being unable to start the Aston because he was borrowing it from a friend and hadn't driven it before. The policeman climbed in, started the car and wished them all a pleasant drive home. John sighed with relief, then started searching for his cocaine, but he couldn't find it anywhere. He became agitated. "This is Mick Jagger's car, and the police are liable to search it at any time," he said. "I can't just leave my coke rolling around the floor of his car; it isn't fair."

As John poked around on the carpet, my cousin was experimenting with the power of the Aston, and at one point he accelerated so hard that John lost his balance and fell off his seat. By then they had travelled to the Warren Street tube station — less than a quarter of a mile from the club. "Stop the car!" shouted John. "We're getting out. I'll walk home if I have to. You find the coke and keep it."

My cousin came back a few minutes later, and I asked him where John had wanted to go. When he told me he'd only gone to Warren Street, I felt really upset.

"You mean," I said, "that he made me send out three people for cabs, then he borrowed Mick's Aston Martin, to travel less than a quarter of a mile?"

"No, no," said my cousin. "He wanted to go further, but he lost his nerve." My cousin never was a very good driver.

Everyone at the party laughed hysterically when they heard the full story.

By one in the morning the entire staff seemed to have vanished. The barman had gone; there was no cloakroom girl and no one left on the door. When Paul McCartney wished me good night, I apologised and explained that he and Linda would have to find their own coats.

"Righto, Tone," he said, "don't worry . . . great party."

As Paul walked into the darkened cloakroom, his feet kicked against someone lying on the floor. His first thought was that a couple of the less inhibited guests were making love on the thickly carpeted floor, but then he looked down into the gloom and realized that there appeared to be only one body — not two. And that one body seemed ominously still. "Tony, come here quick," he called nervously, "I think you've got bad trouble."

I fumbled for the light switch and walked around behind the black Formica counter of the cloakroom. There, lying flat on her back, was my cloakroom girl with her blonde head pillowed on somebody's £1,000 wolf-skin coat, with a beatific smile playing across her face.

"Looks like another hash cake casualty," Paul laughed.

Later there were just four of us left: Mick, Marianne, Robert and I. We sat cross-legged on the floor cushions inside one of the tents around the low Oriental table. Robert slipped a small polythene bag from the pocket of his velvet jacket. "Pure opium, all the way from Thailand," he whispered.

The thick oil was placed into the pipe on the table, and with some difficulty, we set light to it. "You first," Robert said to Mick, "it's your birthday."

Mick drew deeply, then lay back on the cushions with a contented sigh. The pipe was passed around the table until it was in front of me. I had never tried opium before, so I had little idea what to expect. As I sucked deeply, I could feel the acrid fumes burning their way into my lungs. I began to splutter and cough, but then my head seemed to become as light as a helium-filled balloon; I could see Robert grinning at me from the other side of the table, and then I could feel myself floating, like a feather, backwards on the cushions.

A moment later I was conscious again. Marianne's beautiful face was smiling down at me. "Come with me, Tony," she whispered, and grabbed my hand. Robert and Mick were so dazed that they didn't even look in our direction as we walked together across the darkened club hand in hand. "Something marvellous has happened," she said when we reached the other side of the room. "I think I'm going to have Mick's baby."

"Christ," I said, genuinely pleased, "that's fantastic. But what does Mick say? Isn't he afraid of being tied down?"

"Not at all," she replied. "But he keeps on and on at me to divorce John and marry him. He can't seem to understand that I never want to marry anyone. I have learned my lesson; people who are really in love don't need to be handcuffed together by legal contracts. Oh, Tony, I've never been so happy in my life. I wish the world could stop now."

When I crawled into bed at my flat in Maida Vale the room swayed gently from side to side, and it was like being in a yacht anchored in some balmy bay. "It's really all going to work out," I thought euphorically. "I'm going to be really rich, really independent at last."

The 'phone shrilled me into reluctant consciousness shortly before ten the next morning. I picked up the receiver to hear the New York voice of Linda Eastman, the blonde who was now living with Paul McCartney. "Where's the acetate of Paul's record? We want it right away. We must have it now..." she was saying, as I tried to clear my head and work out what she was babbling about.

"Okay," I said. "Your place in St. John's Wood is just around the corner from here, so I was going to bring it to you this afternoon."

"Oh, no, you don't, we want it right now," she said, sounding more and more hostile.

Hell, I thought, she's talking as though she's Paul's old lady or something. "Let me speak to Paul then," I said wearily.

"What the hell's the matter with her?" I asked Paul. "I told her I'd bring the record. As far as I'm concerned, you lent me the acetate and I don't need her shrieking at me first thing in the morning as though I'm going to run off and steal it."

Paul, as always, was the perfect diplomat. "Don't worry, Tony," he said. "Linda just takes a keen interest in my affairs. Do me a favour, and bring the record over to keep her happy."

I drove to their big psychedelic painted house on Cavendish Avenue that afternoon. As always there were a dozen girls hanging around in the street outside for the moment when they would be able to see the most beautiful Beatle of all.

I rang the bell beside the high green painted wooden gates, then shouted out who I was over the crackling answerphone. The gates opened with a buzz, and I slipped inside.

"Thanks, Tony," said Paul. "I'm sorry about the fuss, but Linda had the idea you'd make pirate copies of the record — silly, isn't it? Still, she's a very special kind of lady, and she's the only person I know who really genuinely cares about what happens to me."

9

BRIAN LAY IN HIS CANDY-PINK VELVET SUIT IN A CORNER OF OLYMPIC Studios, curled in a ball, like a sleeping dog. His big red guitar was on top of him. In another room, through a glass partition, I could see Mick and Keith laughing and joking with guitarists Dave Mason and Eric Clapton, who had dropped by to lend a hand with the recording of this album: *Beggars Banquet*. "Come on, Brian," I said, shaking him. "Time to go home."

"Clear off, Tony," he snarled. "Piss off and leave me alone." I could see that his face was wet with tears, as though he had been crying for a very long time.

He had gone into this new album full of hope. The *Satanic Majesties* fiasco had proved that Brian still knew what he was talking about musically. Jagger had promised to make this a rock album, and yes, of course, they would record one of Brian's songs this time. They were even going to put down one of Bill Wyman's numbers.

"But they just don't want to know, man," he told us when I had dragged him to the Rolls. "Jagger-Richard, Jagger-Richard that's all they want to know about. They want all the glory, all the fame and all the publishing royalties from writing songs for themselves. I know that I can write singles that would go straight to number one in the charts, but they won't even listen to them. Sometimes they just shut me into that little booth on my own, and sometimes they don't even bother to tell me they are having a recording session. It's not me they want anymore; it's all Dave Mason this and Eric Clapton that.... They treat me as though I'm a leper. I had a fight with Mick about it the other night, and you know what he said? He said I was a pain in the arse. He said I was a whiney pain in the arse, and I wasn't even a good enough musician to be in the Stones. Christ, man, it's my fucking band. The whole thing was my idea, they'd never have got there without me and now they have taken it all away from me . . . ."

I knew that Mick and Keith hadn't consciously set out to destroy Brian. It was just that they were so, so busy. They knew that everything hung on the success of this album, and Brian was being a self-indulgent pain. While Mick and Keith had virtually given up dope because they knew they had to be really sharp, to give their all for this one, Brian had carried on stuffing himself so full of Mandrax and brandy that he was totally unreliable. He seemed to turn up either late or so stoned that he was no use to anyone. Why the hell couldn't the guy see sense? All he had to do was work for a few months, and then he would be free to blow his mind later.

Brian was back again with his old girlfriend Linda. Although he was fond of her, he still yearned to be with Anita. To compound his problems, a detective had taken to putting the pressure on him. Three times the same officer visited Brian, and he always seemed to be able to find him, no matter how often Brian moved.

Each time Brian had to pay £1,000 to avoid prosecution. "The third time I didn't even have any dope in the place, so he just pulled some out of his pocket and told me he'd plant it on me if I didn't pay over the money," said Brian.

I believed him implicitly. I knew that the officer Brian was talking about had offered to give cannabis to people employed by the Stones in return for information about their whereabouts and their drug habits.

Brian had started to take his problems out on Linda, as he had on Anita, with his fists. It was obvious that Linda loved him deeply. She had had his child, had stuck with him through everything, but in March she, too, cracked and had to be rushed to the hospital from a flat in Chesham Place, Belgravia, where they were attempting to hide from police persecution. The shock had seemed to have a beneficial effect on Brian; for a few weeks he attempted to pull himself together.

John Lennon had helped him. He had huge respect for Brian as a musician and had already persuaded him to play saxophone on two Beatles records: "Baby You're a Rich Man" and "You Know My Name." One night, as we sat in the Ad Lib, John squinted at Brian in his myopic way and roared, "Cut out the crap. It's you who've pushed yourself in to the state you're in, not Jagger. You've got to be tough, very tough, to survive in this business, and if you don't look after yourself, Brian, don't expect anyone else to. If the Stones are blowing you out, fuck 'em, you're still the big star, you're a good looking boy and the girls really dig you. Get out and start a new band and prove you're a man, not a little girl."

"I'm going to do it, Tony," he had said later. "Jonn is right."

But before he could do anything, the police decided to crush him with their size eleven boots once again.

Les Perrin, the Rolling Stones' genial publicist, had been tipped off: "They're going to bust Brian again, and this time they're going to make it stick."

Perrin phoned Brian immediately at his new hideout in Royal Avenue House, Kings Road. "This is real, Brian, they're coming down now, so if you've got anything at all there, get rid of it."

But Brian had told him he never had drugs in his flat anymore. There was no problem.

Within minutes the bell was ringing. "Sod 'em," thought Brian. "I'm not opening the door so those bastards can come in and squeeze another grand out of me." He sat quietly in an armchair as the ringing turned to a thunderous knocking at the door of the flat, but then they seemed to give up and go away.

But soon three policemen pried open a window and climbed into the flat. "Surely you're not trying to avoid us. One said, "Here, read this." The cop proffered an official looking piece of paper. "We've got a search warrant this time."

The police started to pull the place apart, emptying drawers on the floor, disdainfully pulling Brian's silk blouses and velvet trousers out of his wardrobe as though they were handling the garb of a transvestite. Eventually one of the cops called out from the living room, "Here it is, sir."

It was as though they really meant to make this one stick.

"Oh, no, this can't happen again, just when we're getting on our feet," he said, looking at the ball of blue wool the policeman said he had found inside a sock in a drawer.

"Is this your wool, sir?," the policeman asked. Brian had never seen it before.

"Why do you have to pick on me?" said Brian as he began to realise what was about to happen to him. "I've been working all day and night, and now this has to happen." He said the police didn't even show him what was alleged to have been found until he arrived at the police station. Then they placed a small block of cannabis resin in front of him and told him he was being charged with possession. But, in truth, all of us around Brian knew he had not used hash for months.

Madeleine

I had left my wife by then, and was living with a beautiful blonde dancer named Madeleine, with whom I was deeply in love. Brian 'phoned us the evening after his arrest and asked us if we would meet him for a drink at the Revolution club, in Mayfair. I picked him up with his latest girl friend, Suki Poitier, and noticed that yet again Brian had become involved with a woman who was the mirror image of himself. Women seemed compelled to look like Brian; it was as though they were worried that he was more beautiful than they. They'd all cut their hair into long fringes, like his, and they would wear Moroccan clothes borrowed from his wardrobe. Brian had once come out with some garbled theory to me about how he believed most beautiful women were narcissistic and they dug making love to him because it was as close as they could get to making love to themselves. The theory had sounded faintly ludicrous, but I had been unable to deny the extraordinary sway Brian held over women. He once told me he had slept with sixty in a particularly energetic month, and I'm certain he was telling the truth.

93

Brian was completely sober when we arrived at the club, though his shirt tail was out and his fly wasn't completely zipped up. The manager was honoured by the visit of an important star and seated us at the most prominent table in the house, right beside the dance floor. A bottle of champagne arrived with the compliments of the manager, and we sipped at our glasses, nervously trying to avoid the subject of the bust. Brian ordered a bottle of brandy, and after a couple of glasses, he politely excused himself and headed off in the direction of the toilet. Ten minutes later he staggered back toward us, his eyes rolling back into his skull, and crashed semi-conscious across the table, knocking glasses and bottles to the floor. I knew from my own experience that he had swallowed four or five Mandrax sleeping tablets which, though relatively mild alone, have the impact of a howitzer cannon shell if taken with booze. We tried to wake him, but he was too far gone. In the end, we were forced to carry him to the car and drive him home.

He slowed down a little after that, and by May he was rehearsing hard for a guest spot the Stones planned to play when they went to receive their awards after being voted the top British band of the year by readers of *New Musical Express*. The appearance was to be the first the Stones had made on a British stage for two years, and it was important that it should be right. The band played only a couple of numbers, but Brian was sensational, throwing his long golden hair up and down as he zipped his way perfectly through the melodies. And the fans all knew that the rumours about Brian being a druggie couldn't be true.

But still, the police raid hung over his head. They had come close to locking him in a cell for nine months last time. Perhaps this time the people at the top, the ones who had deemed that the Stones were vermin, pests who had to be destroyed, had decided that he should go into jail for a very long time. In June he was committed for trial at Inner London Sessions, but the case wasn't heard until September because of pressure on the courts.

For the whole summer Brian had been obsessed by the thought that he was going to be jailed. "They'd have just asked for the usual pay-off if they were doing it for fun," he said. "This time they really want to nail me. They want to see me locked up for a very long time."

On the stand Brian swore that he had seen neither the ball of wool nor the hashish before. "I have never had a ball of wool in my life. I don't darn socks. I don't have a girl friend who darns socks," he said.

It was revealed that Brian had lived in the flat for only eighteen days and that the previous occupant, actress Joanna Pettet, had told police she thought she might have left the wool in the flat — though she had never had anything to do with cannabis.

As the case drew to a laborious close, Mick and Keith walked into the courtroom to sit among the teenaged girls who had been anxiously watching every second of the trial.

The judge made short work of the prosecution's case. Had Brian been guilty of possession, he could have flushed the hash down the toilet while the police were banging on the door and searching for a window they could pry open. Besides, there was no evidence whatsoever that Brian had been using the drug, and the only evidence against him was purely circumstantial. I heaved a sigh of relief; perhaps when Brian got off this one, he would be left alone. Beside me Mick and Keith grinned, gave Brian thumbs up signs and signed autographs for the fans.

The jury took forty-five minutes to haggle out their verdict, and everyone in the court gasped with disbelief as the foreman pronounced, "We find the defendant guilty." Suki Poitier started to cry. Jagger punched his right fist into his left palm and looked at the jury in black rage. "Even when the courts are just, the dummies who make up the older generation still seem to be out to destroy us," he fumed.

Judge Seaton, his face set in a stern frown, told Brian, "Mr. Jones, you have been found guilty. I am going to treat you as I would any other young man before this court. I am going to fine you according to your means, fifty pounds and one hundred guineas court costs. You will have one week to pay the money. Your probation order will not be changed. But you really must watch your step and keep clear of the stuff."

Brian, who had taken the case so seriously that he was wearing a businessman's grey suit with a white shirt and sober tie, sighed and grinned at his friends in the courtroom and marched down the steps out of the court. With Suki on his arm he climbed regally into his chauffeur driven Rolls and glided away.

"It's hard to believe that the jury could take it into their heads to totally ignore the judge," a reporter was saying to Mick. "The judge isn't stupid. He knew the whole thing stank from beginning to end. Have you got any comment to make about the case, Mick?"

"We're very happy that Brian didn't have to go to jail," he said simply.

But later he told me, "See what you can do to steer him away from dope, Tony. The cops aren't going to let him off with that one. They know he is breaking, and they are just sitting around like vultures until he is so weak that they can swoop in and peck him off. If Brian doesn't get his head together now, he's a dead man."

10

REDLANDS, KEITH'S COUNTRY HOUSE, WAS AS PERFECTLY SET AS ANY JEWEL. Around the rambling thatched main building were glistening, scrupulously manicured emerald green lawns, and around the lawns was a wide, deep moat which had been built centuries before to protect the historic house from attack by highwaymen or pirates. On a hot day the moat sparkled, reflecting the blue of the sky, and guests would often suggest a swim — until Keith told them about the rats. I hadn't believed him at first until one afternoon, as I took a quiet stroll around the grounds, I almost stepped on a family of them nesting in the bulrushes beside the water's edge. Three of the smaller ones scuttled away, but the biggest one, obviously the male, glared at me malevolently, almost challengingly, with his red eyes, and bared his yellow teeth. He was huge, almost as large as a cat, it seemed, and I remembered all the old farm legends I had heard about king rats, which had little trouble biting through the jugular vein of the toughest terrier.

"Yeah," Keith agreed when I talked to him about the rats that evening, "they are beginning to worry me, too. If we don't do something about them soon, they are going to get really out of control. They'll be in the house before long."

The next day he dug out a couple of old pump-action shotguns from the attic. At about seven in the evening it seemed as if the whole world was standing still. It was one of those summer evenings when you could hear a dog barking from five miles away and when there wasn't enough of a breeze to shake even the tops of the trees. Keith dumped a chicken carcass on the lawn, about ten feet from the moat, as bait, and we settled down behind a shrub twenty yards away with our guns. Noiselessly we had rolled a joint and were idly puffing away when Keith nudged me and pointed to a rat crawling from the rushes toward the chicken. "Wait,"

Keith at Redlands

he whispered, raising his finger, "there may be more."

Soon four of the loathsome creatures were tearing at the meat, and Keith lay slowly down in the grass to take aim. I looked along the gun-sights until I had the biggest rat of all slap-bang in the middle. "Go," said Keith, and the report of our guns shattered the still of the evening. All four rats lay, splattered with blood, on the lawn.

Keith picked them up gingerly with a piece of paper and hung them upside down on a barbed-wire fence near the gate because that is what he had seen other farmers do. Later that evening Mick came down to stay the night, and I heard him asking Keith, "What the hell are those things on the fence?"

"They're my fucking rats," said Keith. "We're having them for dinner tonight."

Later I heard the two of them plucking away at acoustic guitars and Keith was singing the chorus: "My friend shoots water rats, my friend shoots water rats...."

"There y'are, Tony, you've got your own song," said Keith.

I hadn't really wanted to work for him. I knew that I had to put my energy into the Vesuvio if I was ever to make any money. But after only a week I had grown bored with the life of a nightclub proprietor. It had always seemed glamorous to be the boss, buying people drinks, shaking hands, telling jokes. But I had rapidly realised that it wasn't quite like that. I wasn't cut out to put on a phoney charm, to pretend that people I loathed were really my best friends. So, when Keith had offered me a steady £150 a week to work for him as his personal assistant, I had asked my partner if he could run the club on his own — in return for an increased cut of the profits — and he had accepted with alacrity.

"You see, man," Keith had confided, "one of the guys who is working for me now is taking liberties. He's been nicking things, swindling me, and I'm pretty sure it was him who tipped the *News of the World* off about the party where we all got busted. But he's very strong, and he's a useful boy, so I've arranged for him to help look after Brian instead."

With friends like that, I thought, Brian had no need of enemies. But I kept my mouth shut. Keith was a good friend, we liked the same things and I knew I would enjoy working for him.

Keith kept a small rowing boat in the moat. Sometimes he would wend his way peacefully around, puffing away on a huge joint until he was so stoned that he dropped his oars into the water and had to scrabble around trying to find them. But he also became obsessed with archery for a spell,

Keith relaxing in Redlands

and since he rarely hit the targets, he needed the boat to retrieve all his lost arrows.

After one particularly arduous session he announced, "This is too much like hard work, man. What I need is a little Hovercraft so I can zip straight across the lawn, into the moat, pick up my arrows and skim out again." If anyone else had made such a suggestion, I would have laughed, but I had learned long before that in the millionaire world of rock superstars every whim rapidly becomes reality, so I agreed that a personal Hovercraft sounded like an excellent idea.

The Hovercraft arrived a month later. It was a circular silver machine, about eight feet in diameter, with a single seat in the middle. When Keith started it up, it roared like Concorde taking off, and he skimmed across the lawn screaming, "*Eeeeee*... out of the way there, clear the lawns," and Anita, I and other friends scattered like ninepins.

Though the bank which led to the moat had proved too steep to traverse, Keith remained undismayed and promptly shot off through the front gates and down the public road outside, like some kind of spaceman.

"Amazing, fan-bloody-tastic!", he said when he came back. After a couple of weeks the novelty wore off, and the Hovercraft was left to rust in the barn like a discarded toy, never to be used again. I suppose it cost him approximately £5,000.

The following weekend he 'phoned me late on Friday evening to ask me to stay at the house with him and Anita. I had a dog, a big, tough Doberman called Caesar, and I decided to take him with me. He needed fresh air and wide open spaces. I didn't arrive at Redlands until three in the morning, but since Keith rarely went to bed before four o'clock, I wasn't worried. As soon as we arrived, Caesar leaped over me to escape from the Alfa Romeo and gambol across the lawn as though he were a puppy and all the world was new again.

Keith heard my car roaring up the driveway, and he staggered out through the back door of the house with his dopey old Labrador, Yorkie. Before either of us knew what was happening, Caesar had flown out of the darkness like a wolf, and he was tearing, roaring and biting at Keith's bewildered animal. Yorkie put up a brave counter-attack, and Keith and I needed all our strength to haul them apart.

I locked the disgraced Caesar in the garage while Keith rolled a joint and surveyed his dog's wounds. "Hell, Tony, poor Yorkie hasn't even got a neck left," Keith said with a grin when I came into the room.

"Yes," I said, slightly proud of Caesar's victory. "I think Yorkie has lost his tail as well."

"Yeah, well your dog didn't play fair. He hasn't even got a tail to start off with," said Keith, and we started to laugh.

Anita was already in bed, and Keith and I were about to go to sleep when from the garage Caesar started a forlorn howling that would have made the hound of the Baskervilles proud.

"Shut him up, can't you?" asked Keith.

I stomped out to the garage and smacked him. Minutes later he started off again. Anita shouted down the stairs, "What the hell is that noise, Keith? Can't you shut that animal up?"

"I know what," said Keith, grinning mischievously, "we could give him a couple of sleeping tablets — a couple of Mandrax. Do you think that'll put him to sleep and keep him quiet?"

"Great idea," I said dubiously.

While Keith held the bewildered animal's mouth open, I rammed a couple of the pills down his throat. We waited to see what would happen. Ten minutes later Caesar tried to run from the garage but kept stumbling over like a canine Charlie Chaplin. Somehow the dog made his way out through the garage door into an alleyway beside the house. He was so drugged that he repeatedly banged his head against the wall, and I worried that he would kill himself.

Keith staggered out of the garage doubled up with laughter. "Oh, terrific," he roared. "Great . . . why don't we do it to Yorkie as well?"

Suddenly we heard a huge splash. Poor Caesar had tumbled into the moat. Keith laughed so hard that tears were streaming down his face, but I was worried. "It's not funny, Keith," I protested. "That poor dog's drowning out there."

"Well, jump in there and rescue him if you're so worried," he said, laughing louder than ever.

"You jump in there. It's your fault this has happened," I said.

We ran down to the water's edge, but it was a dark, moonless night and we couldn't see a thing. We could hear the unfortunate animal splashing around, though, and every few minutes there was a scrabbling noise, as though he was trying to climb up the steep bank.

Keith went for a torch, and I managed to spot the spluttering, desperate creature in its powerful beam. "Here, boy, here, Caesar," I called and whistled to him, but though he came over, he couldn't climb the bank and just slipped back into the water. Everywhere there was so much thick mud and slime that it was impossible for me to get close enough to grab him. I was becoming genuinely upset by then because I knew the dog wouldn't be able to survive much longer. I ran quickly to the garage to grab an old clothes-line. I tied one end in a loop around my waist and told Keith to hold the other.

I started to climb down the bank, convinced all the while that I was about to step on a family of water rats, while Keith guffawed ever more hysterically at my predicament. "Hey, Anita," he was screaming, "come and see the Doberman swimming in the moat — and now Tony's going for a swim as well."

I was up to my waist in the stinking, murky water by then, and from where I stood, the situation had become distinctly unamusing. Poor, drug-dazed Caesar no longer seemed to know what was happening, and he just kept swimming desperate, ceaseless circuits of the moat while I lunged at him each time he passed me.

At the third attempt I managed to grab his collar, and I hauled him toward me. "Okay, Keith, pull us up," I yelled. But my feet had sunk deep into the ooze at the moat's edge, and it seemed for a moment as though the dog and I were doomed to stay in there together. Eventually, however, with Keith hauling hard on the rope, we crawled out together and sprawled covered with slime and mud on the grass.

"Fantastic...fantastic." Keith was still laughing. "We must do it again tomorrow."

"Yeah," I replied, "but with you in the moat this time."

Dogs, at Redlands, always seemed to lead to chaos. Some months later Keith and Anita were giving one of their endless string of house parties, and this time the guests were all actors and actresses from an underground theatrical group called the Living Theatre, which Anita had once worked with. Among them was a tall, turbaned, satanic looking black actor named Joe Monk.

"Mind if I borrow the bike and do a bit of hunting?" he asked this particular afternoon. The "bike" was a tough scrambler motorcycle with wide handlebars and fat cross-country tyres; Keith allowed any of his friends to take it out for spins in the country.

"Sure," said Keith. "Take Yorkie with you, and see if you can get some pheasants for our dinner." He inserted five cartridges into one of the pump guns and passed it to Joe. As he roared off down the driveway, the big black man cut an extraordinary figure, like some murderous Afghan tribesman, with his sheepskin coat flying in the wind and the big gun strapped across his back. Twenty minutes later we heard his first shot

103

Brian at Redlands

echoing across the fields from about a mile away; a long pause and there was a second shot; then a third, a fourth, and a fifth. "That's his lot," said Keith. But suddenly two more shots rang out in quick succession, and we all looked at one another in bewilderment.

"Christ," said Anita, "I hope they haven't shot him."

A few minutes later a police car drew up outside the house; a cop climbed out and walked across to Keith. "A farmer tells us he had to fire warning shots to frighten off a poacher, and the poacher was with a dog that looked remarkably like yours, sir," he said. "Was this man one of your guests?"

"No, no," protested Keith. "He wasn't one of my guests. I don't know where my dog is at the moment, but he certainly isn't out poaching."

"Are you sure, sir?" replied the cop suspiciously. "He was one of those Jimi Hendrix fuzzy-wuzzies, and the only weirdos we ever see in this neighbourhood are the people who come to visit you."

Keith managed to get rid of him. We were relieved, as Keith had hash and cocaine hidden in the house. Two hours later there was still no sign of Joe; perhaps, I thought gloomily, the farmer didn't aim to miss, and poor old Joe had collapsed somewhere from loss of blood.

At last, just as the dusk was deepening into night, Joe staggered to the front door with his coat torn and splattered with blood. "What happened?" I asked.

"I was in such a hurry to get away from that nut with the shotgun that I fell off the bike on a corner and cut myself up," he said. "But here . . . I got these." And he dumped three plump pheasants on the table.

Keith 'phoned for a cab at once so Joe could be whisked back to London before the police took it into their heads to return. "Nice of old Joe to leave us these," said Keith. And we all laughed.

The incident changed the attitude of the neighbouring farmers dramatically. At first they had been tolerantly amused by the goings-on of these glittering young people at the big house. Now they were to become openly hostile. And there were numerous, inexplicable, worrying incidents.

First Yorkie set off for a stroll and never returned. Then Bernie, another of Keith's Labradors, vanished equally mysteriously. And so did Winston, his Great Dane.

"I've had enough of this," said Keith. "I reckon one of those bloody farmers has shot or poisoned them. I'm going to get a really big, vicious dog that they'll have to leave alone."

That was how Syph came into our lives. Syph was a deerhound which Keith had sent down by rail from a breeder in Scotland. We picked him up from Euston Station, and within minutes he had vomited over the back seat. "Christ," said Keith, "he looks as though he's got syphilis." And that was how the unfortunate animal earned his name. Syph seemed to grow uglier with each day, but he was the best hunting dog I had ever seen, and Keith grew dependent on him to flush out rabbits and pheasants. But then, one fine summer day, Syph trotted off to disappear as suddenly as his predecessors.

"If I find out it's that fucking farmer, I'll go round and blast him," screamed Keith. He probably would have, too, for Keith was not a man to issue idle threats. Unlike most pop stars, he would never, ever walk away from a fight. In Keith's eyes any man who killed his dog deserved to take his punishment from the barrel of a twelve-bore. But we could find no trace of any of the dogs on any of the neighbouring farms, and in the end Keith was forced to content himself with merely reporting the disappearances to the local police. The desk sergeant asked a lot of questions and took a page of notes in his big record book, but not surprisingly, we heard nothing more. I suspected the dogs had decided that life with this particular Rolling Stone left much to be desired. Keith was frequently away from Redlands for weeks at a time, and then the welfare of the animals would be left in the hands of an elderly caretaker who lived nearby. The animals probably found themselves more considerate owners nearby. Even hounds have standards.

Another harassment at Redlands was the constant stream of burglaries. There were three break-ins in the space of six months. Keith was driven to linking a burglar alarm at the house to the police station, which I found deliciously ironic, and he also had a nine foot high wall built around the two-acre garden. But then the thieves seemed to get a kick from seeing what they could grab and run off with in the ten minutes before the police could arrive. They always seemed to go for small, silly things like gold discs and clocks — completely ignoring the £5,000 Persian rugs and priceless antiques. Frequently the thieves weren't quite quick enough, and they would end up in court. "Serves 'em right," Keith told me after two boys had been fined £125 each for a break-in at the house. "If there's one thing I can't stand, it's an amateurish villain."

All the Stones were frequent guests at the house. I sensed that Anita had a thing for Mick, and that unsettled Keith. Mick was almost always with Marianne, so the friendship between him and Anita was

never more than a flirtation.

Mick seemed to delight in Anita's sharp mind, her vicious streak that made her somehow very different from Marianne. For a while she seemed to dominate him with the same, almost supernatural hold she had over Brian and Keith. Once I heard Anita listen to a tape of "Stray Cat Blues" as Jagger proudly waited for her to tell him (as all the other sycophants had done) how brilliant it was. "Crap," she said when it had finished. "The vocals are mixed up too high, and the bass isn't loud enough." Mick, with the basic insecurity of every creative artist, was so unused to hearing someone dare criticize his work that he at once went back to the studio and had the number re-mixed.

Anita and I both spoke fluent Italian, and we had always been close friends, though our relationship was that of brother and sister, with never a hint of romance. And so it was to me she often confided. "I feel," she told me one day, "as though I'm rather like the sixth Rolling Stone. Mick and Keith and Brian need me to guide them, to criticize them and to give them ideas."

Brian was constantly invited to the house, but he didn't feel he could stand the strain of being so close to Anita and yet so far away. At one point, though the harassment from the police became so intense that he arranged to meet Mick at Redlands to talk about the whole problem of police persecution. He was awaiting trial after the ball of wool case then, and was convinced that a long jail sentence awaited him and that Mick and Keith would use this as an excuse to squeeze him finally out of the Stones. As Keith and I sipped beers on the lawn, we could hear, through the open window, that Brian and Mick appeared to be having a fairly violent argument. "Come on, Brian, we've all been busted, and none of us have gone to prison yet. Don't be so stupid, why should you be any different?" Mick was shouting.

Suddenly we heard Brian scream hysterically, "I'm going to kill myself! I'm going to kill myself!" and before we knew what was happening, he had burst out through the door, dashed across the lawn and taken a flying leap into the moat — which Keith had often said was about twenty feet deep.

Brian's head disappeared beneath the surface of the water just as Jagger came running out of the house.

"Quick!", he yelled desperately. "Brian's drowning...somebody get a rope... right, get in there after him, somebody."

Keith, Anita and I looked at one another in bewilderment. None

108

of us was a strong swimmer, and we had no desire to be dragged to the bottom of the moat by Brian.

"Is anybody going to save the poor bastard?" Mick screamed.

"Yes, you," said Keith, looping the rope around Mick's waist.

Mick slithered down the bank, waded through the rushes and out into the moat. As he walked closer to Brian, he realized that the moat was, in fact, only about four feet deep, though there was another foot of mud at the bottom. Brian was obviously bending his knees to fool everyone that he was way out of his depth. Mick was furious by then at being so badly frightened, and he grabbed hold of Brian's bell of yellow hair and forced his face under the water. "You want to drown, you bastard?" he yelled malevolently. "Well, I'm going to bloody well drown you then."

He dragged Brian ashore by his hair in a blind fury, and when they were on the grass, he slapped him on the side of his head. "Look at these velvet trousers. They cost me fifty quid, and you've ruined them!" he screamed. "You stupid, stupid bastard. I hope you do go to jail... and for a long bloody time, too."

Brian drove home to London the same night. But the incident seemed to shake much of the self-pity out of him. He virtually stopped taking drugs for a week; then he flew out to North Africa to record the pipes and drums of the Joujouka tribe. He was away for nearly a month, and when he returned, he was lean, tanned and healthy. "Their music is going to cause a sensation," he enthused. "People are becoming bored with rhythm and blues, and they are looking around for something new. I really reckon this could be it. The music has got this incredible, pulsing excitement, and I've got it all down on tape. It's going to make the most amazing album."

"Thank God," I thought, "it looks as though Brian is going to be all right again."

11

EARNING A FEW MILLION POUNDS A YEAR FOR SINGING SOME SONGS AND looking sexy is the ultimate fantasy of every young man. Yet the reality is considerably less glamorous; churning out the same old numbers night after night for months on end can become boring. So it is that, without exception, every singer of talent and imagination — from Sinatra to Sting — seeks to move across to the parallel, but far more demanding (and satisfying), career of acting. Mick Jagger was no exception. He felt that he had done all there was to be done as a singer and that all that lay ahead was a gradual decline in popularity simply because he was growing older. Many of his friends were film makers, and Jagger seemed to find in them an intellectual stimulus lacking in musicians. The Stones had worked with Jean-Luc Godard on a strange avant-garde film called *One Plus One*, and the experience had whetted Mick's appetite for serious acting.

When film producer Donald Cammell, a friend for several years, asked him to play the part of a demented rock star ("you, only more so," Donald had said) who becomes involved with an East End criminal on the run, Jagger accepted immediately. James Fox took on the role of the gangster, and Warner Brothers agreed to put up the substantial capital needed for the film. To complete the preparations, Nicholas Roeg, a young director who had earned much praise but little money from his first film, *Walkabout*, was brought in to co-direct.

"The trouble is," Mick said to Marianne, as they leafed through the script together, "this guy Turner, the one I'm supposed to be playing, is round the twist. He's nothing like me at all."

They were living now in a huge castle in County Kildare in Southern Ireland that Mick had rented so Marianne could rest during her pregnancy. The life they were leading in London was too much of a strain for her, the doctor had said; she was coming to rely too much on cocaine and barbiturates to lift her up and set her back down again. If she didn't get right away, she would lose the baby.

Marianne talked for hours with Mick about his film role; she was a better actress than a singer; she had starred in *The Three Sisters* and *Hamlet* on stage and understood the nuances and subtleties of drama.

"Whatever you do, don't try to play yourself," she told him. "You're much too together, too straight, too strong. You've got to imagine you're Brian: poor, freaked-out, deluded, androgynous, druggie Brian. But you also need just a bit of Keith in it: his tough, self-destructive, beautiful lawlessness. You must become a mixture of the way Keith and Brian will be when the Stones are over and they are alone in their fabulous houses with all the money in the world and nothing to spend it on."

Together they went through the script again and again until Mick was somehow changed. He seemed to Marianne to have become in real life the same person he was on stage. And she didn't think she liked him very much.

In London, Donald Cammell was turning James Fox into gangster Chas Devlin by far more direct means. James was a sensitive, elegant, typical Englishman who had earned a fortune from starring in films like *The Servant*, *King Rat* and *Those Magnificent Men in Their Flying Machines*. But Donald wanted more than competent acting for his film; he wanted a *real* confrontation between a London hood and an effete, decadent superstar. So he engaged a fast-talking underworld hustler named David to transform James into a villain. I knew David from my Soho days, and I was well aware that he was involved with just about everyone — from the Krays to the Richardsons — in one way or another.

He took his task seriously; James bought his suits from the gangster's favourite tailor, a little Jewish establishment near Waterloo Station; he moved into a flat in East London and he trained with muscle-bound thugs at a gym over the tough Thomas A'Beckett pub, in the Old Kent Road, three times a week. One night David even arranged for James to go out with a couple of burglars to see how they carried out a job. They clambered over rooftops together, and though they didn't actually break into an office, they showed him how they would have got in and out if he hadn't been with them.

Like many of the best actors, James was so skilled at his craft that his own identity seemed to have been lost somewhere along the way and he rapidly took on the mantle of Chas Devlin. He was so immersed in the character that he actually became him. From being a polite, charming gentleman he was transformed into an aggressive, snarling, hot-tempered tough who genuinely frightened people. The nastier he became, the happier was Donald; he was after a genuine personality clash between two very different people. The script was intended only as a rough guide; it would need altering again and again as Jagger and Fox developed their own feelings on the struggle that was to go on between them.

The situation was complicated still further by the presence of Anita Pallenberg on the set — she played Jagger's secretary. And Keith knew, I knew, everybody knew, that she still wanted Mick very badly.

The sixty-five lighting, sound and cameramen had been working for nearly a week in the house in Lowndes Square, Knightsbridge, which was supposed to be Turner's mansion, before Jagger arrived. During that time a growing hostility, had developed toward him. "The guy's not even an actor; he's just a silly little pop star. What right has an amateur like him got to be starring in a movie?", moaned one of the technicians — and many of the others agreed with him.

Jagger knew that he was a novice in this business, and he was eager to learn. He was polite and charming to the crew and he listened carefully as Nicholas and Donald guided him into his first scene. He did exactly as he was told, and his lines were word perfect. The scene had to be filmed again and again until it was right, through no fault of Jagger's. Each time he put everything he had into it — never complaining at the monotony of film work, never protesting that he was being forced to repeat the scene because of the laxity of others and, above all, never behaving like the millionaire superstar he was. It became obvious that Jagger wanted to prove he could be as revolutionary an actor as he was a singer.

Fox and Jagger disliked one another intensely, for both had become so deeply the characters they were playing, that it wasn't altogether acting anymore.

Chas, though a gangster, lived a life that epitomized straight society. His flat was pop-art modern; he wore sharp suits and read *Playboy* magazine; only the gun hidden in his spotless bathroom appeared to set him apart from any other young bachelor. He was aggressively heterosexual, though violence and sex were so deeply interwoven in his mind that he took erotic pleasure from beating his submissive girl friend. Crisis befell him when a rival gang wrecked his flat, strapped him down and whipped him almost to death. But Chas managed to grab a gun and blast at his torturers, sensually savouring the bloody murder of the rival gang

112

boss. He was on the run then, and when he heard about an empty flat in Turner's mansion, he disguised himself by dyeing his hair red and set off to hide out there.

Once at the house the gangster became bewildered by the bizarre sexuality of Turner, who wore make-up and pretty feminine clothes; his glossy hair tumbled over his shoulders.

After Anita had agreed to let Chas live in the vacant basement flat, the film showed her going upstairs to climb into bed with a couple who seemed to be asleep. It wasn't clear at first whether the couple were male or female: The girl, Michele Breton, had short hair and a boyish figure; the other person in bed, Turner, had long hair and make-up.

It was apparent to me that Anita, who was a close friend of Donald's, had inspired this scene, for it captured perfectly the confused, heterosexual/homosexual love life she had enjoyed with Brian. He would encourage her to pick up girls and bring them home so the three of them could share a bed together.

Chas was disorientated; he had always felt that he knew who he was, what sex was all about, but now he wasn't quite so sure. After they had eaten hallucinogenic mushrooms together, Turner also began to question his beliefs.

Turner had rejected a society dominated by male violence — the very violence that he knew was at the heart of his success as a rock star. He had cocooned himself in a mystical bisexual, drugged, female-orientated world, but as he taunted and changed Chas, he too was changed. Though both men appeared to be extreme opposites, they found themselves in each other.

I could see the film draining both Jagger and Fox, for they were being forced to question the very roots of their beings. James, particularly, was becoming as dangerously disorientated off screen as he was on.

And Jagger, too, seemed to have become Brian; he was beginning to crack up and lose his identity.

Mick and one of the other actors would smoke DMT together in their dressing room so that they could add realism to the drug scenes. But the drug has the hydrogen bomb impact of a twelve-hour acid trip crammed into the space of fifteen minutes and served only to alienate them still further from the real world. Recently doctors have discovered that DMT can cause irreparable brain damage.

Anita, too, further confused things by seducing Jagger in their dressing room after only three days of working on the film together; she had always found him attractive, but now that he was so much like Brian and Keith — the two most important men in her life — she found him irresistible. Donald saw the passion between them and capitalised on it.

Fox caught Mick and Anita making love in their dressing room during a ten-minute break in filming and was genuinely appalled that Mick could behave so wickedly toward Keith Richard, the man supposed to be his best friend.

Mick and Anita's private dabbling in black magic spilled over on to the set when Donald introduced all sorts of symbols and talismans.

There were other tensions — Anita and Marianne were close friends, yet here Anita was trying to steal Jagger away, while Marianne was helplessly pregnant in a remote corner of Ireland. The affair was sinking Keith into the same kind of depression that Brian had gone into when Anita had left him. Anita was like a life-force, a woman so powerful, so full of strength and determination that men came to lean on her, to become as dangerously dependent on her as a heroin addict is on his drug supplier.

It began to look as if the Stones would not survive the split that was coming between Keith and Mick. During filming, I used to try to talk Keith into coming in the house in Lowndes Square, where scenes were being shot, to wait in the dressing room with Mick and Anita.

Keith refused to go there. He seemed afraid that he would be forced into a confrontation, realized that once he caught Mick and Anita making love, he would lose both of them, and his world would crumble as surely as Brian's had. He would wait in a nearby pub, morosely sipping Bacardis, or he would just hang around for Anita in the back of his Bentley, which I parked nearby.

"This is stupid," I told him once. "There's no need for us to sit in the car. We could go up to the dressing room and smoke a few joints with Mick and your old lady. You could be writing songs instead of just sitting here, twiddling your thumbs."

But he mumbled an excuse and simply asked me to go to the dressing room to see how long Anita would be.

Anita seemed to revel sadistically in being at the centre of so passionate an intrigue; it was proof of her power, her magnetism. Every girl in the world was longing to go to bed with a Rolling Stone, and Anita was holding all three that mattered in her sway. "You know, Tony," she told me, "I'm certain that any one of them would break up the band for me. It's a strange feeling."

114

But she, too, was affected by the strange vibes of the film. She started to steal the props, or to be more exact, she would persuade me to steal them for her. Every time I went to the house she would have something placed on one side for me to smuggle out under my coat. Once it was an Oriental headband with a snake twined around it; another time it was the bust of an Egyptian god. Donald suspected what was happening, and he was annoyed — not because of the value of the props, but because it delayed and complicated the already difficult process of making the film. Frequently the focal point of a half-completed scene would mysteriously disappear from the set overnight. He wasn't prepared to risk upsetting Anita and Mick by complaining. He just discreetly whispered to me that he wished people would leave his props alone. After that I refused to carry out any more smuggling assignments for Anita.

The film took three and a half months to complete, and nobody was quite the same when it had ended. James Fox's father, Robin Fox, who was also his agent, had warned him that the film would damage his reputation because of its advocacy of bisexuality and drugs. But James had ignored him — only to discover when the film was almost finished that his father was dying of cancer. The shock, coupled with Jagger's DMT and amorality and the sheer strain of the film, shattered him. He suffered a nervous breakdown and quit his hugely promising acting career. Later he became a preacher with the obscure Navigators religious sect. When, years afterwards, a reporter from the *Daily Mail* tracked him down, he was to admit, "*Performance* gave me doubts about my way of life. Before that I had been completely involved in the more bawdy side of the film business. But after that everything changed."

Anita went quietly back to Keith to bide her time, for she felt certain by then that Mick's relationship with Marianne was floundering. Mick was left with his mind in a state of turmoil that was quite outside the scope of his confident, organized experience. Later he admitted, "I really got into thinking like Turner. I drove everyone a bit crazy, I think, during that time."

But Cammell and Roeg, though exhausted, were in celebratory mood. "This is going to amaze everyone. No one will ever have seen a film quite like it; it will set a whole new standard," Cammell told me as the film was nearing completion.

His dreams were dashed by the fat men with cigars at Warners. They were so stunned by this vivid, explicitly degenerate work, which was quite unlike anything they had ever seen, that they refused to release it for

115

two years. In that time seven different editors were engaged to cut and change it in a naive effort to avoid offending public sensibility. Eventually, because of international bungling, there were five different versions of the film being shown in various parts of the world. Even the title was changed — from *The Performance* to *Performance*.

The version that Cammell and Jagger saw so incensed them that they sent the following telegram to the president of Warner Brothers:

> "Re Performance: This film is about the perverted love affair between Homo Sapiens and Lady Violence. In common with its subject, it is necessarily horrifying, paradoxical and absurd. To make such a film means accepting that the subject is loaded with every taboo in the book.
>
> You seem to want to emasculate (i) the most savage and (ii) the most affectionate scenes in our movie. If "Performance" does not upset audiences it is nothing. If this fact upsets you, the alternative is to sell it fast and no more bullshit. Your misguided censorship will ultimately diminish said audiences both in quality and quantity."

Warners ignored them, and the row only reinforced the junkie-satanist image that the straitlaced men who finance films had of Jagger. It is significant that once *Performance* was released, Jagger was to be offered no more worthwhile film parts for many years.

Marianne knew that Mick was having an affair with Anita, and the knowledge ate into her as she whiled away her days in the lonely Irish castle. Gradually she became more and more dependent on cocaine as a substitute for the love that had once been so real, so all important to her. When he came back to her after the film, he was cruel and changed, not sure which part of him was the real Mick Jagger and which part was still Turner. They had argued about the cocaine then. Jagger thought it would endanger the life of the unborn child, and anyway, he was afraid to take it himself in case he became as dependent on it as Keith and Anita and Eric Clapton and so many other of their friends seemed to be.

She virtually gave up the drug. The doctor confined her to bed from her sixth month because he feared for the safety of the infant inside her womb. Marianne wanted the child very much, Jagger's child. She was certain it would be a girl and they would call her Carena.

After being misquoted by reporters who had asked him about the subject, Jagger decided to go on the top-rated David Frost television chat show to talk about his attitude: "It's very important that you shouldn't get married if you think that you could get divorced. If you want to get married and you consecrate your union to God, you can't break it, not even with God. You just have to carry on. I think marriage is really groovy."

When Frost became more specific and asked him why he wasn't marrying Marianne, Jagger replied, "Ah, well, the lady that I am with is already married, so it's a bit difficult. I could be a bigamist, I suppose."

After more questions he added, "I don't really want to get married particularly.... I don't feel that I really need it. But if I were with a woman who really needed it, well, that's another matter. But I'm not with that kind of woman."

Mrs. Mary Whitehouse was wheeled onto the programme then: a reactionary, stiff middle-aged woman with starched grey hair and butterfly-framed glasses who had become a self appointed guardian of public morals after founding the National Viewers and Listeners Association.

"The fact of the matter is," she lectured Jagger, "that if you're a Christian or a person with faith and you have your marriage in Church, and you make that vow, when difficulties come you have this basic thing you have accepted, you find your way through the difficulties. And even if you don't get married in a Church, you have this legal thing."

Jagger had crossed swords with this dragonish matron before and knew that he had to be very firm if he was to win the tussle. Brusquely he replied, "Your Church accepts divorce and may even accept abortion — am I right or wrong? I can't see how you can talk about this bond which is inseparable, when the Christian Church itself accepts divorce.

"You really can't, you can't say that. Either you're married and you don't get divorced, and that's it, or you don't bother, and you can't come along with some compromise Christian option on marriage."

For once Mrs. Mary Whitehouse appeared to be dumbfounded.

Four weeks after taking to her bed Marianne lost her baby boy, and as the tears streamed down her face, she felt her heart breaking; life would never be quite the same again. Jagger, too, wept with her un-ashamedly and told her she was still very young, and there was plenty of time for more babies. They seemed very close then, and for a time she forgave his infidelity and his selfishness.

Jagger overcame his misery at the loss of the child by throwing himself hard into his work, totally absorbing himself so there was no time to think of the cot that Marianne had made ready; of his own dashed hopes of playing with a little girl called Carena. He spent his time planning the band's tour of the United States . . . and thinking how he could tell Brian he wouldn't be making this trip with them.

Madeleine, my girl friend, had gone away to dance in Las Vegas for a year then, and Marianne phoned me repeatedly from Cheyne Walk to ask me to visit her when Jagger was out working through the dawn night after night, for weeks on end. We became lovers again, and sometimes Marianne would come to my flat in Maida Vale. All the while we were both snorting coke to give ourselves an instant buzz of happiness. I think she wanted, deep down inside, for Jagger to know that she and I were having an affair. She bitterly resented the way in which their original passionate sexual relationship had drained away; he seemed to be so tired, so wrapped up in his work now that he sometimes wouldn't make love to her for weeks at a time, and it was as if she hoped the knowledge of her infidelity would goad him into possessive jealousy.

I believed, too, that she had other lovers, but my suspicions were to be confirmed in a way that stunned me. I had picked up Keith and Mick from Olympic Studios in Keith's Bentley and driven them to Mick's house on Cheyne Walk. As soon as he walked through the door of the beautiful old house, Mick bounded upstairs to the bedroom to tell Marianne he was home earlier than he had expected.

When he came back into the big, beautifully proportioned drawing room, he was ashen-faced. "Jesus wept," he said to Keith. "She's in bed with a chick."

Keith roared with laughter. "Don't worry, man." He guffawed. "Anita's been like that for years. You ought to get in there with them and teach 'em a lesson."

"I'm not a dyke," Marianne explained to me later. "But I like to make love with young, beautiful people. Whether they are boys or girls doesn't make an awful lot of difference."

12

REVOLUTION WAS IN THE AIR. THROUGHOUT THE WORLD THE SIMMERING DIS-content of youth had reached boiling point, and it seemed certain that the politicians responsible for the constraint of the young were about to be very badly scalded. It started in Paris; students who wore their hair like the Stones, dressed like the Stones, were tearing the city apart like an angry volcano. Then the United States had been ripped by a furious devastating army of blacks screaming, "Burn, baby, burn!", after the assassination of Martin Luther King, Jr. Even the country's complacent white young people were being stirred by the songs of Dylan and the exhortations of radical young reformers to question the war in Vietnam, the power of the big corporations, the corruption in high places. Even behind the iron curtain, in Prague, the Czech kids were battling for a freer society, daring to challenge the might of the Kremlin.

Jagger had become interested in politics when he was a student at the London School of Economics. Brilliant young men and women argued that the world was undergoing a period of change, that the old order would be overthrown and replaced with a new, freer society.

At first he had been sceptical; it seemed ludicrous for students who were living on grants from the government to be plotting to overthrow the very society that had given them their special privileges. But he had talked of Marx and Lenin long into the night so that although he disagreed with their doctrines, he understood the fundamental wrongness of capitalism and accepted that life in Europe and the United States was less perfect than newspapers and politicians told people it was.

He hadn't had time to be an activist, though. He had been more interested in becoming a rock 'n' roll star. Later he had grown rather fond of capitalism as first one million, then the next poured into his bank account. But the farcical drug trials that he and Keith and Brian had endured, coupled with the bubbling anger of their audiences, combined to make him, momentarily, a committed revolutionary.

"The Commandments say, 'Thou shalt not kill,' and half the world is in training to annihilate the other half," he protested to Jack Bentley of the *Sunday Mirror*.

"Nobody would get me in uniform and off to Aden to kill a lot of people I've never met and have nothing against anyway. I know people say they're against wars, and yet they go on fighting them. Millions of marvellous young men are killed, and in five minutes everybody seems to have forgotten all about it. War stems from power mad politicians and patriots.... Politicians? What a dead loss they are.... There shouldn't be any Prime Minister at all.

"Anarchy is the only slight glimmer of hope. Not the popular conception of it – men in black cloaks lurking around with hidden bombs — but a freedom of every man being personally responsible for himself. There should be no such thing as private property. Anybody should be able to go where he likes and do what he likes. Politics, like the legal system, is dominated by old men. Old men who are also bugged by religion. And the law — the law's outdated and doesn't cater enough for individual cases."

He leapt at the chance of joining the revolution when tens of thousands of angry young people stormed into Grosvenor Square to demonstrate their hatred of American Imperialism and the Vietnam War, outside the huge modern American Embassy. At first he was not noticed, and he linked arms with a young man on one side and a young woman on the other as the mob tried to smash their way through police lines and into the embassy. He felt a part of what was happening as though he were really contributing. But then he was recognised; fans demanded autographs; newspaper men scuffled with one another to interview him, to fire off their flashguns in his face. He fled, realising bitterly that his fame and wealth precluded him from the revolution — he was a distraction, not a leader. He suddenly felt impotent — his power seemed trite, meaningless, beside that of a revolutionary student leader like Tariq Ali. He poured this realisation into a new song, "Street Fighting Man," bemoaning the fact that summer has arrived and it's time for revolution, but he's only a rock 'n' roll singer.

The record caused an uproar when it was released as a single in July. All over the world radio stations banned it because they feared it would fan the flames of revolution. To the young the song was a marching song, proof that Jagger's ambition to change society went deeper than mere eradication of the taboos surrounding sex and narcotics. "Really, though," he told Keith at the time, "it is just my admission that there's nothing I can do to help the revolution along. It's amazing the things people can read into a song."

The song was also to be included on *Beggars Banquet*, the new album. But it was beginning to look as though Decca would never allow it to be released. Apparently the fuddy-duddies at the company objected to Barry Feinstein's amusing sleeve photograph of a graffitied toilet wall. I was particularly keen for the picture to be used because it would have given me a mention — albeit cryptic — on the cover. Keith had scrawled across a drainpipe with his felt-tip: "Spanish Tony. Where Are You?" during a period when I had taken a long holiday in Valencia.

Sales of the album would not have been affected if the sleeve had been changed, but Jagger took Decca's stance as yet another example of the authorities attempting to stifle his freedom of expression. The Stones' relationship with the company had long been uneasy; they objected to Decca's orthodoxy and its involvement with the manufacture of weapons of war, and the issue of the toilet wall brought things to a head.

"I don't find the cover at all offensive," Jagger told one newspaper defiantly. "Decca has put out a Tom Jones sleeve showing an atom bomb exploding. I find that more upsetting."

Later Jagger suggested that Decca should put out the album and its sleeve in a brown paper bag stamped "Unfit for children." Decca was not even prepared to consider the idea; as far as it was concerned, the record was never, ever going to be released with that photograph on the sleeve. Eventually, after much public haranguing of Decca, Jagger was forced to back down, and the record was released in a plain white sleeve. "But those bastards won't get away with that one," Mick told me later. "I've got one or two ideas about how we can get our own back on them."

Many listeners, particularly in the United States, saw one track on the album as Jagger's brazen admission that he and his men were working hand-in-glove with Satan. The song, "Sympathy for The Devil," was, in reality, inspired by Bulgakov's classic novel, *The Master and Margarita*. But it was indisputably the closest brush ever between rock 'n' roll and voodooism.

Brian knew by now that his days with the band were numbered. He had hardly played on the album, scarcely spoken to Mick or Keith for months, and he had two drug convictions, which made it impossible for him to visit the USA. The realisation of his position seemed to calm him; he still used drugs but less hysterically now. He bought Cotchford Farm, a beautiful old country house in Sussex, where A. A. Milne had written *Winnie the Pooh*, and he supervised plans for modernising and redecorating the place. "When it's finished," he confided, "I'll have my own little studio, and I can start working on forming a really good new band of my own. I might even go into production. Who knows?"

But for the moment he was content to continue with the charade of being a Rolling Stone. Though he hadn't played on the original recording, he was hauled in to play piano on "Sympathy for the Devil", when the Stones performed it on David Frost's television programme.

Brian was the star of the show when *Beggars Banquet* was launched with a custard pie throwing press reception at the Elizabethan Rooms of the Queensgate Hotel, in Kensington. Keith was unwell, and so it was left to Brian to flirt with the girls and make the reporters laugh. Several people remarked afterwards on the distinctly aggressive way in which Brian had rammed pie after pie into Jagger's face. "Oh, well, you know Brian," said one. "He always does go a bit over the top."

A few days later the whole band was at a BBC television studio in Wembley for the *Rolling Stones Rock and Roll Circus*, a daring film venture conceived by Jagger as compensation for fans who had not seen them in concert for two and a half years. Outside, Elsie Smith, Mick's old school teacher from Dartford, was regaling fans with stories of the days when their idol had worn short trousers. But her ardent listeners turned away, stunned, to ogle in disbelief as John Lennon and Yoko Ono glided ethereally from their huge white Rolls into the studio.

Jagger had 'phoned all his friends, asking them to join him in making this the rock film to end all rock films. The Who were there; so were Jethro Tull, Eric Clapton, real live tigers, a boxing kangaroo, a fire-eater, clowns, midgets and Lord only knows what else. Plans had been made for John Lennon, Keith Richard, Eric Clapton and Mitch Mitchell to play together in a superstar jam session.

Brian knew that Mick and Keith were trying to persuade Clapton to replace him, but he was unperturbed. He was virtually off dope now, and he really, genuinely dug the new album. "Sympathy for the Devil," in particular, had so captivated him that he had dressed in a peculiarly satanic way for the show, silver horns protruded from his top hat, and his trousers were tucked into his high Moroccan boots so that he looked like a satyr. For a moment there was a togetherness of the Stones, the Who and

Bill Wyman (clown) and Brian at the Rock 'n' Roll Circus

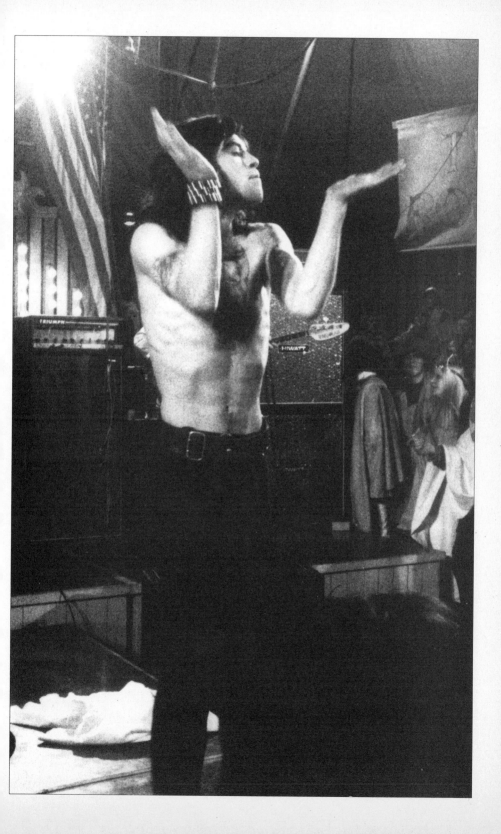

Top: John Lennon talking to Brian Jones backstage. *Bottom*: The first supergroup, Eric Clapton, John Lennon and Keith Richards rock out together.

Top: Keith Richards strikes a pose. *Bottom*: Rocky, a friend, Brian Jones and the late Keith Moon relaxing.

all the other superstars which made all the myths about the beautiful, brilliant people seem true. For that one night all the back-stabbing machinations of big money rock 'n' roll seemed a million miles away. Mick and Marianne were playing leapfrog before the cameras started to roll, while Keith swaggered around dressed as a decadent reprobate in top hat and black eyepatch.

Mick was dressed as a ringmaster, while Bill and Charlie were clowns. "How appropriate," I thought, "they have all put on costumes that directly reflect their roles in the band."

After Jethro Tull had played and the fire-eaters had finished singeing our eyebrows, Marianne stepped alone into the ring, looking fey, vulnerable and exquisitely beautiful, with her long blonde hair cascading over her shoulders. She sang a mysterious, slow song called "Something Better," about her need to live a different kind of life. But that night even she and Mick seemed to be in love, and he squeezed her and made her laugh between takes.

The acrobats bored us, and then it was time for the supergroup to take the stage. Keith and Eric both stuck firmly to the original Beatles version of "Yer Blues," as though not daring to improvise on a number written by the Masters. So it was left to Lennon to inject passion into the song. I'd never seen him singing at close quarters before, and the sheer, emotional impact of being so near someone screaming out all the tortures in his soul overwhelmed me. All the misery of drugs and the coming Beatles break-up seemed to be poured into the song; when John screamed out, "I even hate my rock and roll...", I could feel the hairs at the back of my neck standing on end.

The Who played next, but they were dwarfed by the direct comparison with Lennon's raw genius. A few more dreary acts dragged things out still further, so that it was one in the morning and we had all been in the studio for nearly fourteen hours by the time the Stones were ready to play. They warmed up with "Route 66," then plunged straight into "Jumpin' Jack Flash." During the number, dozens of explosion machines, used in war films, blasted dazzling flashes into the air. "Don't look at them, they will blind you," the floor manager lied to us dramatically.

They pumped through lots of songs from *Beggars Banquet*, and it was like seeing the old Stones again: Jagger leaping and prancing like a dervish, Keith crouched low and using his guitar like a Vietcong machine gun. Though Brian was being carried, he looked beautiful, and very few people in the audience realised he was merely being used to strum the simplest of chords, or even just to rattle the maracas on some numbers. At the climax of "Sympathy for the Devil", Jagger ripped off his crimson T-shirt to reveal a huge, ugly tattoo of Satan on his chest. I began to wonder then if he was perhaps more deeply into black magic than any of us realised.

At five in the morning the filming was over, and all that remained was for everyone in the circus to sit together, swaying from side to side, singing "Salt of the Earth." "Thanks," I overheard Mick saying to John Lennon as they parted for home, exhausted. "That's gotta be the rock movie to end all rock movies. Nobody will ever believe their eyes."

But the show was never to be screened because Jagger didn't like it. And Brian was never to play with the Rolling Stones again.

The *Circus*, *Performance*, *Beggars Banquet* — there had been too much trauma, too much hard work in too short a space of time, and they were all beginning to grow pale, jittery and tired. Jagger had had a nervous breakdown in June 1966 after non-stop touring in Australia, New Zealand and the States, and he recognized the growing symptoms of a repeat attack. "We've got to get away to the sun, somewhere where nobody can reach us on the 'phone," he said.

Keith and Anita, too, were desperate to get away. Anita had had two miscarriages; now she was pregnant for the third time, and she was determined that this child would be born. So the four of them, together with Marianne's son, Nicholas, set off to Brazil by ship. At first they stayed on a vast ranch owned by a cattle millionaire, but to escape the tense atmosphere, Mick, Marianne and Nicholas flew off to a hotel in Rio without Keith and Anita.

Later Mick, Marianne and Nicholas flew on to a straw beach hut, a thousand miles to the north and found blissful anonymity, cut off from the pressures of fame and business. They seemed to grow close then; Mick became a father to Nicholas, and the rift between Mick and Marianne seemed to disappear.

Brian, meanwhile, had flown to Sri Lanka for a break, but things had gone badly. The Sri Lankans hadn't yet learned that even young men with long hair and candy pink suits could be millionaires, and he had been turned away by two of the island's biggest hotels. Furiously he pulled out a ridiculous wad of notes, slammed it down in front of a startled receptionist and yelled, "I am not a beatnik. I work for my living. I have money, and I do not wish to be treated as a second-class citizen."

13

I HAD ALWAYS BEEN WARY OF HARD DRUGS. THEY DESTROYED THE MIND, killed people. But I knew that I was strong enough to use them and give them up at will; there was no way I would ever allow myself to get hooked. It was with some surprise, then, that I woke up one morning early in 1969 to the realisation that I was a heroin addict. And so, it seemed, was everyone around me. Keith, Anita, Marianne, Eric Clapton — they all were strung-out on smack. The swinging sixties had been a time when all that had mattered was instant pleasure, regardless of dire warnings and danger; now, it seemed, we were to pay for our hedonism.

It had started with cocaine. Once I had learned to use it properly, sniffing the white diamanté crystals had transformed my life. If I felt tired or low, a quick snort would be enough to lift me up and to turn me instantly into a sparkling, witty, outgoing person again. And coke had changed my love life, too. On coke I was metamorphized into the kind of lover women dream of, carrying on passionately for ten hours or more until my partner was driven almost delirious with ecstasy.

"What, me a junkie?" I had said to a girl friend. "I'm no junkie. Junkies are dreary, introspective people. I only use coke because it's an upper. It makes me sociable, energetic and as unlike a junkie as it is possible to be." But coke is a strange drug; though non-addictive, it produces a compulsion to keep snorting more and more, so that sometimes I would keep raving for three days and nights before my supply ran out. Scientists have taught monkeys to inject themselves with a variety of drugs and discovered that the animals will go on administering coke to themselves until they drop from exhaustion. There is no unpleasant come-down from the stimulation of coke as there is with other uppers such as amphetamines, so it is a drug that one can become psychologically dependent upon in a surprisingly insidious way.

131

I was snorting so much that I was hyped-up, jittery, paranoid and afraid to sit still. At a friend's flat in Chelsea, I was stalking around, scratching my body and babbling almost incoherently because my mind was racing so fast that my words couldn't keep up with my thoughts. "Here," he had said kindly, "sit down and take a snort of this. It'll calm you down a bit."

I sat on his Moroccan cushions and snorted the powder. It looked exactly like cocaine. Within a second I felt a huge bubble of air swelling inside my brain, the room blurred and I floated gently into unconsciousness. I came to minutes later, feeling as calmed and satisfied as if I had just enjoyed a huge dinner, a few bottles of wine and a couple of hours in bed with a beautiful woman. "What the hell was that?" I asked. "It's amazing."

"That, man," he said, fixing me with a quizzical grin, "was heroin. You've just had your first taste of smack."

Suddenly I felt as though I were about to be sick.

The experience frightened me, and I refused to take heroin again, though I was persuaded to snort speedballs — mixtures of tiny amounts of cocaine and heroin which produce the euphoria of heroin without the drug's tendency to make you first unconscious, then sick. I went on using coke and speedballs intermittently for months until one day, after a couple of really wild evenings, I woke up feeling extremely ill. I ached all over, and my body was covered in a cold sweat. I telephoned a doctor, told him I seemed to have the flu and asked him to come and see if there was anything he could do. He agreed with my diagnosis and prescribed medicine, but it did no good, and I started to feel so chronically ill that I was afraid I had picked up some ghastly disease like cholera or typhoid. Then a friend came to visit and offered me a speedball, thinking it might perk me up. I sniffed the white powder through a tiny gold tube I wore on a chain around my neck, and within twenty minutes, I was completely cured. I felt as strong and fit as a man who has just returned from a summer holiday. "That's fantastic, man," I said to my friend. "I didn't know speedballs cured the 'flu."

"They don't," said my friend. "They just make heroin withdrawal symptoms go away. You're an addict, Tony."

At first I had not believed him. Addicts stuck needles in their arms, and I hadn't been near a syringe since childhood vaccinations. When the "flu" came and went in much the same fashion the next day, though, I realised that he was right. I consoled myself that I could stop at any time.

All I had to do was to steel myself for a bout of chronic influenza and I would be back to normal again.

Marianne and Anita both started in much the same way. They seemed to enjoy the huge, orgasmic buzz of heroin so much that they started to alternate it with cocaine. They would take coke for a day or two to lift them up higher and higher; then, when they started to become strung-out and jittery, they would snort heroin to bring them back down again. They both felt lonely, rejected by their men. Mick and Keith were working every night until dawn in the studio at the end of Mick's garden on Cheyne Walk on their new album, which was to be called *Let It Bleed*.

Keith had never been a particularly energetic lover, and now he was so tired, so wrapped up in his music, that he and Anita seemed to make love as rarely as Mick and Marianne.

Keith also lived in Cheyne Walk now, in a huge Queen Anne house he had bought for £26,000 from Anthony Nutting, the Minister of State for Foreign Affairs. It was just a few doors away from Mick's place, and the two of them became very close. Keith taught Mick to play guitar, and together they were writing songs like the devastating "Honky Tonk Woman," "Gimme Shelter" and "Midnight Rambler." Musically they were at the very peak of their prodigious powers.

The girl who was supplying Marianne and Anita with their dope showed them how to skin-pop it: how to dilute the minuscule heroin jacks, then put them into a syringe and jab them into their bodies. It seemed a sensible thing to do because they needed only a tenth as much heroin if they skin-popped instead of snorting.

I stopped using heroin. Everyone around me was obsessed with the drug, talking and thinking of nothing else, and it frightened me. Anita, too, reverted to nothing more than an occasional snort of coke — after her doctor warned her she was in danger of losing her baby, and Anita wanted to have this child very much.

But Marianne, poor Marianne knew she was losing Mick, knew that, at twenty-one, she was every inch the fallen woman the public made her out to be. Even the Archbishop of Canterbury denounced her from the pulpit for being pregnant by Mick. Though she was brave, beautiful and hip on the outside, somewhere deep inside there lurked the soul of the confused, consumptive little girl who had been packed off to boarding school at the age of eight. Soon she was mainlining four jacks — pills — of smack a day.

"You've got to help me get away from Mick," she pleaded with me after we had made love one evening in my flat in Maida Vale. "He never, ever makes love to me anymore, and I'm going out of my mind — all his energy is sublimated into his work. But when I try to tell him he is destroying me, he just gives me roses, hundreds of fucking roses, and buys me presents and tells me he loves me."

"I just feel I'm trapped and I'm so unhappy that I really need the smack to get me through everything. I'm sure he knows I'm on it, but he won't admit it, even to himself. It's something he pretends isn't happening; he turns his eyes away from it and hopes I will just cure myself and everything will be okay again. If you could only take me away from him, Tony, there would be no more reporters hounding me and people attacking me, and I would be free to be me again, to live my own life. I'm just not strong enough to walk out on my own."

I was in love with Madeleine at the time, and I was looking forward to her return from the States so we could marry and settle down together.

"I'm sorry, Marianne," I said, teasing her. I don't earn enough money for you, and I only live with rich ladies anyway."

"Ah, but I'm rich," she protested. I earned a fortune last year for making that awful film *Girl on a Motorcycle*."

Anita and Keith knew of our affair, but I don't think either of them mentioned it to Mick. Even if they had, he would not have cared very much — just so long as the newspapers didn't get hold of the story, and there wasn't much danger of that.

All the Stones were investing their money in property. Jagger had bought a vast Elizabethan manor called Stargroves, set in forty acres of lush English countryside, near Newbury in Berkshire. Oliver Cromwell had stayed in the house in the seventeenth century, and Jagger set a costly renovation programme in motion with instructions to the builders to "make the house look as good as it did when old Cromwell first saw it." But the house was primarily an investment, and Jagger visited it rarely.

Bill Wyman had become Lord of the Manor of Gedding and Thormwoods when he bought Gedding Hall, an exquisite Suffolk mansion as old as Hampton Court. Charlie Watts had bought an historic manor, near Lewes, in Sussex, from Lord Shawcross, the Attorney General. And Brian was living at Redlands, Keith's place, while the builders put the finishing touches to his tranquil new house, Cotchford Farm.

After the *Rock and Roll Circus* Brian had seen little of the other two. He had been locked away at Redlands in the oppressive 'care' of the chauffeur Keith had been so anxious to get rid of, and for much of the

135

time he felt like a prisoner. The chauffeur had been given orders to keep Brian off dope, and he was carrying them out rigidly; the only drugs Brian was allowed were the sleeping tablets and tranquilisers prescribed by his doctor. But the precautions were unnecessary. Brian was jumpy about being busted again and wouldn't even allow his girl friend, Suki Poitier, to smoke a joint in the house. He knew he was no longer a Rolling Stone; the others didn't even go through the charade of inviting him to rehearsals anymore. He was uncertain of what to do — whether to quit the Stones and form a new band, or just hang on in there a little while longer.

Mick and Keith were undecided about Brian. He hung over their lives like some sad spectre of the past. They were frightened of what would happen to the Stones without him — in Germany and Scandinavia he was still regarded as the band's leader. In most of the rest of the world, too, he had a fan following that closely rivalled Jagger's own.

"We can't just sack him," Mick argued with the Stones' manager, Allen Klein. "He may be just a druggie now but he helped put the Stones where they are. And anyway, it's going to look very bad for the band if Brian goes around screaming to the newspapers that we sacked him. That sort of publicity would be enough to ruin everything."

Klein countered with the unassailable argument that the Stones had not toured the United States or the Far East for three years because of Brian and that they either had to get rid of him or break up the band. "I know, I know," said Jagger. "I just wish there was some other way around it."

A compromise was worked out. Brian would be asked to leave the group for a year or two, ostensibly to work on solo projects. He would be paid £100,000 a year for as long as the Stones stayed together, and if he wished, he could rejoin them at some future date.

"You must be crazy paying him all that money," Klein had said. "There must be a better solution than that...surely we can work something else out."

But Mick and Keith were adamant. A hundred thousand pounds a year was not a great deal of money split between the whole band, and they couldn't just abandon Brian to his fate. They drove together to Cotchford Farm — where Brian now lived — in Mick's cream-coloured Bentley, moving fast, talking little.

"We came to talk about the American tour," said Keith, not looking at Brian's face.

"You know I can't go. I can't leave the country, and I can't possibly go on the road again right now," Brian said. And Jagger noticed that though his voice was steady, his hands were shaking.

It was easier than Keith or Mick had expected. Brian put up no arguments, and he merely nodded when they mentioned the salary.

"I haven't been a Rolling Stone for a very long time now," he said. "Who are you bringing in to replace me?"

"We're not certain yet," said Mick. "It might be Eric Clapton or Mick Taylor. We haven't worked it out yet."

"Yeah, they're both very good."

"Right, then, we'll drop down in a couple of weeks to tell you how things are going."

They exchanged awkward goodbyes, and Brian noticed something strange. Neither would look him in the face. It was dark now and he walked back into the old kitchen through the back door, sat at the table, put his head in his hands, and sobbed like a broken-hearted child.

Anita and Marianne cried, too, when they heard about it. "They have finished him off now," said Marianne, weeping. "Poor, beautiful, bewildered Brian. Whatever is going to happen to him?" In her heart she knew; she believed he would die soon. No one could go through what Brian had and survive.

Keith had been guilty and angry when Anita mentioned Brian. "For Christ's sake," he protested, "the guy's getting a hundred grand a year for sitting on his bum. I don't know what everyone's moaning about."

The police seemed dismayed by Brian's disappearance, and were casting about for fresh suspects. Jagger seemed an obvious target. When a policeman spotted his Bentley driving along Royal Hospital Road, in Chelsea, he gave chase in his unmarked police car and pulled Jagger to the side of the road. "I have reason to believe there are drugs concealed in your vehicle, and I must ask your permission to search your car, sir," he said.

Jagger had long since stopped carrying anything stronger than peppermints, and he had suspected that he was about to be set up. "No way," he replied. "I know all about what you did to Brian, and you ain't doing it to me. You don't come near this car until my lawyer gets here to watch you carrying out the search."

The cop furiously mumbled something about getting even next time and drove off.

In May one of the men who was 'looking after' Brian phoned Marianne to say he could let her have some very cheap heroin. He brought it to the house on Cheyne Walk in two small polythene bags and accepted £40 for it. Less than four hours later there was a ring at the door, and as soon as it was opened, a detective sergeant and his team burst in.

"Okay," said Mick. "Here it is." And he handed over an ornate wooden box containing about a quarter of an ounce of hash.

"We're looking for the real stuff, sonny," said the policeman, with a malevolent grin, and ordered his men to search the house. In a remarkably short time they had found Marianne's heroin, she had taken only one snort so both packets were almost full.

"Talk your way out of this one," challenged a triumphant policeman as he left.

Mick was distraught. The bust meant he would lose his American and Far East visas. It was a catastrophe.

"I just don't know what the hell to do, Tony," he told me over the 'phone that evening. "The guy who sold the stuff to Marianne says he can fix the forensic laboratory test on it for two thousand pounds, but I don't trust him. I think he'll take the money and scarper. You know how he ripped off Keith all those times."

"Let me have a word with Marianne," I said. "You're sure it was smack, aren't you baby?" I asked her.

"No, I'm not sure at all," she said. "That's the funny thing. I was just trying to tell Mick. It seemed to have been so cut it was like snorting talcum powder."

"Yeah, well, I'll bet it was talcum powder," I said.

I surmised that the man had sold Marianne talcum powder, pretending it was heroin. Then he had tipped off the cops that there was heroin in the house, and now he was hoping to collect £3,000 from Mick for bribing the police analyst. Of course, the laboratory would say the test was negative because the powder genuinely wasn't heroin.

"I'm certain that bloody sergeant was in on it, too," said Mick. "He's probably collecting half the profit."

Months later Mick claimed at Marlborough Street Court that he had been asked to pay a bribe for the police officer to "keep his mouth shut." The police officer replied that Mick was lying, and Jagger was accordingly fined £250 with £75 costs. Marianne was acquitted. Later the sergeant started to sue for libel, but he dropped the case; Scotland Yard investigated Jagger's allegation and found the policeman innocent. But he was rapidly shifted to another police department, and the persecution, at last, stopped.

Brian laughed when I told him about Jagger's bust. "Serves the bastard right. I hope he loses his visa," he said with a grin.

Cotchford Farm seemed to be good for him. He had insisted on showing me around the garden filled with statues of Christopher Robin, Winnie the Pooh and all the other nostalgic reminders of childhood. "This place has terrific vibes," he said. "I can see how A. A. Milne felt inspired to write here. It's so peaceful; there's just trees and fields everywhere I look. I even saw a fox dashing across the garden the other night."

I had offered him a snort of coke as we strolled into the huge strange shaped drawing room, crammed with beautiful antiques, dripping with history. "No way, man," he said. "I'm clean now. I'm a boozer again; I just bomb down to the village on my motorcycle and down a few beers with my mates in the pub. They're the real people, Tony, not like all those junkies up in London who will rip you off and flog you strychnine instead of coke if you give them half a chance."

"I got out of my skull in the pub a few weeks ago and crashed the bike into a shop window, but all the guys ran out, cleaned me up and helped me on the motorcycle again so I could clear out before there was any hassle. I thought I was going to be in trouble with the law again, but the whole village helped me to hush up what had happened."

I put away my tiny brown bottle of cocaine, and we sipped chilled white wine instead as we looked out over the garden together. "I've told Keith I won't be coming back to the Stones at all," he said suddenly. "They were going to keep the job open for me, but I don't want that. It would just hang over my head, it would be a good excuse for not doing any work. No, I'm getting a new band together, and we are going to be bigger than anyone would ever believe. I want to go right back to real rock 'n' roll instead of all this commercial crap the Stones have started putting out; the only trouble is that there doesn't seem to be any decent musicians around anymore. I've got Alexis Korner helping me to audition people, and it's working out okay. Give us a few more months, and we'll have the best band you've ever seen."

We had a few more glasses of wine, and then Brian leaned across to me conspiratorially. "Want to work for me, Tony?", he whispered. "That bastard Keith gave me is taking outrageous liberties. I mean he cooks for me all right and everything, but he treats me as though he's my boss. I sent him out to buy some furniture a few weeks ago, and I only discovered quite by accident that he had bought two sets of everything — one for his house, one for mine. But when I mentioned it to him, he just told me not

139

to be so fucking petty. Everyone seems to think I'm a millionaire or something, but I'm not. Mick and Keith get all the money for writing the songs, and they take a larger share of the profits from the records and concerts as well. They're not going to pay me that first hundred grand until next year, and I'm really worried about how I'm going to pay for everything until then. And I don't trust anybody. I know it sounds as though I'm getting paranoid again, but I'm not. It's just that there are a lot of people around who seem to think I'm still so out of my skull that I just don't know what's going on. But I'm not blind. I've got a pretty good idea who's ripping me off and how much they are ripping me off for."

Keith was pleased when I told him that Alexis Korner seemed to be helping to pull Brian together. "He's a good guy, Alexis, Brian's lucky," he said. But when I told him about the incident of the duplicate furniture, Keith scowled. "I warned him not to do that to Brian," he said. "That bastard tried the same stunt with me, and that's why I had to get rid of him."

The announcement that Brian was no longer a Stone was delayed while Jagger tried to persuade Eric Clapton to replace him. Clapton had just broken up with Cream, he had been a friend of all the Stones for many years and, after Hendrix, he was the best rock guitarist in the world. He was the obvious choice. But Clapton had been nauseated at the idea of stepping into Brian's shoes, and he hated the screaming and hysteria that the Stones attracted. He was much more interested in a new supergroup he was forming called Blind Faith. The Stones settled on a prodigiously talented twenty-year-old guitarist from John Mayall's Blues Breakers, named Mick Taylor.

Blind Faith — Eric Clapton, Ginger Baker, Stevie Winwood and Rich Grech — made their debut with a free concert in Hyde Park. "It's amazing," Mick said to Keith as we all stood together backstage. "I've never seen so many people in one place in my life. There must be a hundred and fifty thousand people out there." This was far bigger than any Stones gig had ever been, and Mick knew that the show would attract publicity to rival anything the Stones had enjoyed. He asked at once to speak to the man who had arranged the event.

"Would you be interested in a concert here by the Stones?", he asked Peter Jenner, when they had been introduced.

"Would I!" exclaimed Jenner. It took only a few hours for the concert to be fixed for Saturday, July 5.

"I'm really worried about doing the show without Brian," Mick said later. "People aren't going to like it."

"Yeah," said Keith, "but they are going to like it a whole lot less if we suddenly come out on stage with Mick Taylor in Brian's place and no explanation. We've got to tell the papers now that Brian has left. It's a real drag, but we can't just let it slide any longer."

The brief announcement was leaked to only one national newspaper, the *Daily Sketch*, on June 9.

"The Stones' music is not to my taste anymore." Brian was quoted as saying. "I want to play my own kind of music. Their music has progressed at a tangent to my own musical tastes."

Mick commented later: "Brian wants to play music which is more to his tastes rather than playing ours. So we have decided that it's best that he is free to follow his own inclinations. We have parted on the best of terms. Obviously, friendships like ours just don't break up like that."

Four days later Mick Taylor was introduced to the world at a photo session beside the bandstand in Hyde Park. With his tall, willowy good looks and clear blue eyes, he looked barely old enough to be out of school. He revealed to reporters hungry for an angle that he was a teetotal vegetarian. "I want to be as naturally healthy and aware as I can," he explained shyly.

"Why did you choose him, Mick?" someone asked Jagger.

" 'cos I fancy him, don't I?", he replied campily. And everybody laughed.

"Did you really mean all that stuff about not drinking?", Keith asked incredulously later.

"Sure." Mick grinned. "But I wouldn't say no if you were to offer me a bit of smoke."

The Stones had rehearsed long and hard with Taylor and had been quite overwhelmed by his virtuoso brilliance. If anything, he was an even better musician than Brian. Jagger was excited about the Hyde Park concert; the Stones hadn't given a real show in Britain for three years, and now the newspapers were predicting that more than a quarter of a million fans would be coming to Hyde Park on Saturday. It would be the biggest concert the world had ever seen, they said.

But still, Jagger was worried that the fans would realise that their blonde haired idol had been cruelly mistreated, and he persuaded Keith, Charlie and several Stones employees to phone Brian asking him to come to Hyde Park. Perhaps he could even guest on a few numbers with the band — just to show the world there really were no hard feelings.

"He's still getting more than two hundred grand a year out of us. It wouldn't kill him to come along," moaned Jagger. But many of those close to him felt that there was something slightly unpleasant in Jagger's egocentric desire to parade his vanquished rival before the world.

I was worried about Mick. The strain of the drug bust, his disintegrating relationship with Marianne, the new album, Brian — and now he was scheduled to fly to Australia to begin work on Tony Richardson's new movie, *Ned Kelly*.

"He's really going to crack up under all the pressure if he isn't careful," I said to Keith that night.

14

THE OLD MAN WAS DYING. BLOOD TRICKLED FROM HIS MOUTH, FROM THE gaping wound in his forehead, and he moaned softly, deliriously, as he lay in the dust of the desert road between Fez and Marrakesh. The donkey that had been pulling his little wicker cart had also been hit by the high-sided grey truck, and the dazed creature was trying vainly to struggle to its feet. Across the road the oranges the old man had been taking to market were splattered like squashed rabbits. The few long-robed bystand-ers were arguing so fiercely about whose fault it was, who should 'phone for an ambulance, that they scarcely looked up when a long black chauf-feur driven limousine glided to a halt behind the truck. Even when an exquisitely beautiful blonde, clad in a heart stoppingly short pink mini-dress, climbed out of the back of the car, they merely glanced curiously at her, then continued their furious agrument.

Anita Pallenberg slipped through the crowd to squat beside the old man. She wiped his bloody brow with a small perfumed handkerchief clutched tight in her hand. She plunged the scarlet handkerchief into her expensive leather handbag, climbed back into the limousine and signalled the chauffeur to drive on. That night, in her opulent room, Anita pulled the handkerchief from her bag and noticed that the scarlet had dried to a colour that was almost brown.

Later Anita was to attempt to use the same handkerchief to put a curse on a young man who had angered her. Subsequently, he died.

It was Kenneth Anger who had told Anita of the power of blood taken from a man killed by violence and she had listened rapturously, filing the information away to await her opportunity to obtain this most potent of talismans. Historically the blood of dying men has long been believed to possess magical properties. Spectators at executions, including those of Charles I of England and Louis XVI of France, struggled to dip

143

Brian in North Africa

cloths and handkerchiefs in the dying man's blood before his body ceased quivering.

Anger was a disciple of Aleister Crowley, the heroin addict whom some call the Great Beast and others the most advanced practitioner of magic the twentieth century will see. Mick and Marianne, Keith and Anita, and many others of the new, rich, jaded rock aristocracy listened spellbound as Anger turned them on to Crowley's powers and ideas. Jimmy Page, Led Zeppelin's sensitive leader, was so excited by the stories that he went so far as to buy Crowley's ghastly old mansion on the shores of Loch Ness, in Scotland.

Crowley was born in 1875 and joined a magical brethren called the Order of the Golden Dawn at the age of twenty-three. When he tried to take over leadership of the order from Samuel Mathers, the irate Mr. Mathers allegedly sent a vampire to attack him, but Crowley "smote her with her own current of evil" and defeated her. Mathers was not used to having his vampires treated in this cavalier fashion, so he quickly struck Crowley's pack of bloodhounds dead at a single blow, then sent one of Crowley's servants mad so that he tried to murder Crowley's wife. The vassal didn't give up, apparently, until he had been beaten off with a salmon gaff.

Crowley responded by summoning up the demon Beelzebub with forty attendant devils and sending them off to have a go at Mathers in Paris. When Mathers died some while afterwards, many occultists claimed that Crowley had murdered him by means of black magic. Characteristically Crowley passed the First World War living in the United States writing anti-British propaganda for the Germans, and in 1916 he ascended to the highest magical grade of Magus, going through a depraved ceremony in which he baptized a toad as Jesus Christ and crucified it. Even after he died, at Hastings in 1947, he still managed to upset people by having arranged for some of his followers to recite his orgiastic "Hymn to Pan" at his funeral service at Brighton Crematorium.

Like Crowley, Kenneth Anger claimed to be a Magus, though he refused to reveal whether toad sacrifices had been necessary for his promotion. What is indisputable is that Anger does appear to have certain powers, and he has been linked with some extraordinary incidents. His life's work, for instance, was to have been a film of homage to the devil called *Lucifer Rising*. For the role of Lucifer, Anger employed a good-looking young man named Bobby Beausoleil, who played guitar with the Californian rock band Love. Mysteriously, after many months of filming,

Beausoleil appeared to go berserk and carried out a singularly bestial murder which ended with his writing on a wall with his victim's blood. Much later, when Charles Manson's diabolical 'family' had been arrested for a string of gruesome killings including that of the pregnant actress Sharon Tate — it became clear that Beausoleil had been an ardent follower and close friend of Manson's. Some even whispered that in order to make police believe they had the wrong man, the Tate murder was carried out in a similar style to the killing for which Bobby was being held in custody. The full truth will probably never be known, but what is certain is that Manson was a demonic figure on a par with Crowley himself.

After Beausoleil had been jailed for life, Anger decided that Jagger should play Lucifer. Kenneth had long been intrigued by the rabble-rousing, almost supernatural power the Rolling Stones seemed to hold over their audiences. When he met the head Stone at Robert Fraser's flat in Mayfair, he was surprised by the aura of power that seemed to emanate from him. Close up, Jagger seemed almost to crackle with electricity, sparking off energy to everyone who came close to him. Jagger had been equally fascinated by Anger, by his talk of metaphysical forces and diabolical powers. He agreed to help with *Lucifer Rising*. He wrote music for the film and supervised the sound recording, but Anger wanted more, and eventually Jagger apologetically backed out. Mick's brother, Chris Jagger, acted opposite Marianne Faithfull in Egypt for the film, but Anger was unhappy with their performances. Such was Anger's desire for perfection that ten years after he started work on the film it had still not been completed.

In 1969, however, he put out *Invocation of My Demon Brother*, a bizarre film which flashed glimpses of ceremonial magic against such disparates as the Stones in concert and American GIs leaping from their helicopters in Vietnam. The film included most of the music Jagger had written for *Lucifer Rising* and starred the evil Bobby Beausoleil as Lucifer.

We all were just a little afraid of Kenneth. Again and again inexplicable things involving him would happen. Once, for example, Robert Fraser arranged an opening party for some white sculptures that John Lennon and Yoko Ono had created. It was a zany party with all the guests dressed in white. We were even forced to drink a white mineral water. I saw Kenneth clearly at the party, but when I went across to talk to him, he seemed to have vanished. I thought little of it until that afternoon when Anita, Marianne, Keith and Mick all said that they, too, had seen Kenneth but had been unable to find him when they wanted to talk to him. "Anyway," said Anita, "it's very strange because Kenneth told me he wouldn't be able to come to the exhibition because he was going to be away on business in Germany."

Kenneth didn't return to London for two weeks, and by then numerous other people who had been at the party — John, Yoko, Robert, Jim Dine — all remarked on having seen Kenneth across the crowded room, but having been unable to speak to him. Eventually we asked almost everyone who had been there if he or she had spoken to him — and none of them had.

"Were you there?" I asked him one day. And he only laughed.

On another occasion Kenneth came with Robert, me and a couple of other friends for coffee at a little club called the Costa Blanca, off Tottenham Court Road. We drove there in my Alfa Romeo and walked together to the bar. Kenneth was standing right beside me. "Five coffees, please," I said, then turned around to find that Kenneth had vanished.

"Where is he?" I asked. And nobody knew. So I went out into the street to see if he was there, and though there wasn't a corner for two hundred yards in each direction, he wasn't there either. Even if he had sprinted down the road like Mercury, he couldn't possibly have vanished so quickly. We didn't see Kenneth again for another month.

Much later Anita and Keith talked with Kenneth about their vague wish to marry. "The trouble is it's all such a hassle," said Keith. "Anita's a dual nationality. German-Italian, and I'm English. There are so many forms and things to fill in it just doesn't seem to be worth it."

"You could go through a real pagan marriage ceremony," suggested Kenneth.

"That would be terrific," enthused Anita.

"Of course, there are certain formalities," he explained. "The door of the house where the marriage ceremony is to be held must be painted gold with a magical paint containing special herbs, which represents the sun."

"It sounds beautiful," said Anita. "So much better than a rotten Registry Office ceremony with all those horrid reporters everywhere."

Kenneth went home, and we all went to our beds. I was staying at the house, and before I finally turned in, I checked to ensure that the big, heavy three-inch thick mahogany door was firmly locked.

The next morning I was awakened by Anita yelling hysterically to Keith from the hallway. I pulled on my dressing gown and ran downstairs to see what the commotion was about. "Look, Tony, look," she screamed, pointing to the door. I was astonished to discover that it had been fastidiously painted inside and out in gold. The paintwork was completely dry and was so immaculate that it was obvious that the craftsmen who had carried out the job had removed the huge door from its hinges first.

"It must have been Kenneth, but I can't work out how he did it," said Keith. "The security people put the strongest lock you can buy on that door, and there's no way anyone could have got hold of a spare key. Besides, we would have certainly heard if someone had been taking the door off its hinges in the middle of the night. And how could anyone have carried out such a flawless job in the dark?"

"It must be just another of Kenneth's powers," said Anita. "It means he can fly into the house anytime he wants to."

We all looked at one another, and I saw fear in Keith and Anita's eyes.

"I don't want to go through with any black magic wedding," said Keith. "This thing has gone far enough."

Keith began to shy away from magic then, though publicly both he and Jagger had discovered that satanism sold records, so they continued to foster a demonic image for themselves. Before they cruised off to South America, for example, Keith lied to a journalist from the English *Sunday Express*: "We've become very interested in magic, and we're very serious about this trip. We're hoping to see this magician who practices both white and black magic. He has a very long and difficult name which we can't pronounce. We call him Banana for short."

Anita scowled when she read the story and told him he was a fool to mock powers he was unable to comprehend. She was obsessed with black magic and began to carry a string of garlic with her everywhere — even to bed — to ward off vampires. She also had a strange, mysterious old shaker for holy water which she used for some of her rituals. Her ceremonies became increasingly secret, and she would warn me never to interrupt her when she was working on a spell.

One day I was alarmed by the smell of smoke coming from upstairs. I dashed up to Anita's room to find her asleep in bed with a ring of spluttering candles on the floor around her. One of the candles had started the carpet smouldering as it had burned down. I quickly stamped out the fire and doused the other candles. Anita, who I presumed had taken her customary huge dose of sleeping pills, didn't wake at all. I left her to her macabre dreams.

Tony Sanchez

In her bedroom she kept a huge, ornate carved chest, which she guarded so jealously that I assumed it was her drug stash. The house was empty one day, and I decided to take a peep inside. The drawers were filled with scraps of bone, wrinkled skin and fur from strange animals. I slammed the chest shut in disgust and fled from the room.

Anita insisted on sharing her preoccupation with Keith, despite his reluctance, and he found that the knowledge she gave him was an exciting source of inspiration. The Stones' album title, *Get Yer Ya-Yas Out*, is based on a phrase which recurs frequently in African voodoo.

But as Keith and Anita learned more about the powers of darkness, they grew secretive. They knew the subject frightened me, and they got rid of me when Kenneth Anger or other demonic friends came to call. Keith was impressed when Kenneth ticked off all the great artistic rebels who'd flirted with black magic — Blake, Byron, Oscar Wilde, Yeats and De Quincey. Keith told Robert Greenfield in *Rolling Stone*: "Kenneth Anger told me I was his right-hand man. It's just what you feel. Whether you've got that good and evil thing together. Left-hand path, right-hand path, how far do you want to go down? Once you start there's no going back. Where they lead to is another thing. It's something everybody ought to explore. There are possibilities there. A lot of people have played with it, and it's inside everybody. I mean, Dr. John's whole trip is based on it. Why do people practice voodoo? All these things are bunched under the name of superstition and old wives' tales. I'm no expert at it. I would never pretend to be; I just try to bring it into the open a little. There's only so much you can bring into the open. There's got to be people around who know it all, man. Nobody ever really finds out what's important with the kinds of government you've got now. Fifty years after they'll tell you what really went on.

"... Mick and I basically have been through the same things. A lot of it comes from association and press and media people laying it on people. Before, when we were just innocent kids out for a good time, they were saying, 'They're evil, they're evil.' Oh, I'm evil, really? So that makes you start thinking about evil. What is evil? Half of it, I don't know how much people think of Mick as the devil or as just a good rock performer or what? There are black magicians who think we are acting as unknown agents of Lucifer and others who think we are Lucifer. Everybody's Lucifer."

With his characteristic restlessness, Mick rapidly became bored with the mumbo jumbo of satanism. It was power that fascinated him, the

149

ability to control individuals, audiences, even societies — and he knew
Satan wasn't to thank for his strength in that direction.

"Of course, I do occasionally arouse primaeval instincts," Mick told
a reporter. "But I mean, most men can do that. They can't do it to so
many. I just happen to be able to do it to several thousand people. It's fun
to do that. It's really just a game, isn't it? I mean these girls do it to
themselves. They're all charged up. It's a dialogue of energy. They give
you a lot of energy and take a lot away. Maybe they want something from
life, from me. Maybe they think I can give it to them. I don't know.

"I get a strange feeling on stage. I feel all the energy coming from
the audience. I feel quite violent sometimes. I quite often want to smash
up the microphone or something. I don't feel the same person on stage as
I am normally."

Mick's fascination with power, coupled with his conventional middle class upbringing, led him inevitably to conventional politics, and for
many years, he harboured a deep and secret ambition to become a Member
of Parliament for the Labour Party.

He was actively encouraged by Tom Driberg, the MP for Barking, in
Essex, who later became Lord Bradwell. Like many homosexuals, Driberg
found Jagger attractive, but he also recognised in him the charisma necessary for success in politics. After all, argued Driberg, if show-biz personalities like Ronald Reagan could achieve prominence in American
Government, how much more so could an educated, thoughtful man like
Jagger.

The two were introduced by the American poet Allen Ginsberg,
who was a mutual friend. "He's a terrific guy, really hip." Ginsberg had
said.

"Yeah, I've heard of him," said Mick. "He's the guy who complained in the Commons about the way Robert and I were handcuffed
together at Chichester. And he's keen on legalisation of dope, too, isn't
he?"

They met first at Mick's flat in Marylebone Road and hit it off immediately. Mick didn't guess for a moment that Driberg was gay. Later, when
Jagger did find out, it only increased his liking for the MP. Many of Mick's
closest friends are men who, he knows, long to go to bed with him. The
feminine side of his complex personality seems to delight in the flattery
and admiration they heap flirtatiously upon him. Yet paradoxically, he is
extremely masculine, and any advances are rebuffed.

When Mick and Marianne moved to their big house in Cheyne

Walk, they often entertained Driberg and had long talks about England's rotten Government. Jagger professed to be an anarchist, but Driberg said that anarchy was no solution; it was an ideal that wouldn't be practical for centuries. Driberg wanted Jagger to join the Labour Party and become a left-wing activist who would grab the party and shake it by the neck.

"l really want to enter politics," Jagger told Marianne. "It is so much more significant and worthwhile than just writing and singing songs for the rest of my life."

But Jagger knew that he would have to give up his career on the off chance that he might have a talent for politics. He seemed afraid to take the risk, and realistically, he knew perfectly well that despite his following among the young, he'd alienated the majority of voters.

Although he continued to talk to Driberg about politics in the abstract, he always found an excuse for not actually joining the Labour Party and standing for his local council. Even when Edward Heath's Conservative Government was at its worst, he said. "This time I really want to join the Labour Party so I can help to get rid of that idiot, but I've just got so much work to do, I just don't have the time."

None of the other Stones shared Mick's interest in politics. They had their own toys to spend their money on. Charlie Watts was obsessed with the Civil War and spent thousands of pounds collecting guns, medals, swords and uniforms. When the Stones toured the United States, Charlie spent a week at Gettysburg and other battlefields trying to visualize cavalry charges and murderous hand to hand combat.

Brian's secret passion was the strangest of all. As a kid he'd been an ardent collector of the numbers on British buses and he had an encyclopedic knowledge of bus models and bus corporations. He would sneak out on his own in the Rolls to go bus spotting. Twice he even bought buses that caught his fancy. I was in the office when a call came through from a garage that wanted to know where to deliver Brian's latest double-decker. "There's been a mistake," fibbed the girl who answered the phone. "Someone is going around pretending to be Brian Jones and buying up lots of buses. Please cancel the order."

"Jesus," she said, when she had hung up the 'phone. "What on earth is going to happen to that poor, crazy, mixed-up little boy?"

15

T<small>HE TRANSISTOR RADIO BESIDE MY BED CRACKLED RELUCTANTLY INTO LIFE AS</small> I turned it on to catch the early-morning news bulletin. "Police believe," intoned the announcer monotonously, "that a man found dead at Hartfield, in Sussex, early today was a leading member of the Rolling Stones pop group...."

It was like a bucket of water in the face. "What?" I said to myself out loud, shaking my head in disbelief. Mick Jagger dead? How could he be? Mick, so strong, so full of life, dead? This meant the end of the Rolling Stones... there was no way the group could carry on without him. Mick was the Stones. I had to speak to Keith. I had to know what had happened.

Anita answered the phone. "Is it true?" I asked, speaking in Italian.

"Yeah," she said.

"Really?"

"Yes, really...."

"Couldn't they have made a mistake?" I asked desperately.

"No. They found him in his swimming pool."

I was confused. I'd been to both Mick's house on Cheyne Walk and to Stargroves many times, and I knew that neither house had a pool. "Are you sure?" I asked her again insistently.

"Yes, Brian's dead," she replied.

"Oh, God, I thought they said it was Mick."

"No, thank Christ, it was only Brian...."

And I heard the callousness in her voice. Anita of all people, the one woman Brian had genuinely loved, and she was glad it was Brian who was dead, not Mick Jagger. I could feel sobs beginning to choke in my throat. "I'll be over in half an hour," I said. And slammed down the phone.

When I arrived at Cheyne Walk, Mick was there, and he, Keith and Anita were deep in gloomy conversation. They had been 'phoned at Olympic Studios at midnight by the man who was supposed to be looking after Brian, and he had broken the news to them. "I just don't understand it," said Mick. "Brian couldn't have drowned by himself. Don't you remember that time we were in Australia, how he swam out for a mile through all that pounding surf and we couldn't even see him because he was so far out at sea? The guy was the strongest swimmer I have ever known. There are a lot of people who might have drowned — but not Brian."

But beyond a feeling of stunned disbelief, there was no emotion. No one shed a tear; no one spoke of the tragic irony of Brian dying just as he was beginning to clean himself up and pick up the pieces of his life. "You cold, hard hearted bastards," I thought.

Even then, though, there were little incongruities, tiny details that made us all wonder about the true circumstances of Brian's death.

The chauffeur who had told the Stones about the death, for instance, now said he was at his home in East London when the accident happened. "Strange," said Keith.

"Not really," said Mick. "I expect someone 'phoned him at his house and told him about it."

Keith and Mick nagged everyone who worked for them to try to find out what had happened, and gradually the story that was to be told at the subsequent inquest was pieced together.

On the night of Wednesday, July 2, 1969, Brian had been at the house with at least three people — his new, Swedish girl friend, Anna Wohlin; a builder named Frank Thorogood, who had been on the Stones' payroll for three years, and a young nurse, Janet Lawson, who was a friend of Thorogood's.

Brian had been drinking vodka heavily and dropping downers, and Thorogood, too, had drunk a considerable amount. At about midnight Brian slipped into a pair of swimming trunks. Miss Lawson objected: "Brian, don't go into the pool. You're in no condition to go swimming."

But he ignored her and stepped outside to dive into the warm water. Anna and Thorogood went swimming, but Janet Lawson returned to the house.

The 'phone rang and Anna Wohlin left the pool to answer it, leaving Brian and Thorogood swimming together in the deep, clear water. A few minutes later Thorogood came into the house to get a towel; then Janet Lawson walked back to the pool. Suddenly Janet screamed, "Come quickly — Brian's at the bottom of the pool."

Anna jumped in, fully clothed, to pull Brian to the surface. Thorogood helped heave him out of the water. Anna gave him the kiss of life. Janet placed the heel of her hand on his chest and pumped hard in an effort to revive his heart.

"While we were doing this, I actually felt his hand grip mine," said Anna.

An ambulance and a doctor were called, but Brian was dead by the time they arrived, and they called the police.

The next morning the man who was supposed to have been 'looking after' Brian walked by the pool with Les Perrin, the Stones' publicist, and found one of the aerosol asthma sprays Brian frequently used (though I never saw him suffer an asthma attack) beside the water's edge. Astonishingly the police appeared to have missed this crucial piece of evidence when they had examined the scene of this most mysterious death on the previous night.

At the inquest, held a week later at East Grinstead, the pathologist, Dr. Albert Sachs, surprised none of us when he revealed: "For a man of his age his heart was a bit bigger than it should have been. It was fat and flabby. His liver was twice the normal weight. It was in an advanced state of fatty degeneration and not functioning properly." Dr. Sachs managed to quash the suggestion that Brian had suffered an asthma attack while under the water by stating, "I could find no evidence microscopically that he had had an attack of asthma."

The coroner, Angus Sommerville, ruled that Brian had died "due to immersion in fresh water under the influence of drugs and alcohol" and formally recorded a verdict of death by misadventure.

Immediately the vicious gossips of the pop world — nobody record pluggers and deputy assistants who seek to enhance their own prestige by pretending to be intimates of the stars — pronounced that there was positive proof that Brian had killed himself but that it had all been hushed up. Jagger, according to this malicious and totally untrue story, had stolen away a girl friend of Brian's in just the same way that Keith had stolen Anita. This final ignominy had, they said, tipped Brian right over the edge so that he had committed suicide — but the Stones had paid everyone to hush things up because they were afraid the resultant bad publicity would turn the public against the band. The story was blatantly untrue, but I have heard it whispered, in varying forms, again and again.

Even some of Brian's closest friends felt they couldn't rule out the possibility of suicide altogether.

Alexis Korner, for instance, told journalist Tony Scaduto: "To commit suicide, you have to plan to kill yourself, and I honestly don't believe that Brian planned to die. It is possible that in a moment of paranoia, down at the bottom of the pool, he became aware of how easy it would be to die. But I don't think so. I really think it was a mistake. I don't think he deliberately planned to commit suicide. I would have felt more sorrow for him and less for me if it had been intended, but now I feel more for me and for all of us because he isn't here. Most of the sadness is for me because I miss him, and yet I can't help thinking that if Brian had to die, it was a good time for him to die. Because he was happy at that time. If it had happened six months earlier, it would have been much sadder for him because he was in a state of severe depression. At least he died when he was beginning to feel happy."

But there were certain facts that even Alexis didn't know; within a few days of Brian's death someone entered his front door with a key and loaded his guitars, his Persian rugs, his antiques and everything else of value into a lorry. The things were taken away and hidden, to be sold at a later date. We all believed we knew the man responsible for the theft, but we had no direct proof.

There were other inconsistencies, tiny in themselves but which, when put together, added up to a feeling of certainty that at least a dozen other people were at Cotchford Farm on the night of Brian's death. A lot of people appeared, too, to have taken a lot of dope on that night. And there was the mystery of why Brian should take downers, then go swimming. People take sleeping pills to help them relax, and the last thing anyone who is on downers feels like doing is going for a swim.

The Stones knew that Brian's death was not as clear-cut as it had seemed to be, but avoided discussing the subject.

Eventually, a reporter from *Rolling Stone* magazine pumped Keith about the death, and he said more than he meant to:

Some very weird things happened that night Brian died . . . there were people there that suddenly disappeared. We were at a session that night and we didn't expect Brian to come along. He'd officially left the band. And someone called us up at midnight and said: "Brian's dead." Well, what the fuck's going on? We had these chauffeurs working for us and we tried to find out . . . some of them had a weird hold over Brian. There were a lot of chicks there and there was a whole thing going on, they were having a party. I don't know, man, I just don't know what happened to Brian that night. There was no one there that'd want to murder him. Someone didn't take care of him.

And they should have done because he had someone there who was supposed to take care of him. Everyone knew what Brian was like, especially at a party. Maybe he did just go in for a swim and have an asthma attack . . . . We were completly shocked. I got straight into it and wanted to know who was there and couldn't find out. The only one I could ask was the one I think who got rid of everybody and did the whole disappearing trick so that when the cops arrived, it was just an accident. Maybe it was. Maybe the guy just wanted to get everyone out of the way so it wasn't all names involved, etc. Maybe he did the right thing, but I don't know. I don't even know who was there that night and finding out is impossible . . . . It's the same feeling with who killed Kennedy. You can't get to the bottom of it.

The employee who was supposed to have been taking care of Brian moved on. The next time I saw him, two years later, he was financing a rock 'n' roll television show.

And I never did find out quite what happened to Brian's first £100,000 retirement payment.

16

THE ARMOURED CAR NOSED ITS WAY FROM THE CAR PARK OF THE PLUSH Londonderry Hotel cautiously, as if the driver were foraying among the terrorists of Shankhill Road. But this was Mayfair, 1969 and on heaped mattresses inside the intimidating khaki vehicle were all the Rolling Stones with Michael Cooper and me — who were working as the Stones' personal photographers. As we inched our way towards the stage which had been set up for the huge free concert in Hyde Park, the fans rapidly spotted the armoured car, guessed who was inside and rushed toward us whooping like hill bandits closing in for the kill. Fists rained like bullets on the armour plating, and we could feel the army of long-haired boys and mini-skirted girls rocking the truck from side to side so violently it felt as if we was about to roll over. "Jesus," said Mick Jagger. "This is bloody crazy. I knew we should have forced the cops to let us use a helicopter."

The road crew had expected the journey to take five minutes — but the frightening, sweating mile-long crawl took us three quarters of an hour. Before we climbed out, Keith whispered to me, "Got a snort, Tone?" so I passed him the brown glass bottle, and he took a quick couple of snorts through the tube he wore on a chain around his neck. Jagger, too, was glad of a couple of hits of cocaine to bolster his confidence. The rest of the Stones looked on disapprovingly, like old matrons who have somehow come into contact with wild, young runaways on a bus ride.

"Okay." Mick grinned as the coke flashed into his brain. "Let's get out there and give those bastards the best rock 'n' roll show of their lives. We're gonna blow their fuckin' ears off...."

Brian Jones had been dead for two days. At first Jagger, Richard, all of them had agreed: "We can't play Hyde Park now. It'd be sick. We've got to cancel the gig."

But then, as we sat gloomily in the Stones' office, Charlie had murmured lugubriously, "We ought to do it. Let's make it a memorial for Brian, do the whole show as a kind of special tribute to him."

"Right," said Keith. "Brian would have dug an idea like that more than us making some kind of silly speeches at his funeral. We can put up great big posters of him around the stage and maybe get the kids to have a minute's silence in his memory."

Later a reporter trying to snatch an interview with Keith on the pavement suggested that it was in bad taste for the Stones to hold such a huge concert before Brian had even been buried. Keith punched him on the nose.

Marianne took Brian's death badly. In her fragile, confused condition she interpreted it as a portent of her own doom, and she wept for hours, lying alone on the big bed at Cheyne Walk. Mick emotionally destroyed Brian as surely as he was destroying Marianne. He drains people, takes over their soul, their personality, their whole identity. He took away Brian's self-respect, his confidence in his music. And he was doing the same to Marianne by trying to show that he was a better actor than she. He was going to be playing opposite her in *Ned Kelly* when they went to Australia. "I know that he wants to wipe the floor with me, to subjugate me before the world," Marianne said.

In her misery she started snorting heroin again — even though she had virtually managed to give up the drug in preparation for the film role. Jagger had grown impatient with her; he was facing drug charges because of her habit, and he was under too much pressure to humour a tearful, accusing woman. He had invited black actress Marsha Hunt, one of the many girls with whom he was beginning to have affairs, to come along to the Hyde Park gig.

Marsha, Afro-haired and clad from head to toe in white buckskin, like a beautiful Indian woman, hung around at the side of the stage flaunting herself, delighting in the recognition triggered from publicity surrounding her success in the musical *Hair*.

Huge colour photographs of Brian, looking healthier than I could ever remember seeing him, hung at the side of the stage. Sam Cutler, the master of ceremonies, repeatedly told the vast, half a million strong audience that the Stones wanted to observe a minute's silence in Brian's memory before they began their set. I took up my position at the side of the stage, clipped an 85-millimetre lens into my Nikon and waited for the action. "Christ," I thought, "I've never seen so many people in one place in my entire life."

There was an adulatory thunder from the sea of faces as Mick pounced on the stage. He wore an extraordinary white dress with a dog collar around his neck.

"No," he hollered at the crowd's cheers. It seemed, for a moment, that he really would do as he had promised and ask the audience to stay silent as a gesture to Brian. But he knew instinctively that trying to shut everyone up would be such a downer that it would mar the show. And there were so many people here, so many critics and fans and friends, that this gig had to be a triumph. Besides, he was off to Australia soon, and he needed to zap all the people who were whispering that the Stones would never be the same again without their beautiful, blonde, lead guitarist.

"Yeeeah," he screamed, contradicting himself. "We're gonna have a good time, all right?"

"All right," the crowd chorused back.

"Cool it for a minute," he said camply as his dress billowed in the wind. "I would really like to say something about Brian...." And the crowd was suddenly hushed. Many of them had read so much about Brian, seen him on stage and on television so many times that they really felt they knew him. And they were as genuinely distraught at his untimely death as I had been.

"Peace, peace! he is not dead, he doth not sleep — " Mick began reciting from Shelley's *Adonais*. His reading was heartless, clumsy, awkward. But already hundreds of thousands of girls seemed to be sobbing, and as I looked out at their tearful faces, I could feel my own eyes begin to sting so that I pulled out a handkerchief to pretend I had developed a sudden cold.

> He hath awakened from the dream of life —
> 'Tis we, who lost in stormy visions, keep
> With phantoms an unprofitable strife,
> And in mad trance, strike with our spirit's knife
> Invulnerable nothings. *We* decay
> Like corpses in a charnel; fear and grief
> Convulse us and consume us day by day....

The television crews and the photographers from Fleet Street were going crazy now, shoving and pushing across the stage, capturing this historic moment. And Jagger, instinctively, was playing to the audience, to the media.

Yet the audience seemed to be caught in the spell of some mass heartbreak which made them unaware that they were listening only to the bathos of Jumpin' Jack Shelley.

> And cold hopes swarm like worms within our living clay.
> The One remains, the many change and pass;
> Heaven's light forever shines, Earth's shadows fly;
> Life, like a dome of many-coloured glass,
> Stains the white radiance of Eternity,
> Until Death tramples it to fragments, — Die,
> If thou wouldst be with that which thou dost seek!
> Follow where all is fled! — Rome's azure sky,
> Flowers, ruins, statues, music, words, are weak
> The glory they transfuse with fitting truth to speak.

Jagger seemed hugely relieved when the reading was over. As he finished the poem roadies opened brown cardboard boxes (which had once contained Crosse and Blackwell baked beans according to their labels) at the side of the stage to release several hundred white butterflies, which were supposed to emulate Brian's soul as they soared into the azure sky.

Unfortunately the boxes had been left for too long in the heat of the July sun, and many of the butterflies fluttered only a few yards, then fell, dying onto the heads of the wet-eyed fans, like confetti. But already Keith was pumping into the opening chords of "Lemon Squeezer."

At the front of the stage a couple of dozen skinny, spotty, educationally subnormal Hell's Angels shoved people around and generally upset everyone because they understood that was what Jagger had ordered. A girl keeping time to "Honky Tonk Women" with two empty Pepsi cans had them confiscated by one of the black-jacketed morons.

Mick Taylor tried shyly to hide behind the hair billowing around his shoulders as he played hopelessly out of time. And I became very aware of how much Brian's strutting, mincing, desperate to be loved stance had been a vital part of the Stones' appeal. Mick Taylor appeard to have about as much charisma as Bill Wyman (and you can't have much less than that).

By the time "Sympathy for the Devil" had shuddered to a close screaming girls were tearing and scratching at one another to be close to Mick Jagger. But he only looked the other way as the Angels pushed them from the edge of the stage like rats from a ship's deck.

"Yeah, all right, so the sound was dreadful," he said after we had

been to see Chuck Berry at the Albert Hall that evening, "but no one's ever had a bigger audience. I'd like to see the bloody moptops beat that one."

Mick said he was too busy to attend Brian's funeral. He and Marianne had to fly to Australia the next morning. But he did agree to give an interview in order to propound his views on Brian's demise, which, incidentally, gave him immediate access to mass media exposure. Just before Hyde Park he told an interviewer from Granada Television, "Brian will be at the concert. I mean, he'll be there! But it all depends on what you believe in. If you're agnostic, he's just dead, and that's it. When we get there this afternoon, he's gonna be there. I don't believe in Western bereavement. You know, I can't suddenly put on a long black veil and walk the hills. But it is still very upsetting. I want to make it so that Brian's send-off from the world is filled with as much happiness as possible."

He was more candid, though, to a penetrating interviewer from BBC Radio: "I suppose it was the kind of feeling that if anyone was going to die, Brian was going to die. You always had the feeling Brian wouldn't live that long. He just lived his life very fast. He was kind of like a butterfly, oh, we were very close at one point.... I didn't really understand quite what Brian wanted to do, really, in terms of his songs. He kept a lot of things to himself like that. He never played me a song he'd written, so it was quite hard to know what he really wanted to do. If he'd written — I think he wrote some songs — but he was very shy and found it rather hard to lay it down to us: 'This is a song that goes like....' And because he didn't try to bring it out, it wasn't a question of forcefully sort of stifling him."

When I heard his words, I had at first been angry, but then, on

161

reflection, I realised that Mick was being totally frank, totally honest, telling the truth as he saw it. Brian had aspired to the highest pinnacle in rock stardom; if he didn't have the strength to hang on when he got there, it wasn't perhaps fair to criticise Jagger for giving him a shove instead of a helping hand.

The trauma had thrown Marianne back on heroin, hard, but she knew she would have to give it up if she were to take on Jagger in the movie. Besides, everyone said she'd have more chance of finding gold in the desert than smack in Sydney. Her doctor prescribed Sodium Amytal to help her sleep off her withdrawals when she arrived in Australia. She was already starting to shiver, despite the brilliant sunshine, when the 'plane landed and there were dozens of bullying, pushing reporters and photographers asking them banal questions — "Have you heard that the Glenrowan gang is going to kidnap Mick and cut off his hair?" — and firing off flashbulbs in their faces. By the time they staggered into their room at the Chevron Hotel she was retching, dizzy, and her skin was covered with goose bumps. Jagger was so exhausted by the flight and the reporters' barrage that he ripped off his clothes and tumbled into the big, soft double bed to fall asleep in seconds, like a small boy. They never spoke of her drug addiction; in his peculiarly English way he always pretended not to notice. What she did to her body was her affair.

But Marianne was beginning to hallucinate now. Her cold turkey was worse than she had ever known it, like a severe bout of malaria. She felt death was in the room. In the bathroom she sat on a stool and gazed at the face she saw reflected in the mirror — Brian's face. She had cut her hair short, like Brian's, just before he died, and now it became clear — she was Brian. She swallowed a handful of Mandrax tablets to ease the withdrawal symptoms.

She had been confused about her identity for months. She had gradually become nothing more than an adjunct of Mick Jagger. He had taken over her personality so that she no longer seemed to exist as a separate person. She saw now that he had overwhelmed Brian in precisely the same way — stealing his ideas, his strengths, his character until nothing remained. The shell had been discarded like a lobster picked clean.

The dead eyes, gazing blankly from beneath the long blonde fringe, were Brian's eyes. And then he seemed to wake as though he had merely nodded out after a snort of smack. "Where's my Valium?" he was saying. "God, I feel awful." He seemed to be talking from the other side of the mirror, and Marianne could catch only an occasional word. It sounded as if someone were trying to talk while underwater. Marianne knew what he was trying to tell her: that he had been overcome by cramp and asthma, he hadn't been ready for death and no one had been there to help him this time. It was very cold, and Marianne shivered uncontrollably, her teeth chattering noisily together. She swallowed all her Sodium Amytal tablets, 150 of them, and the shivers seemed to go away. She slipped into the crisp cotton sheets beside Mick, Brian took her hand firmly and she knew she was going through the looking glass.

Brian was twenty-six years old when he died. "He died," said one friend, "as one of the leaders of a generation that was determined to build the biggest monument to itself in the history of mankind even if the monument turned out to be a whirlwind. He died taking the rap for all the drug users of Britain." The Reverend Hugh Hopkins was now burying Brian, and he was one of those who seemed to be quite determined that he should carry that rap to his grave.

After praying for Marianne's recovery — she had been in a coma for two days — he lectured Keith, Anita, Mick Taylor, Bill, Charlie and all the fans who had crammed into his church, on the evils of the now generation: "Brian was the rebel, he had little patience with authority, convention, tradition.... Typical of so many of his generation who have come to see in the Rolling Stones an expression of a whole attitude towards life. Much of what this ancient church stood for, for nine hundred years, seems actually irrelevant to them."

"Wanker," whispered Keith.

17

THE SCENE CONFIRMED EVERY ACCUSATION OF DECADENCE EVER LAUNCHED at the Rolling Stones. It was the best suite in the best hotel in the world, the Ritz. A crystal chandelier sparkled from the ceiling like a duchess's diamond necklace, and beneath it Keith, Anita and I sat cross-legged around an ornate Oriental pipe. Keith was bare-footed and wore trousers the colour of fire that had been made up from a roll of curtain material he had bought in Marrakesh. Anita wore an African caftan, but its voluminous folds were not loose enough to conceal the swelling in her belly. She was five months pregnant. It was early afternoon, and we were smoking pure Chinese opium, the Rémy Martin of drugs. We were intoxicated enough for conversation to be fluid and all the world to be beautiful, but not so far gone that we were watching the room spinning like a whirlwind or nodding out. We all jumped when the knock at the door came but relaxed again when one of the chauffeurs called out, "Keef, it's me, got some good news for you."

"Piss off," Keith called back with his usual measure of tact and charm.

But the varlet was persistent, so, after much discussion and argument, Anita opened the heavily inlaid mahogany door.

"Your car's ready," the chauffeur said. "You know, the big Merc."

"Oh," she asked the driver at once, "can you go and fetch it — bring it here right away?"

Then she turned to Keith and told him they were going to stay at Redlands for a while. "I'm sick of living here just because the builders are at Cheyne Walk," she said. "This hotel gives me the creeps, all the staff make it obvious they despise us and I reckon it's just a matter of time before somebody tips off the cops and we get busted."

164

Tony Sanchez, Anita and Keith

So they began to pack for the big trek. It took them nearly four hours — partly because they were mildly stoned but also because Keith and Anita are the most acquisitive people I have ever met. They only have to take a stroll down Regent Street to spend a couple of thousand pounds on cameras, tape recorders, portable televisions — anything that glitters and catches their fancy. So fabulous is their wealth that every materialistic whim instantly becomes reality.

At length, though, they were ready and they marched outside to Piccadilly, where a crowd had already gathered to admire the huge gleaming car. An army of porters were engaged to cram the suitcases, televisions and guitars into the boot and the back seat. Then they drove off grandly into the night.

Unfortunately Keith still had little idea of how to control a car with a manual gearbox and he repeated his previous error of attempting to drive the car as he would his automatic Bentley. As he roared into a bend on the West Wittering Road, a few miles from Redlands, the car brushed against a kerb at 60 mph, ricocheted across to the other side of the road, somersaulted on to its side, then rolled down a bank and came to rest, miraculously, standing upright in a small copse of oak trees. A passing motorist stopped and rushed to help Keith and Anita out of the huge vehicle. Both were covered with blood and fragments of the shattered windscreen, and Anita moaned softly that she felt her shoulder bone had been broken. "Wait here," said the other driver, "while I 'phone for an ambulance."

"Quick," said Keith urgently as soon as he had gone. "We've got to hide all our gear."

They emptied their bags of heroin, cocaine, grass and opium which Keith put in a polythene bag and hid in the branches of a nearby tree. Seconds later the police arrived, and immediately one of the more officious cops, who had taken part in the raid on Redlands years before, insisted on searching them. He suspected drugs were to blame for Keith's extraordinary driving. He found nothing in Keith's leather shoulder bag, but then he opened Anita's capacious handbag and extracted a string of garlic with obvious distaste.

"I need them for protection," Anita said in response to his quizzical look. Kenneth Anger had warned her that enemies might send vampires to attack her and the garlic would ward off the brutes.

The policeman dug deeper and found three disposable syringes and a dozen phials containing a mysterious substance. "I must ask you to

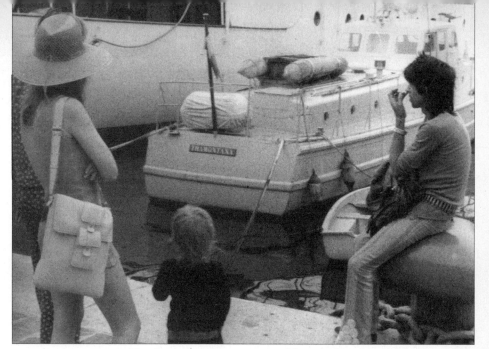

accompany me to Chichester police station," he said, ushering them into a police car before the ambulancemen could tell if they were fit enough to be interrogated.

At the station, Anita explained that the phials contained vitamin B_{12} which she injected with the disposable syringes. A hastily summoned police surgeon confirmed that her story was plausible and that the phials did indeed contain the vitamin. He also revealed, irritably, that Anita appeared to have a fractured collar bone and that she should be taken to the hospital immediately. The police, suddenly contrite, whisked Anita to the nearby St. Richard's Hospital — "an excellent name for a hospital," joked Keith — where they treated Anita's shoulder and sedated her.

By morning the story had leaked to reporters. Keith picked Anita up in the Bentley and took her to the London Clinic. He stayed at my flat in Maida Vale for a week, visiting Anita every day until she was ready to go home. The fracture left a small bump on the front of her shoulder. "I can never wear a low-cut dress again," she said.

We all moved to Redlands. We hunted, walked and drove around the countryside while waiting for Anita to give birth. The baby was born on August 18 at King's College Hospital, and I was astonished at the way Keith took to the child. "He's beautiful, just beautiful," he said. They decided to call him Marlon, and sometimes Keith would pick him up from his cot and whisper to him about all the things they would do together once he got a little bigger. "You and me, baby," he'd say. "We've got the whole world together. We don't need nobody else."

Anita, too, was euphoric, for she had begun to believe — after many

167

miscarriages — that she would never be able to have a child. "He's so gorgeous. We're going to have thousands more," she said expansively.

But later she was to confide, "It's beautiful that Keith is so crazy about Marlon. But sometimes, just sometimes, it seems as though he loves him more than me."

In Australia Marianne believed she was dead, walking through the sky on great white clouds closer and closer to Brian. She wanted to be with Brian, but when she approached him and held out her hand, he floated backwards, away from her. "Go back, Marianne, go back," he whispered, and she knew she was not really dead. "You can't come with me. Go back." Gradually the dream shifted, like a film changing scene, and she was in a white cell-like room with Mick sitting at her bedside, holding her hand, the same hand she had asked Brian to take.

"Don't worry, love," he said softly, and she could see the tears welling in his eyes. Marianne had been in a death like coma for eight days.

"Wild horses couldn't drag me away," she said, and knew she loved him very much, wanted more than anything to live again.

Mick did not tell her that he had left her bedside while she had hovered on the brink of death to go to Melbourne to act in a scene for *Ned Kelly*. Nothing came between Jagger and his career. She had more things to worry about now, in any case: callous detectives and customs men trying to pin a charge of smuggling Sodium Amytal on her. Fortunately her London doctor was able to confirm in writing that he had prescribed the drug. Her mother flew out to look after her, and they spent long days talking together as Mick worked on *Ned Kelly*.

The film didn't seem to be working out. Jagger had no rapport with the director, Tony Richardson, and Diane Craig, the actress who replaced Marianne, hadn't even had time to learn her lines. The script was unconvincing. "People just don't talk like that," Jagger protested to Richardson.

Ned Kelly was an Australian outlaw who had somehow acquired the status of a Robin Hood in the country's threadbare folklore. His story began when his family was deported from Ireland to the land of kangaroos and aborigines in the second half of the last century. He was unjustly sent to jail, and when he was released, he found his sister miserably married, his mother involved with a horse thief and his brother in prison. Persecution by police and a local landowner drove him to crime, and then three policemen were killed by members of his gang. Kelly became the target of a huge police hunt. He devised rudimentary suits of armour for the gang and set out to ambush a train load of policemen at Glenrowan. In the resulting shoot-out Kelly was the only outlaw to survive. He was taken away, tried and hanged.

Jagger tried to avoid the subject of the film when he visited Marianne. "It's boring, not working out," was all he would say. He didn't mention that his hand had almost been blown off when an old gun had back-fired in a scene involving a gunfight with a policeman. The burned and jagged gash needed sixteen stitches, but Mick told Marianne the bandages were part of his costume.

Jagger had known the film would be a turkey, and it was. Though it had been made after the infinitely superior *Performance*, it was released first, and it seemed to the world to be Jagger's acting debut. The critics lost no time in telling Mick he should have stuck to singing.

"When he puts on the home-made armour... he looks rather like a cut rate sardine," one journalist wrote gleefully adding, "He's just about as lethal as last week's lettuce." A less harsh reviewer commented perceptively, "He tries hard... but the script is quite awful." And still another: "Jagger delivers his lines with an almost catatonic lack of expression, battling with an Irish accent in which he would seem to have been coached word for word without yet graduating to sentences."

"They're all right," he admitted. "But it's not my fault. Actors just don't seem to have control over the way films work out. It's so much simpler making music — there I have authority over every tiny detail. And if the record is rubbish, I don't mind carrying the can for it."

Marianne had been weakened by the overdose; her body had been so poisoned that she would never again be as strong and resilient as before. She and Mick took a holiday alone together in Indonesia on their way home from Australia in an attempt to recapture the halcyon days they had spent in the beach hut in South America, but it was too late. Marianne felt that Mick had destroyed Brian, had almost destroyed her, and she no longer loved him. Her reproach irritated him, made him feel guilty, and he knew their marriage — for as such they both regarded it — was over. Yet like many people, he was unable to end a love affair. His relationship with Chrissie Shrimpton had lurched along for years after it should have been dead and buried. And so it was becoming with Marianne. When they returned to Cheyne Walk, Marianne was left at home almost every night while Mick was out "working." Marianne was probably the only person on the London rock scene who didn't know that Mick seemed to be falling deeply for Marsha Hunt. He loved her gentleness and intelligence, which were so like Marianne's. But Marsha loved him, boosted his ego, didn't keep trying to blame him for Brian's death. Brian, for Christ's sake . . . what the hell had he had to do with Brian's death?

He called Marsha Fuzzy-Wuzzy because of her huge Afro hairdo, and sometimes he would spend nights at her flat in St. John's Wood listening to records, smoking grass and making love. He couldn't bring himself to make a clean break with Marianne; he no longer knew just what he wanted.

Marianne never asked him where he had been just as he never asked her if she had started using heroin again. Theirs was not a relationship involving accountability. She knew, however, that if she was to make any kind of life, she would have to tear herself away from him. "You know, Tony," she told me, "I feel as though I've wasted a huge chunk of my life by becoming an extension of Mick instead of a person in my own right. I've got to stand up now and really show everyone that I'm more than just a whore, a scarlet, fallen woman."

And then the Stones were off for the start of their first American tour for nearly three years. Marianne took her little son, Nicholas, and went to live with her mother in her remote thatched cottage deep in the heart of Berkshire.

While Jagger was away, Marianne was not inclined to live the life of a medieval wife awaiting her husband's return from the Crusades. She wanted to regain her psyche, to come alive again. She started to look up old friends, and at Robert Fraser's apartment in Mayfair she met Mario Schifano, a millionaire film director cum artist. She had met him before and liked him, but Mick had always been there, so there had never been any question of an affair. But now Jagger was far away, and besides, Marianne had at last heard about Marsha. When Mario suggested they go to bed together, it seemed the best idea she had ever heard.

He gave her a fur coat, told her he loved her, and flew with her to Rome. Jagger was furious when word reached him in America of Marianne's desertion; that silly cow was making a cuckold of him, undermining his dignity, turning him into a laughing stock. He would not forgive her easily for this.

She delighted in paying Mick back for all the humiliations he had heaped on her. She talked to the newspapers about her new man. "Mario," she said, "is my one true love, my Prince Charming."

The Stones were so big by now that a mere rumour about them, in Germany, could provoke a riot. When "Honky Tonk Women" was topping hit parades in every country, a rumour circulated in East Berlin that the band might be playing a gig on the roof of a building owned by publisher Axel Springer in West Berlin. East Berliners decided it would be possible to see the Stones through binoculars and to hear their music being played live, so more than ten thousand of them marched towards the wall, like a young Red Army. Border guards charged into the crowd of girls and boys, lashing out with clubs, jackboots and fists. Armoured cars were called in to rout the bewildered fans, and more than a hundred were hauled off to jail. The Stones, incidentally, weren't in Germany then and had no intention of playing on the roof of anybody's building.

18

_____

THE KIDS WERE ANGRY. THE STONES HAD SAID THEY WOULD BE ON STAGE AT midnight, but it was after four in the morning, and there was still no sign of them. "Who do you think you are?" a kid with a bubble haircut and khaki shirt yelled at the vast, empty stage of the Inglewood Forum in Los Angeles. His cry was taken up by others, and pandemonium ensued. Their anger was compounded by stories they'd read in the newspapers about the extortionate price of tickets. Jagger claimed the prices were set by the theatre owners. Others speculated that the Stones were saying they were worth more than any other band in the world. The row so angered Bill Graham, one of the most respected promoters in the United States, that he told a reporter, "Mick Jagger may be great as a performer, but he's an egotistical creep as a person."

For the first time in their lives Mick and Keith seemed to have lost touch with reality. They had been so overwhelmed by the adulation of their followers that they were almost beginning to believe that they were Lucifer and God Almighty rolled into one.

The adoration they inspired when they arrived in the States for this tour was heady indeed. The Beatles, America's favourite group, hadn't played the United States in three years, and it was beginning to dawn on the country's young that John, Paul, George and Ringo hated one another's guts. Bob Dylan had become a recluse. The Stones were the last of the great sixties rock gurus still functioning.

From the moment they arrived in Los Angeles they had been mobbed by devoted, exquisitely beautiful girls who sought divine revelation in their beds and by obsequious dealers who proffered pharmaceutical cocaine, pure heroin, potent hash in homage. Mick, Keith or even Bill Wyman had only to walk into the Whiskey-a-Go-Go in Los Angeles for the management to bounce respected customers out of the best seats in the club so that the comfort of the Stones Almighty could be ensured. And always there were girls, beautiful, tanned, wide-eyed, innocent looking blondes, brunettes and redheads whispering promises of blow jobs, orgies and Lord only knows what else in their ears.

At first Mick had realised some of his wilder fantasies like having three beautiful girls in one bed, but the novelty wore off and was replaced with contempt for easy lays. Like Keith, he took up the less emotionally complicated pleasure of snorting those little white crystals. Mick Taylor also started to do coke with them, though mainly to be one of the boys. Newspaper, television and radio reporters fawned over them telling the world sycophantically every time they caught a cold, bought a guitar string or kissed a pretty girl.

Their first gig of the tour, at Fort Collins, Colorado, had been an obvious — almost contemptuous — rehearsal. Now, at the Inglewood Forum, they were four hours late going on. But suddenly all the bitching and the weariness in the audience seemed forgotten as Jagger danced on stage dressed in black like Beelzebub himself, and Keith bent his head low to pump out the rabble rousing opening chords of "Jumpin' Jack Flash."

The exhausted, acid-dazed audience sprang to their feet as one. They were on their seats and dancing. Jagger sensed the pulsing energy of near hysteria from the audience and was galvanized by it, turning up the volume, the dancing and the energy pitch until it seemed the whole building was going to blast apart at the seams. As the band plunged into the hypnotic, voodoo rhythm of "Gimme Shelter," the kids seemed to go berserk, thrusting towards the stage, pushing aside the tired, bewildered security men. But the fans calmed as Jagger talked a little and told them he was going to sing a song called "Midnight Rambler." It was a number the kids were not familiar with, and they seemed almost relieved that the pressure had been eased, that they were being let down gently. Only Jagger had no intention of letting them down gently. For this was the most frightening thing the Stones had ever done — Jagger's own eulogy to the Boston Strangler. He poured himself into the role, thrusting his crotch into the audiences' faces, lashing the stage (only it wasn't the stage at all but every person in that audience) with his huge, heavily studded belt. And as they were still reeling from this sudden and totally unexpected sexual assault, the Stones started piling on the satanism again with the jungle drums and primaeval shrieks of "Sympathy for the Devil."

It was over the top. Way, way over the top, and suddenly all the bubbling fury in the theatre began to erupt. A man in a black leather jacket charged towards the stage to punch in the face a security man who stood between him and the Stones. Suddenly the whole audience seemed to be hurtling towards the stage. The first ten rows were filled with screaming, brawling, crazed people. In a panic Jagger ordered the house lights to be turned on, but this seemed to make everything worse. Police were called, and there were numerous arrests.

The Stones' gross, for the two concerts they played that night, was £150,000; then the largest sum ever made in one evening by any band in history.

Jagger seemed, on this tour, to revel in his ability to bend vast crowds to his will, to excite them and to frighten them.

Behind the scenes, too, he was becoming omnipotent, giving Allen Klein the runaround, phasing him out so that Jagger could take over absolute control of the multi-million pound Rolling Stones money machine. To this end he appointed Prince Rupert Lowenstein as his personal financial adviser.

The Stones' autocratic demands became more and more outrageous. A long list was circulated to all promoters of the dozens of types of food and drink that had to be provided in the band's dressing room, items like iced Blue Nun wine, six bottles of tequila, fresh cold meats, peaches and bread. Ticket prices rose to ludicrous heights, and the Stones were late almost every night. Even the journalists were told by the Stones' actions that they were no longer so important — the Stones were too big now for anything to hurt them. At a press conference in the Rainbow Grill in New York, reporters who stood on chairs to ask Jagger questions were brusquely pushed to the floor by waiters, and scuffles broke out.

Then came the inevitable backlash which was to culminate several weeks later in blood and death. Albert Goldman drew vicious parallels between Mick Jagger and Adolf Hitler in the influential *New York Times* while other writers began to criticise Jagger for the Stones' lateness, greed and arrogance.

Keith carefully avoided the controversy; he was far more interested in the vast quantities of dope that were being laid on him. Sometimes he would snort coke continuously for three days and nights, during which time it was impossible for him to sleep at all. Finally overwhelmed, he would crash for twenty hours with all his clothes on, even his boots.

In direct contrast with the mayhem of this tour there had been

Woodstock: a three-day festival of peace 'n' love attended by 450,000 kids near the village of Woodstock, in upstate New York in the latter half of August. A galaxy of rock talent played for free, but they had to share their glory with the kids, who proved that the population of a good-sized city could gather in a field in the middle of nowhere virtually without incident. The festival had been hailed as the dawn of a new golden age, a time when the hippies really were going to sweep away all the cant and hypocrisy of their elders. And advertisers, who realised that all these hippies were worth a lot of bread, man, started to call the young of the United States the Woodstock Nation and the Woodstock Generation in order to sell them records and films and Coca-Cola.

In reality, of course (as with most events in the rock business), Woodstock was not quite as spontaneous and beautiful as most of the kids believed. Warner Brothers (the same company that had dismissed *Performance*) pumped a fortune into making the event a success in order to create a movie success. And what a movie it was turning out to be; according to the grapevine, Warners were convinced they had a box-office smash.

Jagger heard the rumours and was piqued that his old rivals The Who sounded like the stars of the new blockbuster. It seemed unfair. The Stones had drawn just as many flower children to Hyde Park, yet nobody had made a beautiful movie of the event, and though it was filmed for television, it had been virtually disregarded. He hired his own film makers Albert and David Maysles, to make a full length feature film of the Stones on the road. Jerry Garcia, the Grateful Dead's leader, suggested to Mick, "Why don't you do a free gig in San Francisco when the tour's over? You'd probably get a million people or more along, and it would make an amazing climax to your movie."

Jagger leaped at the idea; it was a chance for him to prove, yet again, that he was the biggest rock star in the world. "Woodstock will seem like a country fete compared with our free show," he boasted.

He asked the Maysles brothers if it would be possible for the Stones' film to be completed before Woodstock. "Sure," he was told. "We can have it ready by mid-March – that's a full month before Woodstock will be out. We'll wipe the floor with them."

Somebody was concerned about the problem of controlling so vast a crowd. "Don't worry," he was told. "Jerry Garcia is arranging for the Angels to take control of that. Don't you remember how good the English Hell's Angels were when the Stones played Hyde Park?"

After the Los Angeles riots Jagger had cooled his act just a couple of degrees so that his audiences came to the brink of hysteria but didn't go over the edge. He delighted in his power to control huge halls full of people like puppets: making them scream, making them cry, making them laugh. For the first time the Stones were making really big money from a tour. In the past all the cash had somehow been siphoned off by the parasites, and the money always seemed to be gone when the Stones arrived home. This time they would be sharing more than a million dollars between them, after expenses.

The astrologers, psychics and warlocks all warned against the free show in San Francisco, and in this, the most ethereal city in the world, such omens were taken seriously. "It's going to be a very heavy day," warned one mystic. "The Sun, Venus and Mercury are all in Sagittarius, and the moon's on the Libra-Scorpio cusp." Another foresaw tragedy: "It's weird, they consulted astrologers before setting the dates for Woodstock, but they couldn't have consulted an astrologer for today. Anyone can see that, with the moon in Scorpio, it's going to be an awful day to do this concert. There's a strong possibility of violence and chaos, and any astrologer could have told them. Oh, well, maybe the Stones know something I don't know." The Stones had heard such warnings before, and things had always been okay on the night. Postponing the concert would have meant postponing the movie, thus relinquishing the opportunity to scoop Woodstock.

Mick was perturbed, though, by a play that had become a minor success in the Californian underground. It was the story of a rock superstar who achieves success of messianic proportions and feels that he has to be killed at the peak of his success, like Christ, if he is to achieve immortality. The singer's name isn't mentioned until the climax – when a youth stabs him to death on stage in mid-concert and the fans cry out, "They killed Mick . . . they got Mick . . ."

"Oh, no," said Jagger when he was told about it. "It only needs one nut to see the play, and anything could happen." And there had to be ten million nuts in California.

Staging the free concert was proving difficult. The show was to be held in Golden Gate Park, San Francisco's equivalent of Hyde Park, but at the last moment the city refused to issue a permit. Four days before the concert the Stones were offered free use of a speedway called the Sears Point Raceway, outside the city. Jagger would have his ultimate ego trip after all.

176

The Stones' juggernaut rolled jubilantly on to the speedway, and Chip Monck, the best rock lighting man in the business, started erecting lighting towers and setting up the Stones' massive hired stage. Everything was working out fine until the next day when Jagger's karma finally began to catch up with him. Jagger was suddenly taken to task for his cavalier treatment of promoters throughout the tour. Aggrieved executives of a company called Concert Associates, who had produced the disastrous and over-priced Los Angeles shows heard about the free gig and realised with delight that their parent company, Filmways, also owned the Sears Point Raceway. One hastily convened board meeting later the Stones were informed that Filmways had thought better of their free offer; they now wanted £75,000 in cash or the rights to distribute the film being made of the tour. Additionally, they demanded a bond of £75,000 against possible damage to the speedway. "We're not going to be ripped off like this," Jagger protested. "We'll hold the show in the bloody road if we have to – but the free gig goes ahead on Saturday somehow." It was now Thursday.

The radio stations carried hourly bulletins on the progress toward the show, and suddenly a businessman called Dick Carter, who owned a stock car raceway called Altamont fifteen miles outside the city, said that he would let the Stones use his track for free. The publicity, he thought, would be good for business. The deal was finally signed twenty hours before the show was scheduled to start, and all the promoters and businessmen and rock people were shaking their heads and warning that it was impossible. Even if only half the expected million people showed up, it would obviously be physically out of the question to arrange sufficient toilets, refreshment facilities, first-aid stations and security for the population of a city in the space of a single day. But this was the sixties, and these were the Stones, the deities of the instant generation, the generation for which hedonism was all and for which happiness, energy, lucidity and fantasy could all be obtained by the selection of the right kind of dope. It was the oldies who said such things couldn't be done; we knew that we had conquered the world, could do anything and the words 'can't', 'shouldn't' and 'won't' had been eradicated from our vocabulary as surely as their ideas about sex with strangers being immoral had been cut out of our life style.

Only the freaks were unhappy. "The Stones are coupling the sinister aspect of the heavens with the use of a place dedicated to destruction through motion. And they are calling on Hell's Angels, the most demonic people on earth, to work for them there," they warned. "Everything bodes ill for this day."

"Bullshit," said Jagger. He ordered Chip Monck to move the stage and the lights to Altamont, while other employees announced details of the show to the media. At two in the morning Mick and Keith flew out to the site to see how things were shaping up. Already the stage was half erected and the forklift trucks were bringing on the Stones' massive 10,000-watt PA system. Amid the wasplike buzzing of the generators and arc lights were great multitudes of people lying in sleeping bags around their camp fires, like Harry's army waiting for Agincourt. Jagger was dressed all in crimson velvet, looking like the Lucifer many here believed he was. A girl ran up to him and planted a kiss firmly on his cheek; a guy with hair to his waist proffered a joint; another girl put a scarf around his throat. Peace 'n' love were everywhere.

"It will be the last and biggest concert of the sixties," said Jagger. Many believed it would be a corroboration of the message of Woodstock: The age of Aquarius had dawned at last

Keith, as always on this tour, was so coked up that he couldn't sleep and wanted only to spend the night wandering around the camp fires talking to the freaks. "You go back to the house without me," he told Jagger. And, to a journalist: "I'm just hanging out, feeling the vibes. It's great. Everywhere I go it's a gas. People sitting around their fires really cool, getting high. Just absolutely beautiful." And it was beautiful. At first. But by mid-morning there were more than a quarter of a million people milling around, and things were becoming chaotic; buying food and drink was almost impossible. The queues for the water taps were three hundred yards long, and a visit to one of the few toilets meant standing in a queue for at least half-an-hour. There were no car parking arrangements – vehicles were abandoned by the roadside for nearly ten miles. There was a lot of bad acid around, and people were freaking out all over the place. Everybody was getting stoned out of their skull to pass the long hours before the music was to start – Mexican grass, cheap Californian red wine, amphetamines; it didn't seem to matter what drug you used as long as you got out of it.

By mid-day virtually everyone was tripping. The intense, hysterical emotive presence of all the thousands of people who had taken LSD became infectious. Everyone in the audience felt as though they too, had just dropped a massive dose of acid. The Hell's Angels were already drunk. The Rolling

Stones had given them vast quantities of booze in payment for their services as site policemen, and now they started dropping acid, whirling their pool cues at fans like the National Guard beating back students with riot sticks. Things were going awry now – the festival of love was becoming a cataclysm, and nobody could control it. A man was almost killed as he tried to fly from a speedway bridge – another acid case. On the other side of the site a young guy screamed for help as he fell into the deep waters of a drainage canal. The stoned freaks looked on bemused as he sank beneath the surface. No one seemed sure whether he had been real or an hallucination. It didn't matter anymore anyway; he was dead. Elsewhere doctors were kept busy delivering babies to girls giving hysterical premature birth.

Fights broke out everywhere. People slashed out with knives and drove cars into crowds – a scene of terrifying mass paranoia. Yet in the midst of this mayhem were flower children dancing naked, their flowing hair entwined with daisies, like cherubim who have inadvertently been sent to Hades and who have yet to realise where they are. Many thought that when the music started, it would bring peace, would settle everyone, bring back the beautiful vibes of the early morning, but it was not to be. Santana started to play – very late because it had proved impossible for their equipment to be set up in the limited time available to them. As the kids started to push toward the stage to take a better look at the musicians, the Angels started to feel threatened by, and just a little afraid of, all these effeminate hippies jostling and pushing towards them. They lashed out murderously with their heavy pool cues, cracking heads, breaking noses, imposing their brand of Gestapo-style martial law. Girls were screaming, crying; guys with long hair were reeling back, streaming blood, too stoned, too confused to know what was happening.

"The fights started because the Hell's Angels pushed people around," Carlos Santana said later. "It all happened so fast, it just went right on before us, and we didn't know what was going on. There were lots of people just fucking freaked out. During our set I could see a guy from the stage who had a knife and just wanted to stab somebody. I mean, he really wanted a fight. There were kids being stabbed and heads cracking the whole time."

By the time Jefferson Airplane went on the area around the front of the stage was like some surrealistic netherworld. One Hell's Angel feinted a karate chop at another and was booted in the groin. Hard. "Don't pull any of that shit on me bitch." muttered the Angel with the steel-toed boots as he strode away. A boy of about fifteen staggered around unable to see where he was because of the blood trickling into his eyes from a scalp wound. There were more Hell's Angels on the stage now than musicians, and they perched like menacing gargoyles with their boots at exactly the same height as the kids' faces.

The Airplane's singer, Marty Balin, was about to start on "We Can Be Together" when a terrified black man leaped on stage pursued by a legion of Angels. He was beaten almost senseless with pool cues as the band, and the half million people in the audience, looked on in impotent horror. Then he was thrown to the ground, coughing up blood and scraps of teeth. He staggered away with the confused gait of an animal in shock, but the Angels jumped him again. This time it was obvious from the hail of blows that this man was going to be beaten to death unless someone intervened. Balin was so appalled that he jumped from the stage and rushed toward the fracas, shouting to the Angels to lay off. One of the thugs turned around, looked at Balin calmly, malevolently raised his pool cue and smashed him in the face. The singer fell to the ground unconscious. On stage Paul Kanter furiously started to berate the Angels, but his microphone was grabbed from his hand. From another mike Grace Slick looked on in disbelief and screamed out in rage, "What the fuck is going down?" All control was lost now, but the Airplane still couldn't seem to believe there was nothing they could do. They wavered their way through one more number, but it was no use – the scene in front of the stage now was one of all-out, primaeval, murderous war with pool cues crashing, knives flashing and blood all around.

It was here that the utopian myth of the *Hair*-Oz/Stones generation was ripped aside to expose the lie beneath. The anarchy these kids espoused worked only with the backup of the straight society they despised. At Altamont there were no war mongers, no businessmen, no oldies – only the pure, bloody murderous reality of anarchy. This was the permissive society that the Stones had so long vaunted, the freedom for all they had tantalized us with from our television sets and newspapers. It was ugly, mindless, blind, black and terrifying.

Down in Southern California, another Rolling Stones fan was busy leading his disciples into a life-style that reflected his concept of the freedom ideal – his name was Charles Manson.

Jagger smiled with satisfaction as his helicopter flew in low over the stadium. "Jeez," he said to Mick Taylor, "have you ever seen so many people in one place in your whole life?" From the sky they could see kids dancing naked, kids in satins and velvets and all around them the arid wilderness of the desert. It was beautiful.

The Angels cleared a path from the helicopter, but suddenly a long-haired, wild-eyed man broke through to strike Lucifer, the man responsible for this debacle, a glancing blow to the face. "I hate you, I hate you," he screamed before the Angels pummeled him into silence. Jagger was visibly shaken, but he was whisked quickly to the backstage trailer that was to serve as the Rolling Stones' dressing room. Someone mentioned briefly that Marty Balin had been knocked out, but the Stones seemed more interested in a bright disc the size of a thumbnail, that had been hovering over the stadium all day. "Looks like even the guys from Mars have come along to see the show," someone said, laughing, to Jagger. Mick and Keith sipped their wine, nibbled on smoked salmon sandwiches and occasionally poked their heads outside the trailer to sign a few autographs.

At the front, the passionless folk music of the Flying Burrito Brothers seemed to calm the crowd. When Jagger strolled anonymously to the back of the stage, no violence was evident. Perhaps the storm was over. He went back to the trailer to sip a little more wine, listen to a few more jokes. Crosby, Stills, Nash and Young went on then, and the excitement of their beautiful music was enough to trigger the Hell's Angels blitzkrieg into action once again. Dozens more confused, uncomprehending young people were beaten to pulp in a hail of pool cues.

In the trailer the Stones were concerned but not unduly worried; everywhere they had played for the past five years there had been an undercurrent of violence and anarchy. Often hundreds of people were arrested before they even set foot on stage. They knew everything there was to know about rioting fans and audience control. When it came to aggravation, they were in a different league to relatively gentle West Coast bands like the Jefferson Airplane.

They behaved exactly as they always behaved, sitting in the dressing room, making the audience wait, letting the kids forget the way they had been moved by the previous band, forcing them to grow hungry and eager for the pile driving music of the greatest rock 'n' roll band in the world. Only this time the Stones tarried even longer than usual; this gig was to be the climax of their movie, and they needed night to fall so that Jagger's swirling costume and dazzling coloured lights could create the thundering, swirling magic of an archetypal Rolling Stones concert.

The crowd had grown even angrier than before. Dusk heralded the bitter cold of the desert night, and the kids, many of whom had had nothing to eat all day, were beginning to shiver in their thin summer clothes. The

Hell's Angels too, were angry; this had become their festival, after all, and now these English pansies were standing them up, making them wait in the freezing, fucking cold, man. There was a limit to how much they were prepared to take.

Even inside the trailer the Angels who had been assigned to guard the Stones started to hassle Mick to get out there and deliver the goods. "Jagger's so vain with the whole scene," one Angel coming from the Stones told a reporter. "We kept telling him, 'Hey you know what? You got a half million fuckin' people out there that made you what you are, and here you are stallin'!' The man says. 'Well, my makeup looks better at night.'"

The Stones waited one-and-a-half hours before climbing onto the stage. Jagger was surrounded by his consort of demonic Hell's Angels, and his satin cape glowed red under the lights. To many, he was Lucifer, By allowing the Angels to stand at his side, he was endorsing all the havoc they had wreaked. The stage was filled with the brutes now, and they jostled around nonchalantly as the Stones attempted to storm into "Jumpin' Jack Flash." They crowded in so close that Jagger was unable to dance, and he stopped the song to move some of the 150 people on the stage back a little. The Angels spotted a young boy, naked, trying to climb on to the platform and kicked him hard in the face, hard enough to break his jaw. He came back for more, so demented that he felt the need to be kicked to death. Out in the audience an Angel was roaring through the kids on his big Harley Davidson, running down anyone who dared get in his way. He was doing it for a bet, it was revealed later.

The next number was "Carol," a good old harmless rocker. But strangely, several of the kids were stripping off their clothes during the song and crawling to the stage as if it were a high altar, there to offer themselves as victims for the boots and cues of the Angels. The more they were beaten and bloodied, the more they were impelled, as if by some supernatural force, to offer themselves as human sacrifices to these agents of Satan. The violence transcended all comprehension. It had become some primaeval ritual; the victims were no longer merely tolerating pain and evil and bestiality but were actively collaborating in it. And now the pounding voodoo drumming and the primitive shrieks echoed out, and the Stones were into their song of homage to the Anti-christ. Another sacrificially naked girl climbed on to the stage, and six Angels leaped on her at once to toss her from the stage like so much human rubbish.

Jagger could ignore what was happening no longer. He broke off in mid-verse to murmur resignedly, "Something always happens when we get into this number…" The Angels ignored him and carried on their tussle with the defenceless little girl. "Fellows, I'm sure it doesn't take all of you to take care of this," he said, breaking off the song for a second time. "Surely one of you can handle her." The Angels were maddened by his sarcasm, but five of them stepped back, leaving one wild-eyed compatriot to pummel the child with his cue.

"Sympathy for the Devil" became the focus of all the evil energy roaring through the crowd.

Jagger danced some more, sang a few more lines, then panicking, turned to Mick Taylor and shouted, "Fuck, man. There's somebody out there… there's a guy pointing a gun at us."

An Angel dived to the floor to make sure he wasn't hit by a bullet meant for Mick Jagger. Some guard! Keith and Mick Taylor, who both saw a black man in a green suit point the gun at Jagger, stopped playing.

In a country where a madman can kill the most popular President of the country, who was safe?

Jagger looked askance, then retreated to the back of the stage. He couldn't see the gunman anymore. He had vanished beneath a legion of Hell's Angels.

Suddenly the Stones stood divested of all authority. They looked small and frightened. Jagger particularly was a fey, delicate, gossamer figure, a fairy prince who couldn't hold out much longer against the hobgoblins. The Californian underground play, in which Jagger was murdered on stage, was about to come true. He had never lost control like this before; things had never gone this far. "Brothers and sisters, come on now!" he said weakly, without confidence. "That means everybody just cool it! We can cool it everybody!" But his hip jargon sounded effete, silly.

On this day hip jargon, flower power and the Age of Aquarius were finished. The great sixties dream was washed up. It would take a little while for the message to filter through to the rest of the world, but this day was the watershed. On December 6, 1969, at Altamont, California, all the beautiful fantasies of the sixties withered and died like flowers beneath a shower of paraquat.

"Okay, I think we're cool, we can groove. Something very funny always happens when we start that number," he added. But he never regained control. The fighting in front of the stage remained bloody and unstoppable. The Angels had tasted blood; death was in the air. Real knives were flashing – the Stones had always toyed with violence, turmoil and the powers of darkness, but now the dogs had slipped their leads

183

and the Stones could only watch in dumbstruck, frightened horror.

"If he doesn't stop it, man . . ." Jagger whimpered toward one particularly bloodthirsty Angel. But he sounded only pathetic.

It was left to Keith to take over. He had always been the strong one, the only Stone who would never run away from a fight. "Keep cool!" he shouted. "Hey, if you don't cool it, you ain't gonna hear no music!"

A Hell's Angel bounded across the stage, tore Keith's mike from his hand and screamed, "Fuck you!"

"A guy's been killed," someone whispered to Jagger, and the show halted as a doctor threaded his way out through the crowd from the stage to see if there was anything to be done. He found a man covered in blood which seemed to pour from stab wounds in every part of his body and face. He was still breathing. Stretcher-bearers ran back to the first-aid station. It was too late, far too late. The man died within minutes.

It was the same guy who had pointed his gun at Jagger. His name was Meredith Hunter, and he was just eighteen years old. No one will ever know for certain why he pointed a loaded gun at Mick Jagger, but it seems likely that he was just another victim trying to frighten away the Angels. The gun was almost certainly pointed in the direction of the stage by the purest chance.

Meredith had come to the show with his beautiful blonde girl friend, and the Angels, whose political beliefs are slightly to the right of Hitler's, don't like to see black men with white women. Especially good-looking white women.

A great six-foot-four grizzly bear of a Hell's Angel had stalked across to Meredith to pull his hair hard in an effort to provoke a fight the black teenager could never win. Meredith pulled himself painfully free, smarting angrily at this humiliation in front of a girl he was trying to impress. A fight broke out, and five more Angels came crashing to the aid of their mate, while Meredith tried to run off through the packed crowd. An Angel caught him by the arm and brought down a sheath knife hard into the black man's back. The knife failed to penetrate deeply, but Meredith knew then that he was fighting for his life. He ripped a gun out of his pocket and pointed it straight at the Angel's chest. "For Christ's sake, don't shoot anyone," somebody screamed. Meredith was only a few yards from the stage now, and he could see the Stones staring in horror in his direction as they continued to fumble their way through "Sympathy for the Devil." And then the Angels were upon him like a pack of wolves. One tore the gun from his hand, another stabbed him in the face and still another stabbed him repeatedly, insanely, in the back until his knees buckled.

When he was down, the Angels stormed in, kicking his body, booting him hard in the face, breaking his nose and jaw. Blood was everywhere. Another Angel ground a steel bucket into his eyes.

Numbed by the violence of the day, fearful now for their own lives, the audience made no attempt to help Meredith Hunter – an astonishing commentary, considering they outnumbered the Angels 10,000 to 1. When the Angels finished with Hunter, several people tried to come to his aid, but an Angel stood guard over the motionless body. "Don't touch him," he said menacingly. "He's going to die anyway, so just let him die." But the Hun grew bored with sentry duty and strolled back towards the stage. Two men ripped off Meredith's bloody shirt, but there were so many wounds it was impossible to know how to even begin first aid. They had screamed out hysterically for a doctor, for the Stones to stop playing, and at last, after what seemed like an age, they were heard. The sombre seventies had begun.

The Hell's Angels were, of course, solely and entirely responsible for the mayhem of Altamont. That was the story the Stones' publicity machine turned out after the debacle. At first they were believed. Said Keith: "Looking back, I don't think it was a good idea to have the Hell's Angels there. But we had them at the suggestion of the Grateful Dead, who've organised these shows before, and they thought they were the best people to organise the concert. The trouble is it's a problem for us either way. If you don't have them to work for you as stewards, they come anyway and cause trouble. This was my first experience of American Hell's Angels. I believe the alternative would have been the Black Panthers. I wouldn't like to say whether they would have been any more vicious. But, to be fair, out of the whole three hundred Angels working as stewards, the vast majority did what they were supposed to do, which was to regulate the crowds as much as possible without causing any trouble. But there were about ten or twenty who were completely out of their minds – trying to drive their motorcycles through the middle of the crowds. Really, the difference between the open-air show we held in Hyde Park and this one was amazing. I think it illustrates the difference between the two countries. In Hyde Park everybody had a good time and there was no trouble. You can put half a million young English people together, and they won't start killing each other. That's the difference."

But others thought the root of the violence was the egomaniacal desire of the Stones to put on a huge concert for their movie at any price.

If the crew had been given more than twenty hours to get ready, they would have built a higher stage, erected barricades, arranged decent food, drink, toilet, parking and medical facilities. Perhaps then the day could have passed without the deaths of four people and the wounding of God only knows how many.

Dave Crosby, whose band immediately preceded the Stones, was the first to voice this growing feeling: "The Rolling Stones are still a little bit in 1965. They didn't really know that security isn't a part of anybody's concert anymore... We didn't need the Angels. I'm not down-grading the Angels, because it's not healthy and because they only did what they were expected to do... The Stones don't know about the Angels. To them an Angel is something in between Peter Fonda and Dennis Hopper. That's not real... But I don't think the Angels were the major mistake. They were just the obvious mistake.

"I think the major mistake was taking what was essentially a party and turning it into an ego game and a star trip. An ego trip of, 'Look how many of us there are,' and a star trip of the Rolling Stones, who are on a star trip and who qualify in my book as snobs... I'm sure they don't understand what they did on Saturday... I think they have an exaggerated view of their own importance. I think they're on a grotesque ego trip... I think they are on negative trips, essentially, especially the two leaders."

Bill Graham, the most respected promoter in the United States, joined the growing chorus of damnation: "I ask you what right you had, Mr. Jagger... in going through with this free festival? And you couldn't tell me you didn't know the way it would come off... What right did you have to leave the way you did, thanking everybody for a wonderful time, and the Angels for helping out? What did he leave behind throughout the country? Every gig he was late. Every fucking gig he made the promoter and the people bleed. What right does this god have to descend on this country this way? It will give me great pleasure to tell the country that Mick Jagger is not God Junior... But you know what is the greatest tragedy to me? That cunt is a great entertainer."

The freaks, too, had their say; this letter to Rolling Stone is typical of many:

> To those who know, it's been obvious that the Stones, or at least some of them, have been involved in the practice of magick ever since the Satanic Majesties Request album. But there at least the colour was more white than black. Since then

186

the hue had gone steadily darker and darker. At Altamont He appeared in his full majesty with his full consort of demons, the Hell's Angels. It was just a few days before the Winter Solstice when the forces of darkness are at their most powerful. The moon was in Scorpio, which is the time of the month when the Universal vibration is at its most unstable. It was held in a place dedicated to destruction through motion. Then Mick comes on only after it is dark enough for the red lights to work their magick. I don't know if they were truly aware of what they were doing or not. I feel they are sadder and wiser from the experience. But an agonizing price was paid for the lesson. And we were all guilty because we have eaten of the cake the Stones baked.

The Altamont tragedy ended in the courts, final symbolic proof that Mick Jagger was no longer a rebellious hippy but had now become a straight-forward millionaire businessman to whom the Rolling Stones was a commodity. He sued the Sears Point International Raceway for more than £25 million, alleging breach of contract and fraud. Californian land-owners with ranches near Altamont countersued the Rolling Stones for £2,450,000.

Nevertheless, the debacle did make an effective movie. It was called *Gimme Shelter*, and true to their promise, the Maysles brothers got it out before Woodstock.

I saw it with all the Stones in a small preview theatre in Soho. After they'd argued about who Meredith had really been trying to shoot, Mick turned to Keith and said, "Flower power was a load of crap, wasn't it? There was nothing about love, peace and flowers in 'Jumpin' Jack Flash,' was there?"

19

Driving sleet hammered at the leaded windows of the centuries-old thatched cottage like the hands of a million dead souls. Inside, huge logs crackled and split in the open fireplace. The small beamed living room seemed the cosiest place on earth. The soothing voice of Leadbelly croaked softly on the stereo, and Marianne stretched out luxuriantly on the rug in front of the fire while Mario put on a few more chestnuts. Upstairs her mother told one of her marvellous stories to little Nicholas. It was Boxing Day, and everything in the world was right.

The 'phone rang, and Marianne went into the dining room to answer it. "Happy Christmas," said Mick. "I'm down at Redlands with Keith, and I'd like to drive up to give you a little present." It seemed silly for him to drive so far, but he was insistent, and she agreed. After all, they weren't children, they could still be friends and it was about time he met Mario.

Mick had flown straight to Switzerland to see his bankers after Altamont and then on to London to arrange a quick series of concerts. All sixty-five hundred tickets for the shows — two at the Lyceum and two at the Saville — had sold out within half-an-hour. He had telephoned Marianne in Rome to remind her perfunctorily that the two of them had to appear at Marlborough Street Magistrates Court on December 19 to hear the final result of the drug bust from the beginning of the year. And when she flew into Heathrow, he met her in a chauffeur driven limousine. But she had been adamant. It was over. She didn't love him any more, and her life was with Mario. Mick had been preoccupied with preparation for the London shows and the inquests on Altamont and had seemed to accept her decision.

So what on earth did he want now?, she wondered. He arrived in his Bentley at about ten in the evening and gave her her present; a tiny, ornate Georgian silver snuffbox filled with the finest pharmaceutical cocaine.

There was nothing Marianne wanted more. Mario had given her valuable jewellery and clothes, but she always left them lying around and lost them; material objects meant nothing to her. But coke, now that was something else.

She snorted some and felt that familiar euphoric rush of happiness and well-being that brought back all the memories of the good times. Jagger was beautiful, his hair shone and he looked like a lithe boy of eighteen. He snorted some coke, too, and they giggled together; they had so much in common, were so close, and she could feel nothing but relief at being near him again. She wanted to be squeezed in his arms, for him to take her to bed with all the passion of the early days. He had always had this overwhelming effect on her, and she knew she could never have broken up with him if he had not been thousands of miles away. Nicholas and Marianne's mother had both gone to bed, and Mick walked into the living room where Mario sat beside the log fire. The men didn't like each other. Jagger believed Mario had stolen his 'wife' behind his back while he had been away on business. Mario knew of Jagger's other affairs, knew he had treated Marianne badly. They started to argue over her — Jagger icily, ruthlessly logical; Mario passionate, waving his arms and shouting so loud he woke up Nicholas.

"Ok, dago," Mick exploded at last, "come outside and fight me for her like a man." But the argument continued raging with both men stubbornly refusing to give in.

"This raises an interesting point," thought Marianne. "They both seem determined to spend the night here, but there isn't a spare bed. I could stop their argument in a moment. All I have to do is choose. But I don't think I know which one I want anymore. I thought I loved Mario, but if only Mick could care about me the way he used to, I'd rather be with him. Anyway, I'm tired. I'll let them sort it out for themselves . . .

She took her usual couple of sleeping tablets, climbed into her big old double bed and fell into a deep and dreamless sleep.

When she woke up, Jagger was by her side, snoring blissfully, smiling as if nothing had happened. Mario had slept in front of the fire and left at dawn, muttering murderous Roman oaths against Jagger, Marianne and anyone else he could think of. Prince Charming had gone forever.

Marianne giggled when Mick woke and started to imitate Mario's passionate Italian arm waving. "Wop in your bed, girl?" he said. "What are you thinking about . . . a bleedin' eyetie. I mean?"

189

Anita was distraught when Keith flew back from the States. "They're trying to kick Marlon and me out of the country," she said. "The Home Office says I can't stay here anymore." He calmed her down and 'phoned the lawyers to see what had happened. The Home Office had apparently confiscated Anita's Italian passport and told her she would probably have to leave the country unless she married a British citizen.

"It's just like living in a police state," screamed Anita. "I think it's disgraceful. I am not going to get married just to suit them." But all of us around the Stones believed that she was refusing to marry Keith because she still wanted Mick. They had been lovers, and Marianne seemed to be well out of the way in Italy now.

Keith told reporters dismally, "It's a drag that you are forced into marriage by bureaucracy. I refuse to get married because some bureaucrat says we must. Rather than do that, I would leave Britain and live abroad. But if I want to continue to live in England, and that's the only way Anita can stay, we will marry. But I don't know when we'll marry. I don't want to rush into anything. I have nothing against marriage — I'd just as soon be married as not."

Eventually the lawyers smoothed everything out. But at this time a shotgun wedding, courtesy of H.M. Government was one of Keith's lesser worries. While the Stones were abroad, Anita had whiled away the long weeks of loneliness with the aid of ever-spiralling doses of drugs so that she now needed saccharin sized tablets of heroin every day merely to avoid withdrawal symptoms. She always injected the dope usually mixed with cocaine to make a speedball, thus avoiding the nausea and unconsciousness that followed the flash of heroin alone.

Keith had been doing a lot of coke in the States with occasional snorts of heroin to calm himself down when he became strung-out after three or four days and nights of looning. But he had never used a syringe — works — in his life. It would all be different when he was back in the womb of Cheyne Walk, he had thought. Then, as before, he would get his withdrawal symptoms over quickly, with the aid of a few sleeping tablets, and he would be clean again. Only this time Anita had made it impossible for him. Their story was one that is repeated over and over again in the rock world — rich, bored wife turns to dope because her old man is away, gets hooked, then hooks him when he returns because she can't bear to be on drugs by herself. It is virtually impossible for one person to be addicted to heroin while the partner is clean. It imposes too much strain on the relationship. Heroin is such an all-consuming, all-satisfying passion that it obliterates all other common interests, even sex. Always the partner either joins in with taking dope or splits. Keith joined in.

I was living with the two of them at Cheyne Walk then, but I would only snort smack and coke, never fix it. My pathological terror of needles had not abated.

Obtaining enough drugs to keep the three of us happy wasn't easy. Through friends in Soho, I arranged to buy heroin and cocaine from registered drug addicts. Getting yourself registered was easy. You gave yourself one fix, staggered into the office of any of the half dozen London junkie doctors and told him you were an addict. Without checking he would charge a handsome fee and prescribe heroin and cocaine for you. (It was years before anyone realised that addiction to cocaine is a physical impossibility). The junkies hit the street and sold most of their drugs at a huge profit. The trouble was that these kids tended to be extremely unreliable, and sometimes Keith and Anita would both be going through the agonies of cold turkey before I could get supplies for them.

Keith and Anita began to change, and I could see that addiction was eating them up, destroying their personalities. Keith would sometimes hide a little stash of dope where he thought Anita and I wouldn't find it, and sometimes the two of them would have screaming rows, largely centered on the fact that heroin had virtually wiped out Keith's desire for sex. I was more determined than ever to keep my snorts small. I had no desire to end up like them, jabbing needles into my arm all day long.

The two of them had never seemed to have many friends, but now the only people invited to the house were drug addicts, people they thought they could score from. One day a well-known guitarist was at the house and told Keith that he knew someone who had a large quantity of dope to sell. I arranged to meet the pusher to examine the stuff he was offering. Drug peddlers are notoriously unscrupulous. They will happily pass off strychnine as heroin if you're stupid enough to fall for it. This man had some first-rate pharmaceutical heroin and cocaine, which Keith agreed to buy for £1,500. "I might be getting some more in," he told me with a wink. "I'll give you a call if I do. And if you tell me what you want, I can get it for you anytime."

"You know what he does, of course," the friend who had introduced us told Keith. "He breaks into chemist shops up north and nicks all the dope he can carry."

"Sounds sensible to me," said Keith.

Ten days later the dealer 'phoned to say he had another consignment of heroin and cocaine. I had a brief word with Keith and arranged to meet him outside Ladbroke Grove tube station. I stood outside on a bitterly cold March evening for an hour-and-a-half, but there was no sign of him so I gave up and drove dismally back to Cheyne Walk.

"He didn't show," I told Keith miserably. But he only giggled and said it didn't matter. He was very high. Higher than I'd ever seen him. Anita was so stoned she couldn't come downstairs. I said nothing. If they had managed to obtain drugs from some other source, good luck to them. Weeks later I discovered by accident that before I even set off for Ladbroke Grove, Keith had telephoned the dealer to ask to meet him somewhere else. Though I was one of his most intimate friends, Keith's greedy drug addict's paranoia made him afraid that I might steal some of his precious dope.

Thereafter the dealer would come to London at monthly intervals to meet Keith at Olympic Studios and hand over small packages of dope for payments of about £2,300 or £2,400 a time. The drugs were of the very finest quality, and Keith was eager to stay friendly with the dealer because he was charging approximately one-fifth of the going rate for his wares. When the dealer suddenly showed up at Cheyne Walk with an unasked for consignment, therefore, Keith quickly wrote him a cheque for £2,300.

Suddenly he disappeared, and the next time we heard his name mentioned was when a boyish plainclothes policeman, who appeared to be overawed by the privilege of speaking to a real live Rolling Stone, called at the house to ask Keith why he had given this man a cheque. "Oh, that," said Keith. "He's a friend of a friend, and I bought a guitar from him."

"Very good, sir," said the policeman. "I knew there would be a rational explanation."

The dealer had been arrested after a raid on a garage; drugs had been found in a steel strongbox in a Mini Cooper. Also in the box was a diary listing his customers along with details of how much they had bought and when. Keith's name, of course, was prominent. At first the police appeared to think they had stumbled on to the magic key to instant promotion, and they had promised the dealer the earth — to say nothing of non-prosecution — in return for sufficient information to nail Keith Richard. The dealer had been helpful, to say the least, and he had given the cops a long and detailed statement: "It all started in February when I got about three ounces of cocaine and a few grammes of heroin. I went down to London and got to know some people who put me on to Keith Richard and I sold it to him for £1,500. Since then about every month I have sold some to him and when he has been away I have sold it through a contact."

The dealer even gave the police detailed accounts of various drug sales to Keith, like: l rang Keith up and we arranged to meet at Olympic Studios at Barnes at midnight. He didn't turn up so I rang his home and he came at about 1:30 a.m. I met him in the corridor of the studio and gave him about one ounce of cocaine and about one gramme of heroin."

Somehow the dealer, who was none too bright, was persuaded to plead guilty to two charges of breaking into chemists and four charges of possession. He got six years at Derbyshire Quarter Sessions, and the police never mentioned the subject to Keith again. I still haven't managed to figure out how he got away with it.

Meanwhile Jagger had become more and more deeply involved in the business side of the Stones. With his London School of Economics training he found it easy to understand the subleties of contracts the band had signed when they had been working at full pelt, too busy even to think clearly.

And what he found did not please him. He decided the time had come to break with both Allen Klein, the band's manager, and with Decca Records. He talked to the rest of the band and they all agreed with him that the time had come to make radical changes.

Decca they disliked partly because it appeared to be run by un-imaginative geriatrics but also because they believed the company had been paying them insultingly minuscule royalties for far too long.

The record company was less than delighted at the imminent departure of their biggest money spinners and forced the Stones to deliver the master tape of one hitherto unreleased song under a condition of their contract that the Stones had misread.

"Here y'are then — that's us divorced," said Mick, handing over a tape to one of Decca's more pompous executives.

"Just a minute," said the man in the pin-striped suit. "You haven't even told me what the song is called."

"'Cocksucker Blues,'" said Jagger. The executive choked on his Havana.

He listened in horror later to a slovenly soporific Jagger whining in a heavy blues voice that he is a schoolboy who is fed up with picking up

strange men and going to their hotel rooms in order to earn enough
money to survive in London's West End.

But there was no recourse. Technically the Stones had honoured
their contract. All Decca could do was to re-package their wealth of Stones
material again and again and again in different sequences and different
sleeves. And it did.

The business hassles took up almost all of Jagger's time. Marianne
was once again being neglected. When he did have an occasional spare
evening, he would always be in St. John's Wood with Fuzzy-wuzzy —

Keith and Marianne in North Africa

Marsha Hunt. Marianne had become such a pain. She was always crying,
always complaining, and she was back on heroin again, spending long
evenings getting off and nodding out, talking to Anita and me. It seemed
obvious that Jagger had been desperate to win her back from Mario not
because he loved her but because his ego had been bruised. Mick Jagger,
Lucifer, Crown Prince of Darkness, couldn't afford to be cuckolded by
anybody.

They never talked about their problems. Jagger seemed to be trying
to delude himself into believing that she wasn't back on dope at all instead
of reaching out with a helping hand. They occasionally had furious arguments, mostly about the way she kept 'phoning him in tears when he was
working so that he was constantly distracted. He was under enormous

pressure in his business fights, and the last thing he needed was to hear Marianne screaming hysterically that she was lonely. She was so fucking hysterical; couldn't she understand he needed help, not an albatross around his neck?

After one of their fights, he told her there was a song he wanted her to hear. He threaded the tape on the player, and she heard his voice singing out the words of another new song. As always, she found it hard to decipher the words, but she managed to make out something about wild horses not being able to drag him away.

She wept uncontrollably. "Wild horses couldn't drag me away" — the first words she'd spoken when she'd come out of her coma. It was a love song of his relief that she had survived. The song was an oasis of brightness in a desert of misery. Things would never, could never be the same again. He didn't love her, and she didn't love him, yet what were they to do?

To add to her misery, John Dunbar was at last divorcing her on the grounds of her adultery with Mick. Everyone she had ever loved seemed to be simultaneously spurning her. There was, however, the solace of heroin — beautiful, all-comforting, all-destroying heroin. Pretty soon she was shooting up a third of a gramme a day. She knew Mick was worried that he could be busted at any moment because of her habit but she didn't seem to give a damn.

The break came at last, inevitably, in May 1970. He said he was planning to emigrate to France because of tax problems. She said she wouldn't be going with him and walked out of Cheyne Walk that night to stay with her mother.

It was over. Marianne was left a hollow, shattered, confused young woman.

20

IRONICALLY THE WORLDWIDE FAME AND FANTASTIC WEALTH OF THE ROLLING Stones had made them the loneliest men I had ever known. One of life's bitter paradoxes is that when everybody wants to be your friend, you end up trusting no one. Mick and Keith had striven so hard for success that all their real friends had been dropped along the way. They had come far. Keith's mother had worked as a washing-machine demonstrator at Dartford Co-op, Mick's father had been a physical education teacher. The suburban kids Mick and Keith had grown up with were married and settled, worrying about paying their mortgages and whether they could afford a new Ford Capri.

The Stones' new friends came from the circle of trendy millionaire pleasure seekers — people like Paul Getty II, Robert Fraser, Christopher Gibbs. These people had been born to money and educated at private schools and universities, and all they had in common with these two amusing cockney accented pop stars was money, unlimited time in which to spend it and a jaded palate for life.

It was easier for the Stones to buy companionship. That way they had absolute control, with no strings attached. Employees had to be there for conversation, commiseration or a good time, to order. Paid companions could be ordinary people who hadn't been to Eton, and you could relax and be yourself with them. That, I am sure, was the main reason Keith was happy to hand me a steady £150 a week for doing little more than getting high with him, talking to him over dinner and listening to his moans about Anita's latest piece of unpleasantness. Keith was a hard-drinking, very masculine kind of man, and he enjoyed male company, and I don't mean by that he was gay — far from it.

Jagger, on the other hand, had always preferred feminine company. As soon as he stopped sharing the flat in Chelsea with Keith and

Brian, he had moved in with Chrissie Shrimpton, and then, of course there had been Marianne. Now, for the first time in his life, he was completely alone.

Marsha Hunt was pregnant, insisting she was going to have his child. He considered asking her to marry him. After all, he was twenty-six, and that wasn't a bad age to get married, but he knew he didn't love her enough to share the rest of his life with her. Marsha was beautiful and terrific company, but she didn't fit his romantic ideal. He had always dreamed that one day he would meet a mysterious, gorgeous stranger who would be as elegant as he aspired to be. Their perfect love would enrapture the world, and they would sail away in a huge white yacht to make love and produce exquisite babies for the rest of their lives. Sadly, Marsha didn't fit the bill. Yet he was lonely. The big house on Cheyne Walk and the Stargroves estate both needed the sparkling presence of a good-looking woman to bring them alive. If he didn't find the right person soon, he knew he would be reduced to pleading with Marianne to come back to him again, and that was something he was desperate to avoid.

Glyn Johns, the Stones' recording engineer, arrived at Olympic for a session one evening in June. He asked if anyone had a job for a really sexy Californian chick he knew.

"Maybe," Mick said, with a wink to me. "I might need a housekeeper. I'll have to take a look at her first."

Jan came to the studio with Glyn after they attended the opening for *Ned Kelly*. Jagger was so appalled when he saw a preview of the film that he refused to attend the premiere as a protest. "It was a load of shit," he told a reporter. "I only made it because I had nothing else to do. Tony Richardson was a reasonable director, and I thought he'd make a reasonable film. The thing is, you never know until you do it whether a film will turn out to be a load of shit, and if it does, all you can say is: 'Well, that was a load of shit.' And try to make sure you don't do anything like it again."

The Rolling Stones were all engrossed in recording their new album, *Sticky Fingers*. It was to be the first on their own record label, and if successful, it would earn more for them than all their previous records put together. They worked through the night, doing take after take of a song called "Bitch" until long after sunrise. At last they were finished, and Glyn pointed Jan out to Mick. She was exhausted after an entire night without sleep, but Jagger came across and started to dance lasciviously in front of her as the music of "Bitch" roared out of the big monitor speakers.

197

Thereafter she appeared at the studio occasionally, but I could sense that Mick hadn't exactly been swept off his feet by her. Then, quite suddenly, after a long difficult recording session Glyn had asked if anyone would give Jan a lift back to London.

Mick said he would and we didn't see the two of them again for a week.

The role of Jan in Mick's life became, for a few months, similar to that which I played in Keith's life. She was always there to talk to him, always around when he needed someone. And just as I would go out to buy drugs for Keith when he couldn't obtain them for himself, so Jan would occasionally go to bed with Jagger when he was too lazy to bring one of his many women home. His relationship with Marsha seemed to have deteriorated since her pregnancy. She had become fiercely independent, told him to stop messing her mind up.

Then along came Catherine. She was an exotic-looking Californian who'd enjoyed a brief affair with Eric Clapton. Eric introduced her to Mick at a party, and a couple of hours later Catherine was tucked in Mick's huge three-hundred-year-old bed in Cheyne Walk. The two of them stayed in bed for the next twenty-four hours, and after that, Catherine moved her things in.

Jan was piqued. She seemed to have fallen in love with Mick. Next to him other men lacked imagination and energy. I had seen other girls, even tough little groupies, entranced in much the same way. Jagger's feminine qualities seem to give him an unusual insight into women, and he uses that insight to give him total power over them. But Jan said nothing — to do so would be uncool, and Mick hated uncoolness in a woman. Besides, she was a paid employee — no strings attached.

The friction between Jan and Catherine sent sparks flying almost every day. Jan hated Catherine because she had won Jagger's body, and Catherine hated Jan because she seemed to have captivated Jagger's mind. The situation was untenable, and when Mick was out, the girls would have bitter, screaming arguments. In his presence they attempted to feign sycophantic devotion. For Mick, it was a perfect set up. He had all the sex and company he wanted without involvement. Neither girl was secure enough to dare complain. Brian was right about chicks, after all — safety in numbers.

Mick loved to pit them against each other until they were at screaming point. It was as if he had become the person he pretended to be

Hair wash time!

on stage; he needed his fans fighting over him, even in his own living room. He was so egocentric now that he couldn't love anyone except himself. He was emulating mad, debauched, oversexed Turner, the character he had played in *Performance*. With Marianne gone, Mick's last link to earth was severed, and his image swallowed him up. Michael Philip Jagger had ceased to exist. Now there was only Mick Jagger, Superstar, twenty-four hours a day.

The farce at Cheyne Walk couldn't drag on forever. Mick's cosy ménage à trois came to a stormy close when he announced in August that the Stones were off on a tour of Europe and that Catherine would not be coming. "Sorry, darling," he told her. "It's a band rule, always has been. I don't take my old lady on the road."

Keith was taking Anita, however. Compounding the hurt, Anita asked Jan to come along with them to take care of Marlon. Catherine wept for days. She knew it was over. Jagger wanted her out of the house by the time he returned from the tour. All her dreams of being the next Marianne Faithfull were flying out the window. When the final explosion came she lashed out at Jagger, kicking, spitting, scratching and trying to tear his hair out by the roots. It was, of course, a very uncool thing to do. Catherine left quietly that night.

Altamont had frightened Mick, made him take stock and ponder what he wanted to do with the rest of his life. At first he had considered quitting rock and taking up politics. He had always been driven by a need to scale new heights, and he knew he couldn't take rock 'n' roll stage performances any further. He had broken barriers, destroyed taboos, and now like an ageing boxer, he was doomed to gradual decline. "But it has become my life. There's nothing else I really want to do," he said. He decided to consolidate his position — keep on as the greatest rock star in the world as long as he could. He knew he would have to stay in perfect physical shape to survive, and he cut down on booze and dope and took up cycling, running and tennis. He wasn't about to end up like Elvis.

The European tour proved decisively that the charisma of the Stones remained undiminished. On the first date, Helsinki, the usual total mayhem ensued. By the time Jagger and his men hit Hamburg ten days later they were pumping it out with the power of an express train. Riot squads had to be drafted to deal with a thousand window smashing fans.

In Berlin all hell broke loose: fifty arrests. On September 20, 1970, the Stones played the first of two shows at L'Olympia in Paris. The Parisian kids had yet to realise that Jagger had long ceased toying with ideas of revolution, and they used the gig as an excuse to bombard the long-suffering gendarmes with bricks and iron bars. There were many arrests.

Jagger was tired and considered skipping the party held in his honour afterwards. But he was very aware of the need to be his own public relations man, and he knew that the French record company executives would be piqued if he snubbed them. So he went along to sip a few glasses of champagne and to be nice to people, hoping he would be able to make a discreet exit after about half-an-hour. And then he saw her.

"Hi, Mick," said Eddie Barclay, a record company executive and old friend. "I'd like you to meet Bianca. She's going to be my wife soon." Mick looked and could not believe his eyes. The girl regarding him with dark, liquid eyes took his breath away. She looked exactly like him — the same full lips, the same high cheekbones, the same look of sophistication and decadence, the same slender, tiny-boned body. She was perfect, and he wanted her.

Bianca was flattered by Jagger's attentions and pleased that the whole room stared at them when they danced. It had been the same when she had been with actor Michael Caine. People had admired her, treated her with respect because she was the woman of a rich, powerful and famous man. Jagger was fastidiously polite to her, treating her in a slightly awed little boy way — like a princess. He suggested an intimate club where they could meet later, and she slipped away without a word to Eddie Barclay. Jagger followed her half an hour later, enormously flattered that she had dropped her fiance to be with him. It appeared that she had fallen as instantly for him as he had for her. Only later was Mick to discover that Bianca was insecure and needed constant reassurance of her charm and power to attract beautiful men who were not always prepared to put up with her selfish ways, and that, in the future, she would feel as little compunction about humiliating Mick as she had felt about walking out on Eddie Barclay.

"I'm a bit destructive," she was to admit later in an interview. "I used to be destructive in a relationship because I was scared of it getting out of hand. It was not really to destroy other people but to protect myself."

But on that balmy September evening it seemed to Mick that he had at last met the mystery woman of his dreams. She was a perfect lady, refusing to sleep with him at first, but telling him that yes, she too had never been quite so happy in her life. He had a few days to spare before the next gig, in Vienna, so they spent every second together, dining in candlelit restaurants, walking around the fairy-tale gardens of Versailles

Bianca Jagger

together, holding hands like kids. Mick offered her a little coke, and she snorted it so clumsily that he thought she had probably never tried the drug before, but he said nothing, thinking only how different she was from the other girls he had known.

But still, they didn't make love, and Jagger was more entranced than ever. Bianca was holding back, making excuses, letting him know that he hadn't totally captured her, and he was as aroused and intrigued by her as he had originally been by Marianne. The Stones flew to Vienna for the next gig, and he arranged for her to fly to Rome a couple of days later, when they played there. He sent a limousine to the airport to meet her and arranged a separate room for her. "This," said Keith, "has got to be the real thing."

He was right. Mick and Bianca made love for the first time that night, and for both of them, it was the best thing they'd known. For the remaining ten days of the tour Bianca travelled with the Rolling Stones, sleeping in Jagger's bed, watching every one of their shows. They were together incessantly, and Jagger scarcely spoke to anyone else.

Journalists covering the tour were eager to find out every detail about this woman who seemed to have replaced Marianne in Jagger's life. Photographers were everywhere. When one of them tried to snap their picture in Rome, Jagger ran towards him and punched him in the face. The photographer called the police at once, and Jagger was fined £800 for assault. In Frankfurt a bodyguard smashed another photographer's camera while Mick and Bianca escaped over a wall, giggling like two kids after a particularly daring prank. When they returned together to London after the tour, the reporters were especially eager to talk to Mick about his love life. Marianne had just been divorced by John Dunbar on the grounds of her adultery with the head Stone. But as newspapermen crowded around them at Heathrow, Bianca would only say, mysteriously, "I have no name. I do not speak English." Jagger, though, couldn't resist his favourite romantic euphemism: "We're just good friends."

Bianca Perez Moreno de Macias was born in Nicaragua. Though she has variously claimed that her father is a wealthy coffee plantation owner or a diplomat, he was, in reality, a small businessman. Her parents live apart and her mother has run a soft drinks shop in Managua. Bianca was an exceptionally intelligent, extremely ambitious child and after passing her high school examinations with honours, she flew to Paris to study political science at the Sorbonne. She was eighteen years old and still a virgin. "I was brought up in a terrible way," she says. "Brainwashed by the sexual repression in Catholic Nicaragua. I was taught that virginity was the biggest asset in life, and I believed it."

In Paris she rapidly surrendered her virginity and found the experience so pleasant that she began to question all the other conservative beliefs her parents had instilled in her. Like Jagger, she moved politically to the far left and began to dabble vicariously with revolution. For a while she was involved in the publication of a violently radical student magazine. Essentially, though, the blood-and-guts reality of revolutionary action held little appeal for her, and she used her fluency in French, Spanish, Italian and English to secure a distinctly un-radical job with the Nicaraguan Embassy in Paris.

Her beauty and style made Bianca popular among the Parisian radical chic set, and she became a fixture at fashionable parties. She moved on to London's Chelsea and there met Michael Caine. When their affair burned itself out, she returned to Paris to work for Eddie Barclay, who promply asked her to marry him.

Soon after Mick and Bianca returned to London, he 'phoned me at my flat to ask if they could come over to say hello. I was surprised because Mick had been slightly frosty toward me ever since my brief romance with Marianne. "I suppose he's having trouble getting hold of coke," I thought cynically. But as soon as they arrived, it became apparent that Bianca just wanted to chat with somebody who spoke her native language, Spanish. "It's such a strain, being with so many brilliant people and having to be witty and charming in a foreign language," she said. I understood why Mick had fallen so hard for her. She was different from the gauche women who hung around the Rolling Stones.

Bianca seemed intrigued when I said I was going to have a hit of cocaine. "Oh," she said when I brought out my ornate snuffbox filled with powder. "It's white."

"Of course," I said. "What colour did you expect it to be?"

"Surely it should be pink," she replied, like a connoisseur of wine who has just been served a Nuit St. Georges when she expected a Blanc de Blanc. "The best coke is always pink." She was wrong, of course. But I smiled and nodded agreement.

I chopped the crystals up on a small mirror, set out two thin lines, and Mick rolled up a five-pound note to snort one line through each nostril. "Ambrosia," he said at last. And he grinned one of those grins that split his face in half like a shattered coconut. Bianca laughed, too, and suddenly it hit me: They were twins. Mick could love this woman because she was he.

She looked the same, thought the same, and living with her was the closest he could possibly get to his ideal: making love to himself.

Anita hated Bianca from the start. She still harboured a deep desire for Mick herself, and the presence of this new woman posed a threat to her relationship with Keith, dreary though it was. Wives are often threatened when a close friend of their husband finds a new woman; it unsettles the husband, makes him question his own relationship. Also, Anita was acutely aware that she and Marianne — now no longer part of the Stones scene — had many similarities. They both were blondes, they both had arrived on the scene at the same time, they both had made love to Brian and they both had become druggies. It was all too possible that Keith would be triggered by Bianca to start searching for someone new.

On the tour, she would borrow clothes from Bianca, and then she would 'forget' to return them or she would just leave the things screwed up and filthy in Bianca's hotel room. By then Anita, like most junkies, had stopped worrying about everyday irritations like baths, and the clothes were frequently in such a repugnant condition that Bianca could only throw them away.

Mick made it clear he didn't want Bianca to fall out with Anita. "You'll have to sort it out between yourselves," he said. "Anita is one of the Stones now. Put up with her as best you can."

Back in London Anita made ever more flagrant passes at Mick. Keith was in the next room when I caught her pinching Mick's bottom and trying to tickle him. When Mick brought Bianca along, though, there was an entirely different reception waiting. Mick wanted to talk to Keith about a song they were working on together the previous night, and he left the girls together to chat, as Anita and Marianne had always done. But Anita refused to look at Bianca and stalked out of the room.

"Why has Anita got it in for Bianca?" I heard Mick ask Keith. "I mean it's so obvious. Bianca is getting really upset about it."

"Oh, don't worry, man," said Keith 'You know what Anita is like. It's just her moods. She'll get over it."

When Keith mentioned Bianca's reproach to Anita, she stepped up her campaign of hatred. "It's up to us, Tony, to get rid of Bianca," she told me. "That chick is going to break the Stones up just like that other chick broke up the Beatles. We've got to do something for the sake of the band."

"Why me?" I asked querulously.

"Because you know her, she trusts you," said Anita. "Let Mick know she's lying about her age. She says she's twenty five, but I'll bet a million pounds she's thirty-five if she's a day. She's just an old bird pretending to be young. I'll bet her tits are all droopy, she's certainly got something to be ashamed of — nobody has ever seen her with her clothes off."

Anita's schemes were truly bizarre. Bianca was a man who had had a sex-change operation, she said. Anita offered to pay me a fortune if I could dig up some proof of the operation from the press or the police.

"That's ridiculous," I said. "There's no way Bianca could ever have been a man."

"Well, get something, damn you," screeched Anita. "Just get something from the cops or the papers that we can show Mick to get him away from this stuck-up, snooty-nosed old bag. If you don't pull your finger out, he's going to fucking well marry her, and that'll be the end of the Rolling Stones and the end of you."

"I'm sorry, Anita," I told her eventually. "I like Bianca. I know she's a bit stuck up, but I don't think it's any of my business to go causing trouble for the two of them."

"It doesn't matter anyway," she said. "I've put a curse on her. She won't be around much longer."

Anita must have been too stoned to say her abracadabras. Bianca stayed very much alive, and Mick confided to Keith that they were getting married. "Good luck, man," said Keith. "If you love her, that's all that matters." It was the first time I had heard him speak about Mick and Bianca's relationship.

Since Mick and Keith sometimes double-dated, it was impossible for Bianca and Anita to avoid speaking. They built up a brittle façade of friendship. Anita used these occasions to feed the fires of Bianca's deep insecurity. For instance, Bianca complained that she got sick after snorting some cocaine I gave her. "Oh, surely you know why that was," said Anita, grinning maliciously. "Tony keeps two packs of coke: one for his real friends and himself — and one for everybody else. The second pack is just rubbish, and that's what he must have been giving you."

"The rotten bastard," said Bianca.

The next time I offered her some coke she turned sharply to me and said in Spanish, "I either want some of the good stuff or nothing. Anita has told me all about the rubbish you give to people you don't like."

The whole story was a complete fabrication. I shared what I had with my friends, and that was that. If I didn't like someone, I didn't give him or her anything.

Throughout this baptism of fire I never once saw Bianca's step falter or her nerve fail. I came to realise that she was in reality two very different people. Outwardly she was a beautiful, gossamer creature who lived for love and pretty clothes. Inwardly she was a person of iron will and determination. Very tough and quite incapable of being shot down by Anita's ragged fusillade. It dawned gradually on Anita, too, that she was fighting a losing battle. She simmered down, smothering her vexation beneath a blanket of heroin. The defeat was to be the decisive event in Anita's life to date. She had always worked hard to stay witty and attractive because that was the way to Jagger's heart. Now she seemed to give up, staying glumly in the house for weeks on end, never going anywhere, never seeing anyone except Keith, me and the few other people who came to visit. She drew deeper into herself; it was almost as though her life's ambition had been thwarted.

The battle ironically drew Mick and Bianca closer than ever, and they started to flit off around the world together like a pair of silly social butterflies. Their faces appeared in every gossip column in the world.

Frequently they would stroll along Cheyne Walk to call on Paul and Talitha Getty. They all were passionate users of cocaine, and frequently the four of them would go on and on snorting until they were so wired that I had to give them heroin (or some of the "naughty stuff," as they now called it) to calm them down again. Paul managed to get hold of my home number, and he would pester me for drugs almost as persistently as John Lennon had. I still refused to sell dope. I had no desire to become drug dealer to the aristocracy. I would, though, often share my stash with Paul, and he would agree to buy me a replacement.

Despite the jet-setting, Mick had still kept his wicked sense of humor. He and Bianca took off with a few friends for a Thanksgiving dinner being thrown by Atlantic Records' millionaire president Ahmet Ertegun in Nassau. They were forced to stop over en route at a seedy hotel in Miami, Rolling Stone reported. Jagger was prowling the lobby restlessly (as was his wont) with guitarist Jim Dickinson, and his circuits of the room had taken him repeatedly past two plump blue-rinsed matrons standing by the door. One of them wrinkled her nose, her face a mask of disapproval. She looked very like Mrs. Mary Whitehouse. Jagger pivoted and announced to the room in general. "These women look like hookers to me." There was a moment of stunned silence, and then Jagger added, "Say, Dickinson, you want a couple of hookers?" Dickinson laughed and shook his head just as a friend opened the lobby door to tell Mick his car was ready. Jagger elegantly took Bianca's arm and escorted her to the door. The women stared at him in stunned fury. As Jagger passed, he bowed.

Mick was desperately keen to impress Bianca with his man-of-the-worldliness. Sometimes he seemed to fear that he was perhaps still a little too suburban for so exotic a creature. He even took her to Marrakesh, to the same house where he had slept and made love to Marianne so long before. Bianca was not particularly impressed.

But she was unable to conceal her surprise when Mick casually mentioned to her in November 1970, shortly after she arrived in London, that Marsha Hunt had had his baby. The child was born in St. Mary's Hospital, in Paddington. She looked remarkably like Mick, and Marsha called her Karis. Jagger collected the two of them from the hospital in his Bentley and drove them to Marsha's flat in Marlborough Place, St. John's Wood. He left after a couple of hours.

Later Marsha told journalist Frankie McGowan, "I fell in love with Mick because I thought he was shy and awkward. I never went out very much with him and his friends because mostly they weren't my scene. He would come to my flat or I would go to his. I used to tell him off for leaving his chauffeur outside for hours. We knew exactly what we were doing when we had Karis. She was absolutely planned. He was very insecure, and he needed the stability of a child.

"For a long time afterwards we were friends. I became his kind of confidante, if you like. If Bianca was giving him a hard time, he would come and tell me. In fact, it was Mick and Bianca who baby-sat for me when I went to audition for a part in the musical *Catch My Soul*. I never married Mick because I knew it wouldn't work. I just couldn't be married to someone who didn't get up till two in the afternoon.

"It's sad now that, for lots of reasons, we're not speaking to each other anymore... I don't think it's so sad for Karis that Mick doesn't see her. I think it's sad for him. Later, when the fame has died down and he's older, I think he may want to know her then. I know people think that Mick abandoned me when I had Karis. But that's supposition. Not many people knew that much about us anyway. But I know, and Mick knows, the kind of relationship we had."

When Karis was two years old, Marsha asked magistrates at Marylebone to bring an affiliation order against Jagger. Mick's lawyers asked for Jagger to be allowed to produce a blood sample. Eventually he settled, furiously, out of court. "I'm not upset for myself," he said. "It's just that my mother didn't know, and she gets so upset about this sort of publicity. Why did Marsha have to be so bloody silly? It wasn't as though I was going to leave her and Karis to starve."

21

EVERYONE SEEMED TO BE ADDICTED TO HEROIN. WE HAD ALL GROWN dependent on H in pretty much the same way: via cocaine. We'd all been astonished when we'd realised that unless we had a few blasts of smack every day, we were doomed to the sickening pain of withdrawal symptoms. No coke user ever fully comprehends at first a very simple fact — every snort of this beautiful, uplifting drug takes him one step nearer heroin addiction. The connection between coke and H is mysterious; the two drugs are diametrically opposite in their effects. Coke brings heightened perception and lucidity; H brings oblivion. Most people say they use cocaine because they want to be as outgoing and energetic as possible, that there is no way they could ever be persuaded to touch heroin. But the more you use coke, the more wired — hyper-energetic, hyper-paranoid — you become and the more your body and mind crave peace and tranquillity. When, at last, someone finally turns you on to heroin, it is like suddenly being on a calm, sunshiny beach after weeks of crashing through a furious ocean.

I was well aware of the dangers because I had been mildly addicted before. But working in the rock world and refusing to use cocaine is rather like joining a rugby club and preaching total abstinence. If you don't accept an occasional snort and proffer one in return, you are an instant outcast. And so inexorably, though I still refused to use a syringe, I had become hooked on heroin once again. Keith and Anita had fallen into the morass far more deeply than I and they both were injecting themselves with about a third of a gramme of smack every day.

Dope was only one of their worries. Prince Rupert Lowenstein, the Stones' financial adviser, spent months combing through the books to discover that although the band had earned almost £100,000,000 during their seven years at the top, so much of the money had gone astray that

210

there was a real danger of their being forced into bankruptcy by the Inland Revenue. "There is only one course of action legally open to you," he told them. "You will have to become domiciled overseas before the start of the 1971 to 1972 tax year."

Bill and Charlie were distraught. They enjoyed their rural gentlemanly lives, and membership of the Rolling Stones had not saved them from premature middle age. Mick and Keith, on the other hand, were thrilled by the romance of being forced to flee their native land. They would go, they decided, to the South of France, following in the elegant footsteps of Somerset Maugham. There would be no more hassles with the cops, no more reporters camping on their doorstep and no more London drizzle. It would be a whole new life. First they would play a quick farewell tour of Britain, record a television spectacular and then try to give up dope completeiy. Re-birth is more fun if you're not strung out on smack.

Marshall Chess came with them on the tour. Marshall is the son of a good Jewish businessman who founded Chess Records in the States, and now he was being groomed to take over as a top executive of the Stones' own record company, like a moth to a flame he rapidly succumbed to the lure of the Stones' exotic lifestyle He came to realise, too, that Bianca was more worldly than he'd thought. She took him for nearly £6,000 when they played a few games of gin rummy to while away their ten days on the road with the Stones. He paid up without complaint. Losing to Mick's old lady could surely do him nothing but good.

Mick Taylor's girl friend, Rose Miller, also came along on the tour. She had given birth to his baby daughter, Chloe, three months earlier. The newspapers had all missed the story.

Keith and Anita were so heavily into heroin that they became a liability, missing trains and planes, turning up late for almost every show and taking their son, Marlon, and dog, Boogie, with them everywhere.

Jagger was ultra-cool, ultra-sophisticated. His hair was cut shorter than it had ever been; he wore tight sweaters and long overcoats, looking more like a French aristrocrat than a rock star. To complete the image, he and Bianca talked almost exclusively in French, baffling and losing everybody else on the tour. They formed their own very exclusive clique — a clique of two. It was obvious to everyone that they were deeply in love.

The tour climaxed with two shows at the Roundhouse in London on March 14. The dressing room was crammed with rock stars and their ladies, but Bianca, clad in a boa of human hair and sporting a peacock feather in her cloche hat, was queen in a way that Marianne and Chrissie Shrimpton never were. She looked very beautiful, but her face seemed almost cruel, like Jagger's, and she didn't seem to have the normal human weakness of needing to be liked. People were becoming just a little afraid of her.

Bianca's carefully contrived awesome persona was completely wasted on a big mouthed groupie called Joyce the Voice, who had somehow managed to slip into the dressing room, journalist Robert Greenfield reported.

"'scuse me, luv," she said to Bianca. "But weren't you with Osibisa in their dressing room last week?"

There were giggles from nearby. Poor Joyce really didn't realise that Bianca was Mick's lady. She had mistaken her for a groupie.

"What," Bianca asked icily, "is Osibisa?"

"Oh, wow," Joyce babbled on. "There's someone around with your exact vibes. I mean, she's like your twin sister. Somebody's walking around with your face."

Bianca rolled her eyes to the heavens. Joyce was hustled out.

The Roundhouse gig was a triumph and earned rave reviews. Jagger always read the reviews, and on this occasion he heaved a sigh of relief. Success in London was no longer financially crucial, but London remained the most discerning city in rock. Success or failure here was always mirrored in the rest of the world.

Decca, meanwhile, got even for the "Cocksucker Blues" fiasco by releasing an album called *Stone Age* without the Stones' permission. The record consisted of twelve tracks, all but four of which had previously been released on other albums. Jagger was so incensed that he paid for full-page black-bordered advertisements in all the British music papers stating: "Beware! Message from the Rolling Stones Re: *Stone Age*. We didn't know this record was going to be released. It is, in our opinion, below the standard we try to keep up, both in choice of content and cover design." All the Stones signed the ad.

Immediately after the British tour I drove Keith to Redlands so he could begin to withdraw from heroin. Anita wanted to come off the drug as well, but they decided that they would have to go cold turkey in turns so that one of them could look after Marlon.

Smithy went with him to administer what she called her morphine cure. Smithy was a tough, no-nonsense, sixty-year-old matron who was so formidable that she had weaned Robert Fraser and many other of the

212

fashionable young ladies and gentlemen of Chelsea off heroin, and she was reputed to be capable of taking anyone off drugs in less than two weeks. Her technique consisted of putting tablets of a morphine substitute under Keith's tongue, gradually reducing the dose day by day. He started off giggling nervously, as excited as a little boy who is about to try smoking for the first time, but then his flesh started to crawl, his nose ran and his stomach muscles were torn apart by agonizing cramps. When he could bear no more, Smithy would slip him a couple of her tablets, and he would grab them with the fervour of a drowning man clutching at scraps of wood.

When I went to Redlands to get him ten days later, he was battered and pale, but he had the exuberance of a man who has just been freed from jail. As we roared through the night toward London in the black-windowed Bentley, he slammed a Bo Diddley tape into the player. Our ears rang to the strains of "Mona," and Keith mischievously switched on the two small tweeter speakers he had had fitted to the outside of the car and the music reverberated through the narrow village streets. I glanced in the rearview mirror and saw a trail of yokels peering curiously after the madmen in the midnight blue Bentley.

"Yippeee... fuckin' great, man," screamed Keith. "Got any coke?" And I knew that his cure was to be short-lived.

The next evening the Stones were due at the Marquee Club, on Wardour Street, Soho, to film a farewell television show for their British fans. Anita had agreed to begin her withdrawal that night. She had a room in a private hospital at Harrow-on-the-Hill called Bowden House, which specialised in the treatment of alcoholism and drug addiction.

A specialist at the hospital told Anita that they had developed a technique which completely by-passed the problem of withdrawal symptoms. "We sedate you with sleeping tablets, and at the same time, we feed you steadily reduced doses of methadone, which is a heroin substitute," he said. "You will feel no pain."

When the car arrived to take her to the hospital, she was fairly calm, although she begged all of us to give her a little smack. "I might get desperate," she said, her voice panicky.

Keith was adamant. "You're crazy," he reproached her. "How are you ever going to give it up if you start smuggling it into the hospital on the first night you are there?"

The television show at the Marquee was an unmitigated disaster. The club's owner, Harold Pendelton, had erected a huge sign advertising his club across the stage in direct contradiction of Mick's instructions. At first, wishing to avoid a row in front of their friends who made up the studio audience, the Stones attempted to ignore the sign. Then the TV director complained that the damn sign was obscuring the view of his cameramen. Keith ordered Pendleton to remove it.

"No," said Pendleton. Keith swung his heavy red Gibson at his face, missing him by a hair's breadth. Roadies charged in and dragged the two apart. The contretemps ended with the entire, bewildered audience being thrown out into the street.

It took half-an-hour for Mick to convince Keith of the importance of the show and a further hour for the Stones to give an extremely sullen performance. The film was never shown in Britain, but it was well received in the rest of Europe, where rock fans are less discriminating.

It was midnight by the time Keith, Michael Cooper, my girl friend, Madeleine, and I walked out to Keith's Bentley. Keith fumbled through his pockets, then asked me plaintively, "Have you got my car keys, Tony?"

"Of course not," I said. "When did you last see them?"

Keith, it transpired, had tossed the keys to a friend called Jean on his arrival at the Marquee and had asked him to park the car. Jean, unfortunately, had omitted to toss the keys back again, and since none of us had any idea where he lived, we were eventually driven to 'phoning the police to see if they could help us start the car. Ironically the two officers who came to our aid were charm itself, and they efficiently managed to start the car by bridging the ignition switch with a piece of wire. Michael Cooper and I hovered in the background, praying that they wouldn't take it into their heads to search us all for dope.

We drove to my flat and put the car in my garage. "Leave the engine running," said Keith. "Then I won't have to mess around calling the police to start it in the morning." We left the car huskily puffing away to itself all night.

Once in the apartment Michael pulled out some heroin — he had become firmly addicted — and offered it around. "I suppose you don't want any, Keith, do you?" he asked.

"You bet I do," said Keith, and that was the end of his cure.

We woke at about nine the next morning, Saturday, and after a couple of cups of black coffee and a couple of snorts of coke, Keith, Michael and I went downstairs to see if we could fix the car. Its engine was still running, but there was only a quarter of a tank of petrol left and the tank was fitted with a locked cap.

"I'll have to go back to H. R. Owen, in Kensington," said Keith.

"They sold me the car. It's up to them to fix it."

I left Keith and Michael and went back to the flat. Almost immediately the phone started to ring. It was Anita, and she was in the midst of what sounded like a hysterical fit.

"Get me out of this place, Tony," she screamed.

"What on the earth is the matter?" I asked.

"They can't put me to sleep. That sleep cure stuff is all a load of bollocks. They've only given me Mogadon, and they aren't even strong enough to put me to sleep at home. I feel terrible . . . I feel rotten. Where the hell is Keith?"

"He's gone to get the car fixed," I said.

"Well, you just tell him to get me out. Tell him to come here right now and get me out of this fucking madhouse."

"How can I possibly get hold of him now? He's in the car."

"Well, if you don't get him right away, I'm discharging myself."

I sympathised because I understood the pain of withdrawing from heroin. The agony goes deeper than the mere physical symptoms, excruciating though they are. There is the constant psychological punishment of knowing that one quick snort of smack would bring the whole nightmare to an end. Withdrawal is like rolling around naked on a bed of barbed wire while you gulp down a bottle of detergent — a ghastly self-inflicted torture.

I asked the Stones' office to help me track Keith down, and at about lunchtime, he phoned me from the rooftop bar of the Hilton Hotel, in Park Lane. He was so drunk that I could hardly understand him. I managed to discern that H. R. Owen had not had a spare key. They had, however, managed to open the Bentley's petrol tank, and now Keith had enough fuel to keep him going for at least a couple of days. He and Michael had parked the car in the underground garage at the Hilton with the engine still running, and they had taken the lift to the top floor, where they had spent the past three hours gulping down margaritas. "I muss zay," he spluttered, giggling, "I do feel juz a lil bit pissed."

"Never mind that. Anita is going to check out of Bowden House if you don't get up there right away. She's going berserk."

"Jesus," he said, sounding instantly sober. "Can't I ever get any peace from that fuckin' woman? The doctors told me she'd be out for three days on this sleep cure and that I wouldn't be allowed to visit her. I suppose I'll have to get up there."

As soon as they climbed into the car, Keith and Michael both took a hit of cocaine. Keith is a bad driver at the best of times, but now the after effects of his withdrawal coupled with the booze and the coke appeared to have driven him slightly crazy as he roared up Harrow Road. An advance copy of the Stones' new album, *Sticky Fingers*, blasted out over the tape player. As Michael Cooper closed his eyes and prepared to die, Keith bounced off kerbs, passed cars on the wrong side of the road and honked at anyone who dared get in his way. They screeched through Paddington, out into Wembley, and then, just as they were about to enter Harrow, Keith saw that he was about to crash into a lorry. He wrenched his big steering wheel, and the car careered straight through an iron fence into the middle of a roundabout. Steam shot out from the burst radiator with a blast like a hand grenade. The front of the car was a write-off, and the chassis was twisted irreparably, but the tape was still screaming out "Brown Sugar" — and the engine was still running.

"Quick," Michael said. "Let's get the hell out of here before the law arrives. I know someone who lives just down the road."

They leaped out of the wreck, scooted through a crowd of open-mouthed onlookers and stopped at the door of a small house. "It's Nicky Hopkins's place," said Michael. Keith looked relieved. Nicky was a musician who had frequently worked with the Stones, and Keith knew he could be trusted.

They bathed their cuts and bruises in Nicky's bathroom while Nicky phoned for a limousine to take them the rest of the way to Bowden House. Keith quickly phoned Anita to tell her what had happened, and she screamed at him hysterically, "Just get me some H or I'm checking out of here right now. This minute."

"Okay, okay," soothed Keith. "I'll bring you some. But just a little bit."

He and Michael hid their drugs in Nicky's lavatory and then left to calm Anita down.

A couple of hours later Keith arrived at my flat to tell me the whole story. Astonishingly he still appeared to be drunk.

"So what happened about the car?" I asked. "Who towed it away for you?"

"Sod the car,;' he said. "I don't care if I never see it again. If I go near it, they will nick me, and then they are going to start going into all that business about my driving licence and everything."

He staggered back to Cheyne Walk to sleep off his exhausting day. The next day was Sunday; at 10:00 a.m. I was wakened by a ferocious thumping at the door.

"Quick," I screamed at Madeline, "it must be the law. We're being raided. Flush everything down the toilet."

After five minutes the thumping was so loud that I was convinced the door was about to be smashed in. With all our dope gone I could saunter casually across and open up. It was Anita.

"For Christ's sake," she screamed in Italian. "What took you so bloody long?"

I explained, and she waved her hands above her head in exasperation. "That's why I'm here. I'm really ill, Tony, the cure isn't working. You've got to get me some heroin right away."

"Stay here," I said, and I drove off to see what I could score. When I returned a couple of hours later, she had been sick and her hands were trembling constantly, as if her body were being racked by a series of electric shocks. Seconds after snorting, she nodded out into a deep, childlike sleep.

That evening she returned to Bowden House for the night, but she was back on my doorstep the next morning pleading for heroin, and so it continued for the next four days. At last her exasperated doctor, a Dr. Maurice, could stand it no longer. He phoned Keith to tell him that his wife had more heroin in her blood now than upon admission; there was no point in attempting a cure if she wasn't prepared to stay in the hospital all day.

Keith lectured Anita until she agreed to stay put for the rest of the course. The doctors also insisted that Keith not visit her. They blamed him for upsetting her and supplying her with drugs.

The onerous task of visiting Anita fell to me. Keith sent a limousine for me the next morning, and I took her a huge bunch of flowers. I was searched for drugs at the entrance to her wing, but the attendants failed to find a tiny packet of cocaine I had secreted inside my shirt.

I gave her the flowers, hugged her, kissed her and allowed her one tiny snort. "That's just a comforter," I said. "Keith made me promise not to let you have smack, so you'll just have to make do with coke." She insisted I should return with more of the drug that afternoon. The ritual continued with me scooting up to Bowden House in the big limousine twice a day for the next week.

When she could stand the strain no longer, she discharged herself with a habit only fractionally weaker than the one she'd had. The doctor prescribed heroin substitute tablets for her to continue withdrawal. A forlorn hope indeed.

217

It was April now, and the Stones were fleeing with their women, their children, their diamonds and their videotape recorders to the South of France. Fleeing Britain's punitive taxes, fleeing the pressures of police persecution, fleeing hostile newspapers. Jagger and his men had at last been routed. The street guerrillas who had once menaced the fabric of society had been destroyed by money. They were running away, deserting the kids to whom they had once offered salvation. Defectors to the lure of indolence and wealth beyond measure.

218

22

THE TINY WHITEWASHED CHURCH OF STE. ANNE IS PERCHED ON A HILL IN St. Tropez overlooking the vast azure sweep of the Mediterranean. The white yachts of the jet set sparkle on the water, and to the north are the mountains and the lush, cool forests of pine and tumbling streams.

Mick and Bianca stumbled upon this holy place by accident as they ambled around the town one day, hand in hand.

"Marry me here, and we'll sail away in a big white yacht and spend our lives making love and looking after our beautiful children," he said.

"I love you," she replied, kissing him on the lips with sisterly tenderness.

Mick was bubbling with excitement when he called Dartford to invite his parents to the wedding. "You must come," he told his mother. "I've booked a suite for you at our hotel in St. Tropez." On the other end of the line Eva Jagger sobbed at the thought that Mick was finally going to get married and settle down. "Oh, I'm so happy, Mick," she said. "So happy."

"Just one thing," Mick added. "Don't tell anyone about the wedding. We're trying to keep it very quiet."

Marrying in the little church proved more complicated than they'd expected. Ste. Anne's was Roman Catholic, and Mick was Church of England. He studied Catholicism four weeks under the guidance of the church's pastor, Abbe Lucien Baud, to prepare for his marriage. "It's not a question of him becoming a Roman Catholic," Father Baud said. "He is merely acquiring an understanding of our faith. He is a very serious, intelligent man. He is an Anglican, of course, and I don't think a practicing one. He has a great sense of religion, that boy. He really has a feeling for it."

Rumour of the impending nuptials spread rapidly, but when Mick and Bianca were photographed leaving a boutique in St. Tropez on April 18, Mick said, "We're definitely not getting married. No way." The wedding was scheduled for May 12.

Mick wanted only close friends at the ceremony: Keith, his brother Chris, Roger Vadim, Nathalie Delon. Bianca insisted on an occasion, however, and they chartered a jet to fly in seventy-five friends from London. Mick phoned to invite me and swore me to secrecy. "We don't want the whole place swarming with reporters," he said. "That would ruin everything." I was amazed at his naivete. Did he really suppose that he could stick the cream of Britain's superstars and aristocrats on a special charter jet without the press finding out?

Mick phoned me again at my flat the night before the wedding. "How are you getting there, Tony?" he asked. You will be coming on the plane tomorrow, won't you?"

"Sure," I said. "I'm really looking forward to it. I'm going to bring Madeleine along. By the way, I know it's a bit late, but we were wondering what you would like in the way of a wedding present. I've got a little surprise for you but if there's anything special you really want, don't be embarrassed about asking for it."

"Well," he replied, "you know what I'd really, really like, don't you, Tony?" And I knew he meant cocaine.

"It might be just a little tricky, Mick," I told him. "But give me an hour or so, and I'll phone around and see what I can do."

"I'd be very grateful, Tony. A guy needs a little c-o-k-e to get him through his wedding day."

I didn't know what to do. There was no coke in London the cops had just wiped out three of the biggest dealers. I had a friend who was a dentist in the Midlands, and he'd swapped me coke for advance pressings of Rolling Stones albums in the past. Though he had to keep a strict record of the cocaine he used, he got around the problem by giving patients another type of anesthetic but entering in his record book that he had given them cocaine. In this way he usually managed to stash away at least a gramme of cocaine a week.

When I phoned him to explain the problem, he was eager to help. "Sure," he said. "I've got about three grammes here. You can have it right now if you like. But you'll have to pay me for it. I'm not going to just swap it for a record this time."

"No problem at all," I said. "I'll happily pay you the going price."

I 'phoned Mick at once in St. Tropez, and he was ecstatic.

"Fantastic," he said. "Look, I'll send a private jet across to Heathrow to pick you up, and you can bring me my present tonight. I'm not going to get through this gig without it."

"You're joking," I said. "That'll cost a fortune. It's ridiculous."

"No," he said. "I want you here straightaway, and I'm not taking no for an answer."

"Hang on," I said. "I'll just double-check that I can get everything arranged that quickly."

The dentist panicked when I asked him if I couid send a friend of mine to the Midlands that night to pick up the package. "No, definitely not. It's in my office," he said. "I'm coming down to London tomorrow morning anyway, so I can let you have it at ten a.m. — but not a second earlier."

"Fuck," Mick said when I told him.

A veritable Who's Who of superstars boarded the jet at Gatwick — Paul McCartney with Linda, who had now become his wife; Ringo Starr; Eric Clapton with his aristocratic girl friend, Alice Ormsby-Gore; Keith Moon; Peter Frampton; Donyale Luna; even Robert Fraser. The press laid siege to the airport, and everything that moved got interviewed (I was caught by CBS).

We drank champagne all the way to Nice, and at the other end a bus waited to whisk celebrities to the wedding. As the dope bearer I got special treatment. A chauffeur with a mile-long Cadillac held a placard with my name on it. When I approached him, he said, "Yes, sir, Mr. Jagger asked me to collect you. He wants me to take you to him as soon as possible."

This posed a slight problem. I had paid a friend to carry the coke for me, and he was now ensconced in the bus. We finally caught up with it and flagged it down on a busy road, much to the merriment of the assembled celebrities.

There was much jeering from McCartney and Clapton as I grabbed my smuggler and pushed him into the limo. We arrived eventually at the Hotel Byblos, which is where all the Stones were staying. Situated between the ocean and the forests, the Byblos is one of the great hotels of the world. Guests stay in small villas around a central, sky blue swimming pool.

Keith grabbed me the second I climbed out of the car. "Thank God you've made it," he said. "I haven't had a snort for days. Anita's only got her heroin substitute tabs, and she's going balmy."

221

He half dragged me into their villa, and I pulled out some coke that I had brought for myself. They both took huge snorts from my bottle, and then Keith lolled back on the bed. You didn't just bring this little bit, did you?" he asked. "Where's my stash?"

You didn't ask me to bring anything for you," I said. "Anyway, you can keep the rest of my bottle if you're really desperate. I've got to nip out for a minute."

I knew only too well that Keith and Anita would have no compunction about grabbing the £1,500 stash of coke I had hidden in my trousers for Mick if I didn't beat it before they talked me into giving it to them.

Mick was alone in his room. We chatted about marriage; and he seemed pensive. "The whole fucking thing is more hassle than it's worth," he said.

Together we snorted a couple of lines of coke and then he confided that he had had a furious row with Bianca. He told me there had been a tiff over the terms of their French pre-nuptual agreement. Bianca had been so forceful, he said, that he had had to tell her he would call the wedding off unless she agreed to his terms.

They were unable simply to marry in Ste. Anne's after all. They had to go through a legal ceremony in the town's council chamber before their union could be blessed in the church.

The longer Mick and Bianca delayed, the more crowded the council chamber became. Fans, reporters and photographers were milling about, buzzing, waiting for the show to begin. Mayor Marius Estezant, the man who was to conduct the civil ceremony, proved to be a pretty good warm-up act, preening like a peacock as he fielded a hail of questions and posed for photographers. But when Les Perrin, Mick's press officer, called the hotel to warn Mick about what to expect at the council chamber, Mick blew up. "Get rid of them," he yelled. "If there's going to be all that crowd I'm not going to get married."

It was now four-twenty, and the wedding had been scheduled for four o'clock. Perrin tried to clear the chamber but to no avail. Under French law weddings are open to the public.

"If the bride and groom are not here by four-thirty, I shall go, and there will be no wedding," M. Estezan announced.

Perrin phoned Jagger to explain the situation. "Fucking hell," said Mick. "I wish to God I'd never said I was going to get married in the first place."

He relented at last, Perrin persuaded the mayor to stay on and the guests began to arrive. Keith was wired and fighting everyone who got in his way — one photographer had his camera smashed, and an autograph hunter had his book hurled to the floor. In the midst of the mayhem Joe and Eva Jagger, Mick's parents, arrived, looking frightened. They sat uncomfortably between Lord Litchfield and Ronnie Wood, trying hard to appear inconspicuous.

Then Mick and Bianca drove up, almost an hour late by this time, and as soon as they stepped from their car they were captured by camera lights and riddled by a volley of questions. "Fuck this," Mick muttered. "I'm not going through with it." And Bianca, wearing a V-cut wedding dress that almost bared her nipples, began to cry — much to the delight of the gathered reporters.

Perrin whispered in his ear, "You've got to get it over and done with," and Jagger relented. He told the press to take their pictures and leave them in peace, but he was just as ineffectual with them as he had been at Altamont. They got their pictures and stayed anyway.

The ceremony was over in minutes. Mick and Bianca signed the register, and their signatures were witnessed by Roger Vadim and Nathalie Delon.

As the hapless couple left the council chamber to climb into the Bentley for the drive to the Church, Mick was again mobbed by photographers. There was also a small group of student revolutionaries who were staging a protest at the extravagance of the wedding. The man who had promised to blast apart the status quo was spending his loot on a bourgeois bean feast for the indolent rich. The kids kicked his car and showered him with insults. Jagger didn't care anymore; he had cut himself off from the debacle.

At the Church Perrin was determined to prevent the press from ruining this part of the ceremony. So tight was security that Mick and Bianca were accidentally locked out. The bridegroom thumped at the heavy oak doors as autograph hunters pulled at his clothes. "Les, Les, let me in, dammit!" he screamed to no avail. At length, the door was opened, and the dishevelled couple slipped inside.

It was not the usual crowd you would find in Church — girls in see-through tops, micro-skirts and hot pants — and Father Baud was obviously unhappy about this flagrant indecency in his house of worship. As he spoke, the organist played a schmaltzy medley from the film *Love Story*. The tunes had been selected by Bianca.

Lord Patrick Litchfield led Bianca down the aisle and gave her away.

The priest liked Jagger, and he smiled paternally as he told him, "You have told me that you believe youth seeks happiness and a certain ideal and faith. I think you are seeking it, too, and I hope it arrives today with your marriage. But when you are a personality like Mick Jagger, it is too much to hope for privacy for your marriage.'

In the evening there was a party for a thousand people at the fabulous Cafe des Arts. I stared as Brigitte Bardot undulated through the crowd. As a beauty Bardot was in a class by herself — just as dazzling off screen as she was on. I am used to beautiful women, but this one left me speechless.

Bianca wore a diamanté turban with a diaphanous waistcoat that made her effectively naked from the waist up. Boobs were in in St. Tropez that season.

The party was decadent in its extravagance — all the caviar and lobster and champagne you could consume. A local band played, dismally, but then there was a reggae set from the Rudies and a few songs from Terry Reid. At last Mick went up on stage, to sing with Doris Troy, P. P. Arnold, Steve Stills and a stageful of stars. They were magnificent.

Bianca was piqued at the way Mick was pointedly ignoring her and slipped back to the Byblos. Alone. Joe and Eva Jagger had also found it difficult to speak with their egocentric son. They had wandered around all evening, waiting for a chance to hand him his carefully wrapped wedding present. They left still holding the package. Mrs. Jagger told a reporter, "I hope my other son doesn't become a superstar."

At four in the morning the bus arrived to take the London contingent back to the airport for a dawn flight home. Only Eric Clapton and Alice Ormsby-Gore, Lord Harlech's daughter, decided to stay on. Heroin addicts, they were starting to shiver and shake as the withdrawals began to bite. They had anticipated a brisk junket, but the circus had gone on for hours, and now they were caught without their heroin, which they had been afraid to smuggle out of London. I took them back to the hotel and persuaded Anita to let them have some of her methadone, the drug that stops withdrawal symptoms.

We talked into the night, and the two of them told me how they had become hooked. "The guy I was scoring coke from would only sell it to me if I bought smack as well," Eric said. "So I kept stashing it away in a drawer. I just didn't want to know about it. Then, one day, there was no coke around, so I thought I'd take a snort of smack, and it was quite nice. A lot of fuss about nothing, I thought. But gradually Alice and

224

I started using it more and more. Now look at the state we're in." And he laughed.

Eric has a theory about the link between musicians and smack. "Musicians live on a very intense plane of emotional necessity," he said. "And heroin is probably the strongest pain-killer you can get."

The next morning dawned with the crickets playing their string concerto for the sheer joy of being alive and with Eric and me rubbing our heads and saying, yeah, man, that was some party.

And suddenly it dawned on me; nobody there had guessed what I already knew. Mrs. Bianca Perez Moreno de Macios Jagger was four months pregnant.

23

WILLIAM BURROUGHS HAD BEEN A HEROIN ADDICT FOR YEARS. HIS WIFE, Joan, consumed enough Benzedrine every day to shove a hippopotamus through the four-minute mile. One night at a party at their home, when everyone was flying about eight miles high, she placed an apple or an apricot or something on her head and challenged her husband to shoot it off. Bill, usually an excellent marksman, pulled out his Colt .45 and blew a neat little hole in the center of her forehead. It was accidental homicide, the jury decided. Bill went on to write *Naked Lunch*, hailed by some as an important novel and denounced by others as a tiresome fraud. He was in his mid-fifties now, still using smack after more than thirty years. Keith liked him very much when we met him in Villefranche. It was through Bill Burroughs that we were to meet Johnny Braces.

Keith and I were standing by the harbour, next to Errol Flynn's schooner, when Johnny Braces strolled over with another man and introduced himself as a friend of Bill Burroughs. Keith and I chatted with him for half-an-hour; then we all departed with vague, insincere invitations to drop in if we were passing one another's villas.

We lived now — Keith, Anita, Madeleine, I and a constant floating population of house guests — in a white palace called Nellcote. It dominates the fishing village of Villefranche as dramatically as the Acropolis crowns Athens. The stately rooms are crammed with antiques, and the gardens running down to the private jetty are lush. Peaches, grapes, oranges and bananas grow next to the spiky palms and leathery green rubber trees. Nellcote is a pinnacle of man's architectural, horticultural and imaginative skills; nowhere on earth have I seen a more gracious place to live. The mansion cost Keith £1,000 a week to rent with the option to purchase for a modest £1,000,000. He decided not to buy for a few months. At that price he needed to be certain that he

226

Tony, Keith, Madeleine, Marlon and Anita

would be happy living in France.

We had been there for ten days. The first flush of novelty had worn off, and Keith and Anita were bored. A pretty house is fine, but for the two of them now the only happiness in life was inhaled or injected. And when you are a stranger in a strange land, it is hard to know how to go about scoring.

I was lolling on the wide front steps, watching the yachts scudding across the bay far below, when I noticed the Bentley gliding effortlessly up toward the house. It crunched to a halt on the gravel road, and Johnny Braces stepped out. His real name was Jean Briteul, but since he constantly wore fiery red braces, the nickname came about.

"Hi, man," he said. "I was just passing by, and I thought I'd take up Keith's invitation to drop in."

"Well, I'm very sorry," I replied, looking away. "But Keith's in a bit of a mood today. He and Anita don't really want to see anyone."

"Oh, well, it doesn't matter. It's just that I've picked up some rather good smack, and I was thinking of offering to turn them on."

"Hold on a minute," I said. This was worth disturbing Keith and Anita for.

The two of them were lying listlessly on their big four-poster bed

227

reading. When I told them Johnny had dropped by, Keith was furious.

"Who does he think he is?" he exploded. "The cheek of the guy coming round here. Who gave him an invitation? Kick his arse, man... tell him to piss off."

"Keith," I said, "he's got some smack."

"Why didn't you say? Tell him to come in. Give the man a drink. Don't keep him waiting. Why didn't you tell me sooner, Tony? We've been waiting upstairs for something to happen and the guy's downstairs with all the gear. Why the hell didn't you come up more quickly?"

But Keith and Anita still refused to go downstairs. "Go down and get all you can off him," he ordered me.

Johnny was pacing back and forth in the living room. He commented on the exquisite beauty of the house, the wonderful spring we were enjoying, until finally I could stand it no more, and I just blurted out, "Hey, man, when are you going to give us a turn-on then?"

"Oh," he said. "Does Keith want a snort or something? Where is Keith anyway?"

Keith and Anita swooped down the ornate staircase like a pair of ghastly vultures when I told them Johnny would turn them on only if they came down and talked with him. Keith was suspicious, and his suspicion was compounded when Johnny pulled a woman's powder compact from the pocket of his slacks. "Here it is," he said, proffering what looked and smelled like pink talcum powder. Keith greedily inhaled through a gold tube I'd given him that he wore on a chain around his neck.

"Here, Tony," he whispered in my ear. "I think this joker's taking the piss. Giving us bloody talcum powder." But a couple of minutes later the effects of pure Thai heroin hit his brain, and he passed out on his seat — along with the rest of us.

When Keith regained consciousness, he treated Johnny like a long-lost friend. "Say, man, why haven't you dropped by before? You know you're always welcome here. By the way, any chance of getting hold of some more of that stuff? There is? Well, why don't you just leave that little powder compact here with us for safekeeping?"

Johnny was hesitant, though. He was on his way to London, he said, and picking up more heroin would involve traipsing all the way back to Marseilles.

"You want to go to London?" said Keith. "Well, you can stay at my house in Cheyne Walk. It's a terrific place, and you can stay there for free for a couple of weeks if you let me have that powder compact."

The deal was agreed; I would go back to Chelsea with Johnny to show him how to operate the numerous alarm and security systems, to take an inventory and to show him around the house. Then I would return to Villefranche. Johnny could stay at Cheyne Walk for as long as he liked, but once his two weeks were up, he would have to pay £300 a week rent. Johnny was so grateful that he phoned his dealer in Marseilles to ask him to drop in at Nellcote next time he was passing to arrange a regular supply of drugs for Keith.

Errol Flynn's schooner had been one of the finest ships to grace the Mediterranean — a huge, sleek vessel of teak, with an ebony-coloured hull, two big timber masts and billowing white sails. But the old lady had seen better days. Her hull was waterlogged now, one of the masts had broken and she was kept afloat only by grace of two electric pumps which emptied her bilges as fast as the sea could fill them, twenty-four hours a day. No one had set foot on her for years.

Keith had always been a fan of Errol Flynn, whose swashbuckling, outlaw arrogance was similar to his own. He developed a fixation about the yacht. He would stroll down to it with Anita and I when the harbour was quiet, and we all would climb aboard to explore her.

He talked with the harbour master about buying her, but it was explained that owing to the tragic death of Flynn's son in Vietnam, mooring fees had not been paid on the boat for many years. More than £100,000 was now owed, and the harbour master was desperate to keep her afloat until probate was settled and he could sue for his money.

Keith and Tony on the
front steps of Nellcote

"What would happen if she just sank one night?" asked Keith.

"Why, then, sir," he was told, "she would belong under maritime law to whoever salvaged her."

"You realise what that means," Keith said when we were out of earshot. "If we sink the boat, we can arrange with the salvage crew to buy her for about fifty grand. I'm going to leave it for a couple of weeks; then I'll nip down one night and just unplug those bilge pumps. She'll be in forty feet of water by the morning."

When the time came, he decided he was too well known to risk performing the evil deed himself, so he ordered me to do it. I refused. I had no desire to get involved in £100,000 worth of sabotage — the frogs don't take kindly to that sort of thing. Keith asked me to pay someone else to do it. I merely told him I couldn't find anyone prepared to take the risk, and the fantasy fizzled out.

Johnny Braces was luxuriating in the splendour of the house at Cheyne Walk. His pleasure increased a thousandfold when I mentioned that Paul and Talitha Getty lived just a few doors away. "Oh, yes, I know Talitha," he said. "She and I are old friends." Unfortunately their friendship was to have deadly repercussions.

Johnny's Marseilles contacts arrived shortly after I returned to the Riviera. They were two burly Corsicans, perspiring profusely in their Daks lightweight suits and carrying identical black fiberglass executive attaché cases. After a brief exchange of pleasantries the stouter of the two clicked open his case to reveal a polythene bag approximately as large as a twopound sack of sugar. "Pure heroin from Thailand," he said. "Uncut and the very finest quality."

Keith said he would have to snort it to ascertain its quality before

230

Keith and Marlon strolling around the harbour

they could discuss money, but the second Corsican held up his finger dramatically. "It will have to be cut with glucose first or it will certainly kill you," he warned. In his case were three bags of ordinary glucose, and he fastidiously mixed a few grains of the H with about three times as much white glucose powder.

Keith cautiously snorted the mixture and, after a few minutes, lapsed into unconsciousness. When he came to, he said, "Okay. I'll take the lot. How much?"

"Four grand," said the man. Keith went upstairs, counted out the cash and handed it over gratefully. The supply lasted us slightly under a month.

Drugs were only a fraction of Keith's living costs at Nellcote. Since I had to help deal with the Stones' accountant, who made weekly visits to the house, I knew that he was spending, on average, £500 a week on lobsters, caviar, steaks and other fine foods, and £500 a week on alcohol. The food and drink were consumed with locust-like avidity by swarms of visitors who descended on the house. Marshall Chess stayed for a while; so did Eric Clapton, little Michele Breton from *Performance* and numerous passing strangers. Keith enjoyed having people around him, even though he knew that the impression of friendship and bonhomie they produced was purely illusory. Most of the houseguests were interesting, creative people with stimulating conversation — and,

231

of course, generous gifts of dope.

The only visitor I took a dislike to was a man called Tommy. He claimed to be an Old Etonian and, if ludicrously exaggerated accents are anything to go by, he probably spoke the truth. He also said he was an ex-racing driver, which impressed Keith.

They went to the Monte Carlo Grand Prix together and staggered drunkenly around the track with Anita, swigging tequila from a bottle and singing ribald songs, while I took photographs of them and of the race. Tommy's wife was withdrawing from smack at Bowden House, so he had brought their two small boys with him to Nellcote. Never one to waste an opportunity, Tommy had flown to France via Amsterdam, where he had picked up a kilo of cocaine, which he strapped in money belts underneath the children's clothes. "What a great way to do it," Keith said admiringly. "Perhaps I can get Marlon to do that for me when he gets a bit older." "You would, too," I thought.

My instinctive dislike of Tommy crystallised one night early in June. There were six of us in the house; I, Madeleine, Keith, Anita, Tommy, Michele and myself, and we took it into our heads to unwind by gulping down a few Mandrax sleeping tablets followed by hefty swigs of Courvoisier. The combination produces oblivion almost as quickly as a bang on the head from a cowboy's gun. In less than an hour, all six of us had flaked out on my vast Louis XIV bed.

We were all heaped on top of one another, but we were beyond caring about details like that. At about five in the morning I began to surface slowly — like a submarine cautiously coming up for air. In my bleary state I could hear whispers and faint gigglings from two people on the other side of the bed. At first I thought the voices belonged to Keith and Anita, but then I realised that it was Tommy and Anita — Keith's foot was just in front of my face, and it was quite still. Anita started to moan gently, and I tried to force myself to go back to sleep; it was all a dream. I would wake up in the morning and know it was all a dream. For a dream, though, this was getting pretty realistic. I could feel the bed shake as Tommy climbed stealthily onto Anita, and then they were making love, gently at first and then violently. All the time Keith and Michele snored on in blissful, drugged unawareness. I was about to mutter, "Hey, what's going on?" but thought better of it. It would be horribly embarrassing for all three of us, much better just to lie here and pretend it wasn't really happening. Cowardly, I suppose, but it really wasn't any of my business, and Keith surely knew what Anita was like.

232

Anita

When the bed had stopped pounding, I slipped back to sleep and woke to find Keith and Michele stretching themselves and gradually coming to. The two little lovebirds had flown. "Where's Anita?" Keith asked. When I said I had no idea, he didn't seem particularly perturbed.

Anita and Tommy turned up sheepishly for breakfast, and nothing was said. We were off to the neighbouring harbour of Beaulieu. Keith had heard of a turbo-powered speedboat for sale, and he wanted to take a look at it. He climbed into the driving seat of his Carmen red Jaguar E-type convertible, and I sat beside him with little Marlon on my lap. Anita, Tommy, Michele and a French photographer who had dropped by were travelling in a hired grey Dodge with Keith's chauffeur, David.

As we roared through the green countryside, I thought back on the previous night and wondered whether to stay silent or give Keith a word of friendly warning.

"Er, Keith," I said timorously at length. "There's something on my mind. I don't really know if I should tell you or not."

"Come on, tell me," he said brusquely.

"Well, I don't know. I'm not sure I should tell you something like this. Perhaps we'll have a talk about it later."

"Come on now, man," he said. "We've been friends for a very long

233

Messing about in boats

time now. There's nothing we should keep from one another anymore."

"Well, it's Tommy,' I said. "When we were all out on the bed last night, something woke me up and I saw that though Anita was still unconscious, Tommy was taking a liberty with her. He had his hand up her dress and he was fondling her. It wasn't anything serious, but I thought you should know just so you can tell the guy to piss off when we get back to the house this evening."

I had minimised the incident because I had no wish to force Keith into a corner where he would be forced to leave Anita through pride.

"Just one thing, though, Keith," I added. "Do me a favour and don't tell Tommy what I said."

"Sure, man," said Keith. "You can trust me."

We arrived at Beaulieu in a shower of warm summer rain and drove slowly along, trying to find the harbour master's office. We knew he would be able to direct us to the person selling the boat. At length we pulled up outside a small whitewashed building and sat looking to see if there was any sign to indicate that it was the right place.

Suddenly a gleaming brand-new Jaguar XJ6 tried to squeeze past us, but the driver misjudged his vehicle's width in the narrow road,

234

On the patio at Nellcote

and there was an ugly ripping sound as his bumper scraped the side of the E-type. All of Keith's pent-up anger seemed suddenly to explode. "What do you think you are fucking well doing?", he screamed through his open window to the genteel Italian couple in the XJ6. Ignoring their spluttered apologies, he yelled on, "You fucking stupid fucking foreigners. I'll smash your fucking heads in." And before I could stop him, he pulled a huge German hunting knife out of his leather satchel and jumped out of the car. I chased after him as he screamed at the old man, You stupid fucking idiot."

The Italian's wife was pleading with me now. "It's an accident, an accident. These things happen. What's wrong with your friend? Is he a madman?"

The harbour master, a broad-shouldered six-feet-two giant of a man, was drawn out of his office by the furore.

He ushered the Italian into his office but waved Keith away. This sent Keith totally over the top, and he started yelling at the harbour master, "That's right, you fucking foreigners stick together. What the hell do you think you are playing at?"

The harbour master spoke no English, and Keith spoke little

French, so I tried to sort things out. Everyone was beginning to blow their top by now, and suddenly Keith pulled his knife out. I'm sure Keith was merely trying to intimidate him — he had no intention of stabbing anyone. But the harbour master had no such assurance and consequently threw a straight right into Keith's face, knocking him to the ground.

Before I knew what was happening, Keith screamed out, "Get him, Tony, fucking kill him." And the harbour master charged over to punch me in the chest. I instinctively swung back and hit him in the face, knocking this Goliath on to a table.

In a blur Keith dashed out to the E-type and grabbed a toy Colt .45 from Marlon's hand. He swaggered menacingly outside the office, calling to the harbour master to come out and face him. Not realising it was a toy, the harbour master pushed the Italian couple to the floor, yelling, "Pistol, pistol!" And he pulled out his own — very real — revolver.

"Non! Non!" I yelled, terrified he might take it into his head to shoot me first. I dashed outside, grabbed the toy from Keith's hand and hurled it across the road.

"Non! Non! Il n'avait pas de pistol. Il n'avait pas rien!" I screamed as the big man took aim at Keith.

The harbour master went across to his telephone then, and I saw him make a quick call. Seconds later I heard the sirens of approaching squad cars and realised he had telephoned for reinforcements.

I was afraid then — if the police didn't shoot us, they'd certainly lock us up. I dashed over to the cars. "You take the E-type, I'll go with the others," Keith shouted to me.

"Strange," I thought. "Keith will never get away in that old bus."

But I guessed his evil logic seconds later as the harbour master pointed at me as I sat in the Jag. It was obvious he was telling them, "That's the man. He's the one who tried to shoot me!"

I had no intention of hanging around to give the Riviera gendarmerie target practice. I slammed the powerful car into first and screamed away in a cloud of blue smoke. I overtook the Dodge in seconds, but I was the one the police were after, and I could hear their two cars screaming back there somewhere behind me. Their cars were no match for the E-type, though, and I hurtled back to Nellcote with the speedometer needle bouncing between 140 and 150 mph. Once inside the grounds I bolted the big wrought-iron gates so that nobody, not even Keith, would be able to come in after me. I put the Jag in the garage.

I had completely lost the police. When I heard Keith's voice over the intercom at the gate a quarter-of-an-hour later, I went down to let him and the rest of them in.

"Jesus, man," he said admiringly. "That made the Monte Carlo Grand Prix look like a practice session."

Keith 'phoned the Stones' lawyers, and three of them raced over to the house in minutes to plot our best course of action. They contacted the police, and later that evening an officer came to hand us a summons to appear at the police commissioner's office the following morning at ten a.m.

As soon as the formalities were over, Keith pulled Anita into their bedroom, and I heard him yell at her, "You fucking had it off with Tommy last night, didn't you?"

"What do you mean?" she asked plaintively.

"Oh, don't think I don't know — Tony told me."

When Anita came back into the living room, she began to mumble strange, incomprehensible phrases toward me, and I suspected from the rhythmic cadence of her voice that I had become the focus of her latest spell.

"Look, Anita," I pleaded in Italian, "I don't know what Keith told you, but I didn't tell him anything. All I said was that you were unconscious and the guy was taking a liberty with you.".

"Filthy squealer," she hissed.

Later Tommy came up to me, and he was none too pleased either. "Thanks a lot, mate," he said. "I know what your little game is. You're trying to get rid of me so you can have her, aren't you?"

'You filthy bastard," I said, totally blowing my cool. "If she was my old woman, I'd knock your head off."

"Yes?" he said.

"Yes. And as it happens, I feel like knocking your head off anyway."

Keith walked into the room then, and I was so furious that I yelled at him. You should be doing this, Keith, not me. It's your woman he fucked."

There was an icy silence. "Well, you know what I mean, don't you?" I said, desperately trying to cover my indiscretion.

"I know exactly what you mean, Tony," he said.

"Well," I urged, "if you know what I mean, why don't you do something about it? There's the guy standing right there." Keith turned on his heel and stalked out of the room. He had had enough of brawling for one day. Besides, Tommy was four inches taller than him.

Keith swaggered down to breakfast next morning, beaming. "Guess what?", he said. "I was reading about Errol Flynn in an old French newspaper last night. It seems he got caught up in a punch-up just like ours down here, and they ordered him to appear before the police commissioner. But he refused, and in the end the commissioner had to come up to the house to see him. Don't you think that's amazing?"

"Yeah, fascinating," I said. "But don't you think it's about time you got changed? You ought to at least put a proper jacket on and a pair of shoes so that you make a decent impression.

"No, Tony, you don't understand. I'm more important than some petty local cop. If he wants to see me, he can come up here himself."

I could see in his eyes that he was terrified the police would lock him up, just as he had been locked up in Brixton after the Redlands fiasco. Arguing with him was useless — the only way he was going to leave Nellcote was with a gun at his back. I set off glumly for the police station by myself. To my relief they merely wished to check my papers and charge me with assault. I would be notified, I was told, of the date of my appearance in court.

The police came to the house that afternoon for Keith. But he explained that Marlon had banged his head on the ground because of the harbour master's unprovoked attack and that he was now suing the man for assaulting the little boy. There was much discussion between the lawyers and the police, which ended that evening when the chief of police joined us for dinner at Nellcote. Keith gave the flattered officer a few autographed Rolling Stones albums, and that was the end of that little problem as far as he was concerned.

Since I was the person who had actually hit the harbour master, the lawyers urged that I take the blame for the entire incident. Arrangements were made for me to flee the country weeks later, when the case came to court. The lawyers pleaded guilty on my behalf, and Keith paid my £6,000 fine.

Tommy's wife died five days later. "I'm very upset about it," he said, dry-eyed.

"Hard luck," said Keith.

24

HAVING HER HUSBAND WALK OUT ON HER SEEMED TO BE THE BEST THING that had happened to Talitha Getty for years. Paul was fighting a serious drug problem so a lady friend went to his home in Rome to nurse him through complete withdrawal, and they became fond of each other. Paul told Talitha he would not be returning to Cheyne Walk.

After the first tears dried, Talitha determined to rebuild her life. She stopped using drugs, cut down on booze, started to eat proper meals again and took a lover — Johnny Braces. She was beautiful in the exotic mode of Bianca; her long hair shone with the colour of burnished mahogany, and her cat's eyes flashed green. Her father was the Dutch painter William Pol, her step-grandfather was Augustus John and she was born on Bali. She was an extraordinary lady.

Johnny was an old friend, and less than a week after he arrived at Cheyne Walk, she started to spend occasional nights with him; it wasn't exactly love, but they seemed to make beautiful music together.

The only cloud on her horizon was the matter of custody of her three-year-old son, Tara Gabriel Galaxy Gramophone Getty. She placed the whole business in the hands of her excellent lawyers, and she was not allowing it to hamper her enjoyment of the very beautiful summer of 1971. She was fun, and I enjoyed sipping champagne, telling jokes and laughing with her and Johnny in Keith's living room one night in July. "You're getting really chubby," I teased after joking about Rubens' ladies.

"Yes, I know." She laughed. "As soon as I stopped using smack, I started putting on weight. If this keeps on, I'll have to go on a blasted diet."

I'd suggested we all drive down to the coast the following day, but no, she said, she had to fly to Rome to straighten something out. She'd be back in less than a week, she said. She slept with Johnny that night and left early, without saying good-bye. I never saw her again.

Talitha Getty, thirty-one-year-old daughter-in-law of the richest man in the world, was found dying in her husband's penthouse apartment in Via Della Ara Coeli, Rome, on Sunday, July 12, 1971. A doctor was called, but she died in a nearby clinic without regaining consciousness.

"Mr. Getty said his wife arrived in Rome alone last Saturday to discuss either a reconciliation or the arrangements for a divorce," the *Daily Telegraph* reported when news of the death broke four days later.

> "He said he was strongly opposed to a reconciliation and that they had had an argument. Talitha had gone to bed after midnight on Sunday. He went to bed about half an hour later after getting something to eat. When he awoke at midday he was surprised to see her still sleeping and tried to wake her. When she did not respond he noticed that something was wrong."

Other newspapers reported that an empty sleeping-pill bottle had been found by her bedside. Doctors who signed her death certiflcate claimed Taitha had died from poisoning caused by barbiturates mixed with alcohol.

Johnny and I tried frantically to find out details of the funeral, but to no avail. Talitha was buried on the same day the newspapers reported she had died, July 15. Only one friend, a woman, attended the bleak ceremony in Rome, and not a single flower was sent.

"Talitha had no reason to kill herself," Johnny told me. "She didn't use sleepers anymore, and she certainly wouldn't have been dumb enough to mix them with booze. The whole business is very, very odd."

"Don't be so daft," I said. But less than a month later Luigi, Keith's caretaker at Cheyne Walk, told me Johnny had died.

Two years later the *Daily Mirror* reported:

> "Paul Getty Junior was ordered to return to Rome for questioning yesterday after a shocking report on the death of his wife. The medical report revealed that she was killed by a massive injection of heroin . . . The new medical report, prepared by experts from Rome University, has been handed to an investigating magistrate. He will sift all the evidence to find out exactly what did happen on the night of July 11, 1971."

240

After that I saw nothing more reported. I have not seen Paul since. But drugs and mysterious death are familiar bed-fellows.

The deaths had no effect on Keith and Anita's voracious appetite for smack. They were subsidising their regular supplies from the Corsicans, with drugs sold to them by the Cowboys, local Hell's Angels, who rode motorcycles and lived on the waterfront. They wanted even more cocaine and heroin, so Keith despatched me to London with orders to send some of the dope he had hidden at Cheyne Walk out to him.

I was frankly scared. International drug smuggling is taken slightly more seriously than mass murder in most of Europe, and I had no desire to spend the rest of my life rotting in a French jail.

I spent days puzzling over the best way to handle the chore, and then it dawned on me — toys. No customs man in the world would be heartless enough to smash up a child's toy to look for dope. At Hamley's huge toy store in Regent Street I spent hours looking for toys with hollow insides. I bought a walking doll, a toy piano, a one-man band and several other beautiful and expensive playthings

I decided to use the piano and spent hours taking it apart and reassembling it with an ounce of cocaine hidden inside. Keith had a regular van which came from London once a week with bits and pieces from Cheyne Walk — records, rugs, furniture and anything else to make life cosier at Nellcote. On this day, I simply slipped the piano in among the other things without saying a word to the driver.

Two days later Keith phoned me from France at 3;00 a.m, "You didn't send me that stuff, Tony," he shrilled accusingly.

"Yes, I did," I replied.

"Well, where the hell is it then? I've ripped everything in the van apart, and it's just not there."

"Just gently unscrew the little piano I sent for Marlon," I said. "And you'll find it underneath the keyboard."

The 'phone crashed down, and Keith ran to smash the beautifully made little instrument to the floor. Sod the piano — dope was more important.

We arranged a few more consignments, but then the Corsicans called again, and Keith asked me to return to Villefranche. He was getting lonely.

"Let's go and buy that speedboat," he said suddenly one morning. "You know, the one we were going to get at Beaulieu when that mad harbour master tried to shoot us all."

We agreed that this was an excellent idea, except for Anita, who hated boats. Keith set off with me, Marlon, Dave the chauffeur, and a new houseguest named Oliver Cromble whose father owned a distillery in Holland. We rapidly located the man who was selling the boat, and he greatfully accepted Keith's £1,000 and handed over the keys. Since Dave the chauffeur, professed to be the world's greatest living expert on motorboats, Oliver agreed to take the car back to Villefranche and wait for us there.

When Oliver had gone, Keith turned to the man who had sold the boat to him and asked, as an afterthought, "The sea's OK to go across the bay to Villefranche, isn't it?"

"Oh, no, Monsieur," the Frenchman protested with a frantic wave of his hands. "It is not safe to cross the bay today."

"It looks all right to me," Keith said. Indeed, the sea appeared as calm and blue as stretched satin. So we sought a second opinion from a gaggle of local fishermen who were quaintly mending their nets on the quayside.

"No, no, no," they said. "Is very rough out there today."

But it was decided the sea must have calmed down since they had last been out there, so we filled the tank with petrol and set off on the three-mile run to Villefranche.

As we roared our way out of the harbour, we whooped with exhilaration, but then the sea became progressively rougher until we were merely bouncing from wave top to wave top like a skimming stone. With each bounce, there was a jolt so bone-jarring that it felt as though the boat had smashed against a rock. Marlon began to cry.

"Hey, cool it, man," said Keith. "You're frightening the kid." Neither Keith nor I cared to admit that we were just as scared as Marlon. Dave pulled back the throttle, and we started rolling over four-foot high waves with a sickening motion.

Unfortunately our new pace was so slow that we were being carried by the tide farther and farther out to sea. Dave insisted he would have to go a little faster or we wouldn't stop until we reached Algeria, and he proceeded to push the throttle lever gingerly forward.

Suddenly it was as if the boat had decided to have a hysterical fit — we started to scream across the tips of the waves like a torpedo. Every bounce threatened to smash the boat to kindling.

"Slow down, damn you! Slow down," screamed Keith as he flew from his seat to the floor.

"I can't," Dave called back helplessly. "The throttle control has broken off!"

Dave crawled along the floor to a toolbox, fished out a pair of pliers and finally managed to drag the furious engine reluctantly into neutral. The boat wallowed furiously as he tinkered with the transmission in an effort to repair the gear-stick, but after an hour of swearing and cursing, he turned to us and sighed. "I'm sorry. It's impossible."

Evening was coming on now, a fresh breeze had sprung up, the sea was growing rougher by the second and Marlon was bawling as if the end of the world was at hand, which perhaps it was. I pulled out some distress flares that had been stowed at the back of the boat and carefully read the instructions printed on them in French, English and German. It seemed simple enough; there was a device at the top which had to be un-taped and struck against the bottom section. But the rockets were old and damp, and not one of them worked.

Keith threw our tiny anchor overboard to stop us from drifting any further out to sea, but it seemed to have no effect. After what seemed an eternity but was probably nearer three-quarters of an hour, a small fishing boat came out of the crimson sunset chugging like a railway train. We waved frantically toward the crew and yelled for help, but they only waved back and called, *"Bonsoir,"* to us as they headed for the distant diamond-sparkling lights of the harbour.

"Hell," said Keith. "We're all going to die out here." Marlon's wailing promptly increased by ten decibels.

After another hour a second boat came by, and this time we screamed like banshees — there wasn't going to be a third chance tonight. The fishermen seemed amused by our predicament, and they spoke little English, but when I asked them in French to tow us in, their linguistic talents were sufficient for them to call back, *"Oui,* monsieur — three hundred francs (£30)."

Like most rich people, Keith lived in constant terror of being exploited, and he actually began to haggle over the price. "Christ," I said. "You couldn't even get your car towed off the motorway for that. If you want to argue with these guys, you can at least wait until we get back to the harbour to do it."

Reluctantly Keith took their rope and made us fast to their boat. We were within half-a-mile of the shore when another boat, a huge Coast Guard launch, swept toward us. In the bow stood Oliver waving a huge red flag. "We've come to rescue you," he called.

"Quick, Tony," called Keith. "Untie us from these thieving fishermen, and let Oliver tow us in for free." But I talked him out of this ludicrous piece of meanness — I also knew the fishermen were hard people who wouldn't tolerate such nonsense — and in a few minutes we were safely back in port.

When we climbed out of the boat, we realised that we had only a few francs between us — certainly nowhere near the 300 francs the fishermen were demanding. Keith was in an ugly mood and recklessly told one of the gesticulating Frenchmen, "Go fuck yourself, froggie." After all we had been through, I had no desire to be pummeled into fish bait; I grabbed Keith's wrist, slipped off his Rolex and handed it to one of the fishermen. "Here," I said. "Tomorrow we will bring you the money, and you give us back the watch."

"*Ah, oui, merci,*" he said — and stayed well hidden until we left the country. The watch was worth £1,000.

The French didn't like the Rolling Stones. They were flash, they were brash, they were trouble and, worst of all, they were English. The French and the English have always made uneasy bedfellows. Both believe themselves to be the most cultured and sophisticated people in the world. Both flatly refuse to make a serious effort to speak the other's language or even be civil to each other. Yet the Rolling Stones not only had become France's most popular band but had also exerted more influence on fashion than Cardin and Dior put together. In France with the Stones, however, there was always hostility in the air wherever we went. Another squall in the gathering storm blew up when Shirley Watts, Charlie's brilliant sculptress wife, was provoked into hysteria by punctilious airport officials at Nice. She hit one of them, swore eloquently at the rest and was promptly charged with assault. The lawyers arranged for her to be immediately freed on bail, then advised her to leave the country until the case was heard. On June 2 she was sentenced to six months' imprisonment and fined £35. On appeal, in August, the sentence was reduced to fifteen days, suspended. And Shirley returned to France.

Meanwhile, drugs continued to wreak their trail of havoc around the Stones. Photographer Michael Cooper and his wife, Ginger, had, like me, been friendly with the Stones for so long that they both had become addicted to heroin. Suddenly Ginger died in Bowden House while she was trying to withdraw, and Michael took such huge fixes to blot out his misery that he had to be pushed around in a wheelchair. He died eighteen months later. Keith and Anita were bitterly upset.

Ginger's death didn't interfere with the fun and games at Nellcote. Nor had the deaths of Talitha, Johnny Braces or Tommy Webber's wife. Junkies die. So what?

Anita's latest game was slipping sleeping pills into the Pimms cocktails Keith drank after dinner every night. Usually he collapsed within twenty minutes on the water bed on the verandah, and we left him out there until the morning. After a week of waking up bathed in morning dew Keith began to grow suspicious, and one day he came out and openly accused Anita of her crime. I discovered later that she had told him I was knocking him out so that I could borrow his E-type to roar into town where I seduced every dolly-bird in sight. Keith was certainly glowering at me every time I offered to get him a drink. One evening, he turned to me and snarled, "You know what Anita told me, don't you? She told me you're putting knockout drops in my drinks. Don't think I don't know what's going on. You're after my woman, aren't you?"

"No way," I said. "But if you feel so strongly about it, I won't make you any more drinks." Two nights later Anita decreed that it was time for Keith to have another Mickey Finn, and he spent one more lonely night on his water bed. He knew then that I couldn't have been responsible; I hadn't made him a drink for days. The subject was not mentioned to me again.

Anita's other little game was turning people on to heroin for the first time — if she was going to be a junkie, so was everybody else around her. I thought she went a little too far, though, when she persuaded the teenaged daughter of the chef at Nellcote to accept an injection of smack. The child was violently sick, and I worried that she would complain to her father. "Don't worry so, Tony," Anita said. "A little bit of smack never hurt anyone. Surely you of all people should know that." And she grinned.

Anita was pregnant, but she steadily chugged on with her three daily hits of Henry — her new name for heroin. She was placid and less dangerous these days, but the troubles at Nellcote continued. We had two bad burglaries, and in one of them thieves stole Keith's entire collection of guitars — Gibsons, Mustangs, Les Pauls, Humming Birds were all carried out the front door while we slept. Keith notified the police and filled in his £22,000 insurance claim the next day.

The Corsicans called again with half a kilo of smack. The price went up to £6,000, and the gangsters treated Keith with a new aloofness.

"I'm worried about these guys," he said. "Do you think they've got any funny ideas?"

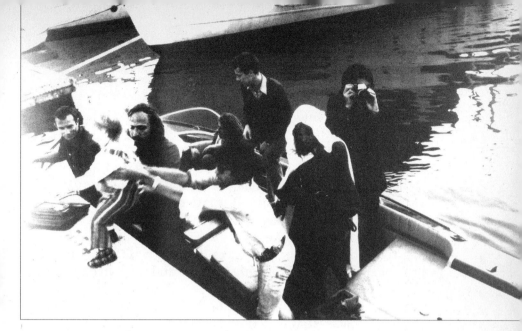

Down by the quayside

"Funny ideas about what?" I asked.

"Kidnapping. You know that's the favourite game of those French and Italian crooks, and they must know from the house that I'm loaded."

"Who on earth would want to kidnap a shrivelled up junkie like you?" I asked, laughing.

"Not me," he exploded. "My son. We'll have to get some guard dogs and cover the whole place with video cameras."

I told him it wouldn't do any good. He would be far better off giving the Corsicans £25,000 to 'protect' Marlon against kidnapping. "They are men of their word," I said. "And what's more, no other gang in the world is going to risk crossing those guys."

At first Keith thought this was an excellent idea. But the notion of parting with so much money for something as vague as protection struck a discordant note in his nature, and he decided it would be better for the two of us to apply for gun permits and carry arms with us at all times. Naturally, owing to our earlier contretemps at Beaulieu, our applications were refused.

The Stones wanted to get a double album together to coincide with a tour of the United States planned for 1972. They built the world's first mobile recording studio — £125,000 of sixteen-track recording equipment packed into an enormous truck that was painted flat khaki to attract a minimum of attention. The original plan had been to rent an isolated farmhouse outside St. Tropez and cut the record there, using the equipment from the truck. Keith didn't like the idea. "I've got huge,

247

really quiet wine cellars underneath Nellcote," he said. "Why don't we work there?"

And so it had been agreed. But after a week went by, we all knew it wasn't working out. Mick, Bill, Charlie, Mick Taylor and the engineers had to travel to the house from so far afield that at least half of every day was wasted waiting for people to show up. It was decided that everyone would stay at Nellcote. "That way we can put in three solid weeks of work and get at least a few tracks down," said Keith.

Bianca refused to go near the place. "I never want to see that cow Anita again," she told Mick. "I'm staying in Paris, and you can do just what you like."

Mick would fly down for a couple of days' recording, then back to Paris to be with Bianca. It was a ridiculous arrangement, and he was obviously upset. Keith appeared not to notice. He was more concerned over the increase in housekeeping bills since the Stones and their wives had come to stay. After a week he sent a secretary to their rooms to present bills for £100 each for 'board and lodging.' Everyone was stunned, and they all tumbled downstairs to ask Keith what was up. "It is a joke, isn't it, Keith?" Bill Wyman asked innocently.

"No, it's not," Keith snapped. "You're getting accommodation dirt cheap at that price. If you were in an hotel, your bed alone would cost you that much, let alone all your food and booze. As a matter of fact, £100 was the wrong figure. I'm going to make it £125. And anyone who doesn't like it can piss off to a hotel."

They all knew that an irate Keith Richard was not a man to be argued with and sheepishly handed over their cash.

Mick had lost Bianca. He was caught up with recording a particularly intricate track at Nellcote and stayed there for three days, 'phoning her in Paris each night. On the third night she told him to return at once or else not to bother. "Come on," he said. "Don't be silly. I'll only be another day or two at the most." She slammed the 'phone down, and when he tried to ring her after that, there was no reply. Five days later he flew back to Paris, but she wasn't there, and none of her friends knew where she was hiding. At length, though, she returned to their suite at L' Hôtel — the intimate, opulent hotel on the Left Bank favoured by Oscar Wilde — and the ruction was forgotten.

On October 21, 1971, their baby daughter was born in the Belvedere Nursing Home in Paris. They called her Jade "because she is very precious and quite, quite perfect," said Mick. Thrilled by the child, he 'phoned Keith to say he would not be back at Villefranche for at least three weeks.

"She's such a beautiful baby," he raved. "She looks a little like Bianca and a lot like me; I really feel now as though I might be able to settle down just a little bit. Bianca and I are getting on so well together you just wouldn't believe it. We want to have loads more kids. We'll probably have at least four of them."

"And I thought you said they'd be divorced within a year," Keith said to Anita.

The chef had found out about his daughter's fix now, and he was starting to make life difficult for Keith. "I want thirty thousand pounds, or I'll go to the police and tell them you held her down while Anita forced the needle into her arm," he said.

"Fuck off," said Keith. "You're fired."

The next day the police arrived in force, taking statements, asking questions, mentioning certain Corsicans who had been observed visiting the house.

"We've got to get out of this place, quick," said Keith. "They're going to sling us inside and throw away the key. I can feel it coming any day now."

The rest of the Stones were equally jumpy. Police followed them everywhere; they were about to bust everybody. They decided that in November they all would fly to Los Angeles to prepare for the American tour.

The police made things even more difficult for Keith and Anita. They would have to stay in France untill investigations were completed, they said. The band's high-powered lawyers explained that Keith would continue to rent Nellcote for £1,000 a week while he was away, and this was adequate proof of his intention to return. Grudgingly the police were forced to let them slip away.

A year later Mick, Charlie, Bill and Mick Taylor went back to the Riviera to refute, successfully, allegations that they had used drugs at Villefranche. Keith and Anita refused, and warrants were put out for their arrest. On October 17, 1973, in their absence, they were given one-year suspended jail sentences and fined £750 each for throwing parties at which drugs were used at Nellcote. Keith was also banned from entering France for two years.

"Thank Christ that's over," he said when the lawyers told him the outcome of the case. "Now, at last, I can stop paying that grand a week rent for that bloody house. It's cost me more than a hundred grand already just to keep it going so the cops wouldn't try to extradite me." He earned something like £12,000 a week. Using the old rule-of-thumb that rent shouldn't exceed a quarter of your salary, I guess Keith could afford Nellcote.

Mick, too, was disenchanted with France. "I don't like the people or the weather in France, and the food's greasy," he told newspapermen. "They're all thieves down there too. They've had a hundred fifty years living off tourists. All they try to do is steal from you. Never treat you as anything other than passing tourists."

25

"WHEN I'M FIVE MONTHS PREGNANT, I'LL GIVE IT UP, ANITA PROMISED, AND in fairness to her, she did stick out withdrawal symptoms for nearly three days. Her retching, fever and delusions became so chronic that she feared for the safety of her unborn child, and she took 'just one little snort' to see her through. That, of course, was the end of that cure. She tried the same thing at seven months, but again it was useless. Perhaps if she had gone into Bowden House, she could have actually stuck out her cold turkey, but the place was linked in her mind with death and pain; she would never go back there again.

Her gynacologist warned her that the life of the baby was being severely endangered by her recklessness, but the more she worried about it, the more she sought solace in heroin like an alcoholic drinking to forget cirrhosis of the liver. In the final days a specialist recommended an exclusive private clinic in Montreux, Switzerland, a place where doctors specialised in discreet handling of delicate situations.

She flew there with Keith and two-year-old Marlon. The steward-esses commented on what a beautiful family they were. When Anita settled in the clinic, Keith took Marlon to a lavish suite in the historic Montreaux Metropole Hotel on the shore of Lake Geneva. The doctors were patient and sympathetic, for which they were well paid at £50 a day. Anita, they explained, would be given the minimum possible dosage of methadone until the child was born. Dandelion Richard arrived in the world red-faced and squawling on April 17, 1972.

Keith phoned me in London to tell me of the birth. Before I could finish congratulating him, he brusquely interrupted me. "Look, Anita's coming out of hospital tomorrow, and she's going to be screaming. I want you to fly out here with all the stuff you can get."

"You're the best mate I've got, and you know I'd do anything for you

251

and Anita," I said. "But as I've told you before, I will never sell drugs and I'll certainly never smuggle them."

"Okay, okay," he said, riled. "Get someone else to carry the dope for you, and you come out as well I'll pay whatever it costs."

I got hold of half an ounce of heroin and a similar quantity of cocaine. I offered Johnny, a friend of mine, £500 to carry it to Switzerland. Everything was going smoothly. Johnny sat four seats in front of me on the flight to Montreaux and we didn't acknowledge in any way that we knew each other. Keith was waiting for me at the airport in his big limousine. As arranged, Johnny proceeded alone to the taxi stand to take the short ride to the Montreaux Metropole.

We followed in the limo. I waited until Johnny checked in before I went to his room to collect the stash and take it up to Keith and Anita's suite. They both took deep, grateful snorts, called me their lifesaver and

Keith and Marlon in a café

passed out. By the next morning their euphoria had worn off, and they got obstreperous when I told them I had promised Johnny £500 for his trouble, and he was eager to take his money and return to London. "I'm sorry, Tony," Keith lied. "I've only got £250. He'll have to take it or leave it."

Justifiably this boy, who had risked a hefty jail sentence, was displeased. "Don't ever ask me to do anything like that for you again," he said. The look of contempt in his eyes made me so guilty that I gave him another £100 from my own pocket. "Look," I said, "Keith's very worried about the baby. He's not usually as mean as this."

In five days' time, Keith and Anita had used up the cocaine and heroin and asked me to arrange for Johnny to bring more drugs. "You must be joking," I said. "After the way you refused to pay him what you owed him last time."

"Go on," pleaded Keith. "I'll give him £500 this time plus the other £150 from last time."

Johnny reluctantly accepted the commission and flew over with a little more heroin and a bag of grass. Keith and Anita devoured it greedily and arranged for Johnny to bring dope every ten days or so.

Anita, meanwhile, had become introspective and reclusive, refusing to leave the suite. Keith and I would take the children out for walks, joyfully breathing the Champagne air blowing down from the mountains, but Anita languished in solitary splendour, smoking her joints, jabbing needles in her bottom and musing.

Whenever the maids came to clean the rooms, she'd snarl at them from behind locked doors, sending them away. After three weeks, the place stank of dirty socks and stale cigarette smoke. There were empty bottles everywhere, cigarette burns on most of the mock Louis XIV furniture and the sheets were an uninviting shade of grey. "We can't go on living in this pig-sty,' Keith announced at last. He buzzed the manager to ask for another suite on a different floor. The maids stuck with the onerous task of cleaning out the abandoned suite insisted on defumigation, I discovered later.

It was almost time for the Stones to begin their first tour of the States in three years — their first since Altamont. Jagger was afraid; he'd quietly visited America several times to discuss plans for the tour, and he came back critical and afraid of the place.

"Where is it?", he asked Robert Greenfield from *Rolling Stone*, referring to the radical political zeal of the young that had made the States such an exciting place to be only three years before. "It's nowhere. It's just a lot of people dopin' up now. All the doping has got to stop before anything else. All that smack and everything. If that's their thing, if they wanna take smack and downers and two gallons of some chemical wine, okay; you're never gonna do what I thought people were gonna do.

l don't blame people for wanting to get fucked up. Everyone likes to get fucked up once in a while, but you can't go through life like that. You can't blot it out. It keeps coming back, man, and in the end you just kill yourself trying to blot it out.

"People say all the dope on the street has stopped people from being active... and I wonder... which is the best thing to do? Whether it's better... aw, fuckit, I just wanna be naïve about it. I think you have to make your country a better place to live and bring kids up in and think in, and sitting at home taking smack and listening to records just ain't gonna do it. That's old-fashioned, maybe, but you got to take the bull by the horns, and it's a huge fuckin' bull, America... and the horns are very nasty."

Many believed Jagger's propounded fears for the United States masked far greater fears for himself. "His nerve has gone," went the whispers. "He's afraid this is going to be the tour where one of those hordes of crazy assassins finally gets to him." Jagger spent hours dwelling on security and finally decided that the Stones would play only small theatres — no arenas — where he could communicate with the audience, so things wouldn't get out of control. The economic realities of taking the Stones to the States dashed such fantasies. After a series of stormy meetings with Marshall Chess and Prince Rupert it was reluctantly agreed — the band would spend fifty-four days touring the biggest stadiums in the United States.

"But this time it's got to be right," Jagger said solemnly. "There are a lot of people who are still bitter about the last tour. I don't want high-priced tickets, delays, riots or any of that crap. We're going out there to make a lot of money and win a lot of friends."

Peter Rudge, a soft-spoken university graduate who organised perfect American tours for the Who, was hired to ensure that Mick's decree was carried out. Every detail of the tour was calculated with the precision of a military campaign. Canadian film maker Robert Frank would make a movie of the tour, writer Robert Greenfield would turn it into a book. This time there would be no mistakes.

Rehearsals started in an atmosphere of secrecy more appropriate to a CIA operation. They were held in a small cinema in Montreaux, the passed out. By the next morning their euphoria had worn off, and they got obstreperous when I told them I had promised Johnny £500 for his trouble, and he was eager to take his money and return to London. "I'm sorry, Tony," Keith lied. "I've only got £250. He'll have to take it or leave it."

Justifiably this boy, who had risked a hefty jail sentence, was displeased. "Don't ever ask me to do anything like that for you again," he said. The look of contempt in his eyes made me so guilty that I gave him another £100 from my own pocket. "Look," I said, "Keith's very worried about the baby. He's not usually as mean as this."

In five days' time, Keith and Anita had used up the cocaine and heroin and asked me to arrange for Johnny to bring more drugs. "You must be joking," I said. "After the way you refused to pay him what you owed him last time."

"Go on," pleaded Keith. "I'll give him £500 this time plus the other £150 from last time."

Johnny reluctantly accepted the commission and flew over with a little more heroin and a bag of grass. Keith and Anita devoured it greedily and arranged for Johnny to bring dope every ten days or so.

Anita, meanwhile, had become introspective and reclusive, refusing to leave the suite. Keith and I would take the children out for walks, joyfully breathing the Champagne air blowing down from the mountains, but Anita languished in solitary splendour, smoking her joints, jabbing needles in her bottom and musing.

Whenever the maids came to clean the rooms, she'd snarl at them from behind locked doors, sending them away. After three weeks, the place stank of dirty socks and stale cigarette smoke. There were empty bottles everywhere, cigarette burns on most of the mock Louis XIV furniture and the sheets were an uninviting shade of grey. "We can't go on living in this pig-sty,' Keith announced at last. He buzzed the manager to ask for another suite on a different floor. The maids stuck with the onerous task of cleaning out the abandoned suite insisted on defumigation, I discovered later.

It was almost time for the Stones to begin their first tour of the States in three years — their first since Altamont. Jagger was afraid; he'd quietly visited America several times to discuss plans for the tour, and he came back critical and afraid of the place.

"Where is it?", he asked Robert Greenfield from *Rolling Stone*, referring to the radical political zeal of the young that had made the States such an exciting place to be only three years before. "It's nowhere. It's just they stayed at Hugh Hefner's vulgar mansion. They were using each other — Hugh Hefner wanted to polish up his image with some of the Stones' hip prestige, and the Stones were happy enough to fuck his bunnies, use his dope and smash up his furniture. They left after a few days, and everybody was pleased with the way the reciprocally beneficial arrangement had worked out. Even Hef.

He wasn't the only one hoping that some of the Stones' sparkle would rub off. Just about every ageing youth seeker in the States is scratching to get close to this elixir of youth, and a few of them made it. People like Princess Lee Radziwill, who was mostly famous for being famous, and writers Truman Capote and Terry Southern. Insiders knew they didn't really fit in. Only Andy Warhol, who was slightly mad, was accepted, and that was mainly because he was Bianca's favourite artist.

On stage and off the show was getting wilder. At the International Sports Arena in San Diego fifteen people went to the hospital, and sixty to jail. In Tucson tear-gas grenades were thrown at vociferous fans. In Washington there were sixty-one arrests. In Montreal maniacs blew up the Stones' equipment van with dynamite and three thousand fans who had been sold forged tickets rioted. In Boston the Stones were arrested after a fight with a photographer.

Some of this insanity was getting to the road crew. Their pranks began to show it. After "Street Fighting Man," Jagger always sprinkled a bucket of rose petals over the audience like a priest spreading holy water. Chip Monck, who was in charge of special effects, decided it would be fun to hide a chicken leg among the rose petals to see what would happen. Jagger didn't even notice it, and he hurled it straight into the crowd, bonking a singularly ecstatic girl on the head. That was in Detroit.

By Philadelphia Chip had plucked up courage to hide a raw pig's liver in the bucket, and Jagger — still too rapt to realise what was happening — hurled it in a graceful arc into the crowd. Seconds later it arched back again, hung suspended momentarily in the glare of the spotlights and then splattered, bloodily, on the immaculate white stage. In Pittsburgh Chip decided to go all the way and bought a pig's leg complete with hoof and blood and stuck that in the bucket. Fortunately for Pittsburgh Jagger found the thing before the show started and hurled it at Chip instead.

By the time this circus rolled into New York for the last three shows of the tour at Madison Square Garden they were slick and perfect. Far from destroying them, their fifty days of drugs and debauchery on the road had brought the Stones to the peak of their career.

256

Tony Sanchez

The tour climaxed on July 26 — Mick's twenty-ninth birthday — with a final show at the Garden. Chip, determined to make the event unforgettable, hired a circus elephant to walk up to the stage to present Mick with a single rose from its trunk at the end of the show. "No," said the men who run the Garden, no doubt envisaging a maddened pachyderm running amok and squashing teenyboppers. Chip compromised by buying five hundred live chickens, which he planned to flutter gently on the heads of the audience. The management sealed off the roof. In desperation he settled for a routine custard-pie fight. But even that was out of line, decided the grey men, and they confiscated Chip's crates of pies. They didn't realise, however, that Chip had hidden reserve supplies backstage.

The last show was the best of the tour. After "Street Fighting Man", Chip wheeled a trolley with a birthday cake and champagne onto the stage. Bianca danced out to hand Mick a huge panda and kiss him. Chip stealthily crept up, pie in hand, and wopped the superstar in the face. Jagger grabbed a pie to throw at Charlie Watts, and suddenly the whole stage was transformed into something out of a Laurel and Hardy movie. The crowd started to roar out "Happy Birthday" with Charlie banging out the rhythm for them. Ian Stewart crept up behind Watts and gently screwed a pie on each of his ears, where they hung suspended for a moment like giant headphones.

The end-of-tour party was held at the St. Regis Hotel. Bob Dylan had his picture taken with Zsa Zsa Gabor, Woody Allen with Carly Simon. Other guests included Lord Hesketh, Sylvia Miles, Dick Cavett and Tennessee Williams drawn as much by the lure of Ahmet Ertegun, head of Atlantic Records and much else besides, as by the Stones. A nude girl climbed out of a huge birthday cake swinging the tassels on her nipples in opposite directions at the same time. But the party wasn't fun. Just another cold celebrity bash, a far cry from marching with revolutionaries. The Stones were now officially just a great vaudeville act.

Robert Frank, at forty-seven, was the oldest person on the tour. His films were not intended for mass consumption — they starred people like Allen Ginsberg and Gregory Corso — and the Stones had seen none of them. They had seen Frank's haunting book of black-and-white photographs called *The Americans*, which captured the feeling of the country's broken dream. The book had inspired Jack Kerouac to write: "To Robert Frank, I now give this message: You got eyes."

The Stones allowed Frank total freedom. This would be the first

257

honest rock film. Image and mystique were to be thrown out the window, and he was given access to bedrooms, 'planes and dressing rooms. For Robert Frank there were no boundaries. His only brief was to tell it like it was.

It was with a tingle of anticipation that the Stones and I settled down in our plush seats in a Soho preview theatre to watch the rough cut of Frank's movie. Since many Stones had screwed many women on the road, all their wives had been excluded from the screening.

As soon as the title flashed on the screen, I knew it wasn't going to work out: *Cocksucker Blues*. How could a film with a title like that stand a chance of being released?

After the credits we were in a jam session with the Stones building "Can't Always Get What You Want" into a thundering number with ten times the power of the recorded version. Then Marshall was introducing a song called "Cocksucker Blues," the number the Stones had recorded as a gratuitous insult to Decca years ago.

Jagger snarled away at a grand piano, and it was a great, tough number. But even Keith cringed each time Jagger sang the chorus about getting your cock sucked and getting your ass fucked. Then it was Keith's turn to play piano while Jagger wandered around a swimming pool with his hand inside the front of his brief trunks, unsubtly fondling himself. A quick couple of shifts of scene, and we were treated to the ludicrous spectacle of the very straight, very brash disc jockey, Emperor Rosko, attempting to interview Mick and Keith while they calmly rolled joints and mumbled incoherently in reply to his inane questioning.

More everyday scenes, and then the Stones thundered through "Brown Sugar" on stage like a flat out Ferrari. A shift back to the everyday world, and they climbed into their private jet which carried them around on the tour. Three busty groupies — Margot, Mary and Renee — trailed along behind them.

With the 'plane twenty thousand feet above America one of the road crew lifted Mary off the floor and pulled off her tight sweater and jeans. She was wearing nothing underneath. Then Margot was stripped, protesting and giggling at the same time. As the roadies prepared to enjoy themselves, Jagger and Richard danced down from the front of the 'plane like evil dervishes. Mick playing tomtoms, Keith a tambourine, their heads bopping in time to the action. Someone turned Mary upside down and thrust his face into her crotch. Bobby Keyes poured orange juice over both girls as Mick and Keith speeded up the rhythms. It was voodoo time again.

258

The Stones at their most unattractive and perverse. Renee, the other girl, screamed and struggled away. She was frightened and obviously wanted out.

Then it was gone, and the movie flashed to a black guy in a cocaine T-shirt selling black-market Stones tickets. In the dressing room now: Keith, wearing a Moroccan prayer rug around his neck, is having his make-up applied and eyedrops administered by Janice, a black woman whose task it was to keep him looking human for the couple of hours a day he was on stage. Jagger, meanwhile, is snorting coke through a $100 bill, getting wired to give his all on stage.

They stroll off toward the arena, but at the last moment Jagger returns for more coke. Then they are in mid-performance with Jagger transformed into the demoniac Midnight Rambler.

Backstage once more, and writer Terry Southern is snorting and mouthing banalities about coke. If you had a million dollars a week to spend on coke," he propounds, "you could probably develop a habit. I mean coke is so expensive . . ."

In another bedroom are Keith and a scantily clad, good looking blonde. They are sieving and cooking up heroin. Slowly, with relish, she plunges a syringe filled with deadly nectar into his arm. Slowly, slowly he nods out.

Later Keith speaks thoughtfully about some young musicians he had met: "Those kids were saying if you really want to be a good band, get out of Switzerland and starve." Their words are demonstrably nonsensical, of course. Almost all the best bands nowadays consist exclusively of cosseted millionaires.

Then there is Ossie Clarke, the designer, camping it up in a white suit with a red rose in his hand. He is helping Bianca try on a low-cut gown, and for a split second Bianca's breasts spill out much to her very obvious embarrassment. More domestic insight comes when she reminds Mick they have a dinner date. "I don't want to see that awful, awful woman," he whines petulantly. "And I don't want to eat her shitty food." Tantalisingly we are not told exactly who this awful lady is.

More mundane scenes as the Stones and their ladies drive around somewhere in the Deep South, bemoaning the shortage of decent places to eat, and then, suddenly, back to the flash of the stage show, with Stevie Wonder and the Stones roaring together through "Uptight" and then on into "Satisfaction."

Another hotel, and this time there is a new, completely naked girl lying on a bed with a couple of roadies. She is rubbing herself and murmuring about how she's just seen fireflies. The mind boggles.

A cut to Keith, who is playing poker while George Wallace screams out his message of hate from the television screen. And then back to the fireflies lady, who is now sharing a joint with an awkward Mick Taylor. "I've never seen a hotel room blessed with such limpid ecstasy," he jokes.

More strange scenes: Keith so stoned that he can't persuade room service to understand that he would like a bowl of fruit. The girl who fixed him last time is jabbing needles into some new people now; and then Keith and saxophonist Bobby Keyes are giggling inanely as they hurl a colour television from the balcony of their umpteenth-floor hotel room.

The movie alternates the flamboyance of the stage with the inanity and debauchery of the road: another town, another hit, another fuck. The film closes with the Stones leaving the stage in slow motion as the malicious poetry of "Brown Sugar" is deliberately read in indictment.

"Whooee..." breathed Keith. "It certainly brings it all back to me. It's going to be the most amazing rock movie the world has ever seen."

"I don't think so," said Jagger. "We'd be busted from here to Timbuktoo the minute that movie hit the cinemas. It'd cause a public outcry, and the law would be after us again just like they were before.

"No, we'll have to leave it five years at least to cool down before we can even think about releasing it. And even then it could still be dangerous. Maybe we'll never be able to release it while we are still a working band."

Five years later he had completely lost interest. "Well, it wasn't much of a film anyway, was it?" was his only comment.

26

JAMAICA WAS EVEN MORE IDYLLICALLY BEAUTIFUL THAN ANY OF THEM HAD imagined: rivers roaring through palm tree jungles, hurtling over falls and then soaring out across flour-white sands into an ocean as blue as Marianne's eyes. The sun shone hot most of the time with an occasional flashing, smashing storm every few days just to keep everything interesting. They had come here to record at Byron Lee's Dynamic Sound Studios. It was November, an excellent month to escape the European cold.

It should have been perfect, yet Keith could sense there was something nagging at Mick, preventing him from giving his all to the toil of writing and recording. "Here, Keith," he said one evening as they sat by the pool at the Hotel Terra Nova sipping Red Stripe beer and watching day slip into cerise night. "What do you think of all this?" And from his pocket he pulled a crumpled envelope. "Go on — read it."

The letter purported to be from a student of the occult, living in California. At great length and with obvious sincerity the writer set out all the reasons why Jagger was doomed to be the next rock star to die. Though ridiculous, his reasoning was eerie enough to be unnerving; all the rock stars who were doomed to die in the sixties and seventies had the letters *I* and *J* in their names — like Brian Jones, Janis Joplin, Jimi Hendrix and Jim Morrison. Moreover, the order of deaths fitted in with a formula which indicated that the next to die would have *I* as the second letter in his first name and *J* as the first letter in his second name. Additionally the seventeenth-century Dutch artist, Frans Hals, who was a celebrated warlock, had painted a picture called "The Merry Lute Player" — the central character of which was Jagger's double.

Somehow the Californian had put all these coincidences together and had worked out a date when Jagger would perish. "But he says you're

261

going to die tomorrow," said Keith, stabbing at the letter with his finger. "What the fuck are you going to do about it"

"Stay in my room, I guess," said Mick. "I mean I'm sure it's all a load of crap, but I don't want to push my luck by going swimming or anything."

"Yeah, sure," said Keith seriously. "I'll get the security guys to keep a special eye on you. I'll tell them no one is to come near you."

There were other hassles, too, as they worked on their new album, *Goat's Head Soup*. The French were rumbling about taking out extradition orders against the band because of the dope Keith had consumed at Nellcote. Jagger, Charlie, Bill and Mick Taylor flew to France to swear statements.

Once again there was friction between Bianca and Anita, so much that Keith and Anita eventually were driven to live in a separate place. They rented Tommy Steele's hillside bungalow overlooking Cutlass Bay, at Ocho Rios. Keith was fascinated by the islanders — their guns, their knives, their ganja and the hypnotic reggae music that boomed out from every corrugated iron shanty town. He helped a young Jamaican singer, Jimmy Cliff, get a starring role in the movie *The Harder They Come*, an international success. He and Anita got high with Bob Marley and his fellow Rastafarians. The Rastas are a strange, little-understood Jamaican religious sect that worships Ras Tafari — Haile Selassie, the Lion of Judah. One day, they say, they will go home to his land — their land — Ethiopia. But mostly they just blot out the misery of their abject poverty by smoking ganja and growing their hair in glorious, fearsome dreadlocks. Their fellow Jamaicans, not surprisingly, fear them slightly and hate them a great deal.

All the Stones flew back to London for Christmas, though Anita had fallen so deeply in love with the island that she was reluctant to leave. "I want to live here always," she told Keith.

"Maybe we will," he replied. "Maybe we will."

For Mick and Bianca there was to be no Christmas. On December 23, 1972, an earthquake tore through Managua, Nicaragua, killing six thousand people and cutting off communication with the outside world. Bianca was hysterical when the news was flashed on the television screen at Cheyne Walk. "Oh no, Mick, no," she screamed. "My mother — all my family — are there. They must all be dead."

Though Jagger and his aides tried frantically to find out what had happened to Bianca's family, it was to no avail. "We'll have to fly out there," he told her soothingly. "Don't worry, the odds are that she is almost certain to be okay."

It was impossible to fly directly to Managua by scheduled airline. Mick chartered a private jet and ordered one of his employees to arrange for the purchase of all the anti-typhoid serum he could buy, together with other desperately needed medical supplies

Bianca wept as they drove into Managua from the airport. Devastation was everywhere, the world of her childhood had been swept away as though by the hand of some malevolent giant. Gracious Spanish colonial mansions lay in heaps of brick and mortar. Jagger, dressed brashly, inappropriately, in an American baseball shirt, was saddened and humbled. No one knew or cared who he was — a rare taste of the normal life he'd known as a teenager, before fame.

They found Bianca's mother, Señora Macias, shaken but unharmed. She had clawed her way out of the rubble, she said, sobbing silently. But how lucky she was. See how many good people, good friends had died.

"They need money so badly," Bianca whispered to Mick. "To them it means life."

"Don't worry," soothed Mick. "I'll give them money."

On January 18 the Stones played the Los Angeles Forum. Ticket prices were higher than they had ever been for any rock concert, and the place sold out instantly. More than £250,000 was raised, and it all went to help the Nicaraguans.

Japan's extraordinary economic miracle had turned the country into the biggest record-buying market in the world after America, yet the Stones didn't mean a thing there. In an effort to break into the land of the rising yen the band arranged to play five consecutive concerts in the biggest stadium in Tokyo. The publicity machine ground into action; hordes of Japanese journalists were flown to Jamaica to photograph and interview the Stones. Already fifty-five thousand tickets had been sold, and then, suddenly, the Japanese government announced that Michael Philip Jagger would not be granted an entry visa because he had been convicted of possessing cannabis. And that, despite the protestations and pleadings of lawyers and journalists, was that.

In Australia six concerts had been sold out when the Immigration Ministry announced that one of the Stones would not be granted an entry visa. "I just don't believe it," steamed Jagger. "One stupid, petty cannabis conviction, and I'm banned from entering half the world. You'd think I was the Boston Strangler or someone."

Luckily Australia was more amenable to reason than Japan, and at length, after a hard battle, the Stones were allowed to slip into the country. As always the Stones' base animal magic cut through all the apparent social barriers, and the band provoked their customary scenes of insanity and rioting. Even in staid, reactionary Adelaide there was a pitched battle between police and five thousand fans.

As well as Australia they played New Zealand, Hong Kong and Hawaii on this tour; then Mick, Keith and their ladies jetted back to Jamaica once more.

They began to talk about money, and they realised how very rich they were. Each member of the band had taken home about £200,000 after expenses, from the American tour alone. Royalties from their records poured in regularly. They had twenty different albums in stock in the record shops, all steady sellers. Mick and Keith had written almost all the songs and they collected about 15p each per album in writing royalties as well as their cut of the 20p per album which was split among members of the band. Most of their records had crashed through the million sales barrier. They guessed that they were averaging out at about £1 million a year each from records and gigs. "It makes me sick to even think about it," complained Keith, but he went out the next day and paid £75,000 in cash for Tommy Steele's bungalow. Jagger, too, made plans to get rid of some of his cash. He flew to Washington and gave the Senate £400,000 for the Pan American Development Fund. It clinched Jagger's burgeoning friendship with several powerful American poliiticians, including Walter Annenberg, the United States ambassador to Britain.

In Jamaica, meanwhile, Anita's fondness for the Rastafarians was beginning to upset her colonial neighbours, who had no objection to blacks so long as they stuck to polishing shoes and cutting sugar cane. Anita went dancing with the Rastas and invited them to stay at the house. "I think you should have a word with your wife, or she is going to find herself in trouble," a local businessman whispered to Keith one evening.

"I don't think it's any of your business," Keith replied. But he had been hurt badly, and a few days later he flew home to London, leaving Anita to her pleasures.

With Anita out of the way he started to live, once again, like a rock 'n' roll superstar. He hired a yellow Ferrari Dino and started to make nightly sojourns to Tramp, in Jermyn Street, London's most fashionable night spot. Every night at midnight we would take huge snorts of coke, then set off to the club to listen to the music and chat with friends. On our third visit a long, slender, elegant blonde came over to kiss me on the cheek and tell me how wonderful it was to see me again.

"Who's that?" asked Keith when she had gone back to her table.

"That's Chrissie Wood — you know, she's the wife of Ronnie Wood, from the Faces."

"Cor," said Keith. "I really fancy her. She's not bad, is she?"

I was flabbergasted. Though I had known Keith for many years, it was the first time I had ever heard him admit to fancying anyone. Sex, for Keith, has always lagged far behind music and drugs in the hedonism stakes.

"No," I said. "But she's not just his bird; she's his wife, you know."

"I couldn't care less about that," said Keith. He strolled over to offer her a drink. They left together an hour later in the Ferrari. He drove her to Richmond, and she invited him in for coffee. Keith was impressed with the opulence of the house. The Wick is a perfect Georgian mansion set at the pinnacle of Star and Garter Hill with views for twenty miles along the snaking River Thames.

"Come downstairs to the studio, and say hello to Woodie," she said when they were inside the door. Keith began to panic; he hadn't figured on being introduced to his new girl friend's husband so early in their relationship. Worse was yet to come. Working away in Woodie's lavish recording studio was Mick Jagger.

They were polite and awkward, both wondering what the hell the other was doing in the house. They went upstairs to the magnificently proportioned, balconied oval living room to sip Courvoisier. Suddenly the door opened, and a great beauty walked in. She was a blonde German model with wide, guileless blue eyes and a body that stretched every seam of her simple white dress. Her name, Keith was told was Ushi. It was obvious that Mick wanted her, but she ignored him and gave Keith all her attention.

He spent every night at the house after that, and I saw no more of him. A week later, however, he phoned me at home to ask if I could bring him some coke to the Wick. When I arrived, it was mid-afternoon, and the personal assistant who opened the door told me I'd find Keith in a room on the third floor, beside the sauna bath. I walked upstairs, knocked on the door and strolled in. Keith and Ushi were in bed together. Keith merely took the coke without a hint of embarrassment, thanked me, and I headed for home again.

A few days later Ushi was offered a modeling assignment in Germany. Keith came home to Cheyne Walk, and that was the end of the romance. It was also the begining of a significant relationship with Ronnie Wood.

One of Keith's favourite games was whipping out the knife he had bought in Jamaica. You could pull it out and flick it open in one swift movement, like a switchblade.

"That's a very dangerous toy," I warned him. "You should only pull out a knife if you really are going to use it. Otherwise, someone is very likely to panic and stab you first."

"Don't worry about me, Tony," he said. "I can take care of myself."

Nevertheless, I was frightened when two Italian hooligans started to stare at Keith in a distinctly menacing way when we went to Tramp a few nights later. But I was there, and so was Woodie and several other friends, so Keith could afford to handle the situation with bravado. "Who do those cunts think they're looking at?" he exclaimed in a voice loud enough for most of the club to hear. I knew, though, that Italians are not so easily cowed as British thugs. Any kind of threat or intimidation is invariably interpreted as a challenge to their manhood. It becomes a macho thing, a matter of honour.

"Look, man," I whispered to Keith, attempting to defuse the situation. "They're just looking at you because you're Keith Richard and they are curious. They're looking at Woodie as well, and he's not making a big fuss about it. Besides, I know that if you upset them, they're going to pull knives or guns, and you'll get badly hurt."

"Fuck that," exploded Keith. lf either of those guys looks at me like that again, I'll throw my glass of scotch in his face."

I left them to visit the lavatory, and the second the Italians saw me leave Keith unprotected, they came to his table and called out, "*Ciao, bella*" — hello, darling — to a pretty girl sitting beside him. Keith completely flipped out at this insult and leaped across the table, spilling drinks everywhere. He flicked out his knife and charged at the Italians with a roar like an angry bull. As people started to scream and run in all directions, one of the Italians kicked Keith in the crotch, while the other picked up a chair and smashed it over his head.

By the time I returned it was all over. The club's manager was helping Keith to his feet while the waiters saw the two Italians out the door. "No, no, don't worry about calling the police," said Keith. "We can all live without that hassle and publicity."

To me, later, he whispered, "I want those two sorted out — there's no way they are going to get away with that.

"Okay, okay," I said. "But it's going to cost you."

I knew that having the boys beaten up would be disastrous. It would be the start of a vendetta that would end with Keith looking up the wrong end of a sawn-off shotgun. I managed to track down one of them — a boy named Willy. "Look," I said. "That guy you beat up in Tramp's has got a lot of dough. Just to avoid any more trouble, I'll pay you a hundred pounds each if you'll just go to another club for a week or so. It would be a personal favour for me."

I advised Keith that the two had been dealt with and collected £200 from him. The next night he arrived at Tramp with a small sword in his satchel and four heavy guards at his side. "Let's see if they want trouble tonight," he crowed. "Let's see if they still feel like staring at me."

Of course, the boys weren't there. Keith came back for the next few nights, but still, they didn't turn up. "See," I overheard him boasting to Woodie. l don't play games. Anyone messes with me they're dead."

These petty intrigues were forgotten when Keith received a phone call from Jamaica to say that Anita had been arrested on a drug charge and was being held in prison. Keith wanted to fly out immediately, but he was worried the Jamaicans might be holding on to Anita as a trap for him.

"Much better," counselled his aristocratic friend Count X, "to let me sort it all out for you."

Count X contacted one of the island's most influential businessmen, a man who'd had many dealings with the Stones. He revealed that it would be possible for Anita's immediate freedom to be purchased for a bribe of £6,000. "Tell him to pay straightaway," said Keith. "I'll give him the money back in any country he likes."

And thus Anita came home. I scarcely recognised her when she arrived at the airport. Her hair hung lank and greasy about her face, her clothes were filthy, there were boils on her neck and she looked as though she had been beaten within an inch of her life. When she saw Keith, she ran into his arms, sobbing like a lost little girl.

With Count X's help we gradually pieced together the full, horri- fying story of what had happened to her.

Local disapproval of Anita's fondness for the black community had reached flash point the day that she attempted to stroll calmly into the very uptight, very white Hilton Hotel with six Rastafarians in tow. The manager asked them all to leave, Anita refused and a vicious screaming fight ensued. When word of the incident spread, the white community around her home in Ocho Rios pressured the police to find some pretext for her deportation. The police, who were well aware who paid their wages, leaped into action. A kilo of ganja was found in the house, and Anita was driven straight to the local jail to be locked in a cell with half a dozen demented black men. There was only a single slop jar in the corner of the dingy room.

Anita was repeatedly raped and beaten by both prisoners and guards. A doctor who examined her at Cheyne Walk when we returned from the airport confirmed that there were signs of multiple rape.

Further investigations by Count X revealed that the businessman who paid over the £5,000 for Anita's release and subsequent deportation had been the prime initiator of her arrest.

"That dirty bastard," said Keith. "He knows me, and he knows Anita but he was willing to put her through all this just to keep those harmless Rastas out of his stinking white neighbourhood. That guy is so two-faced, so evil that he just doesn't deserve to live anymore."

A week later the gentleman in question blithely rang Count X to announce that he would be in London the following week, and he was keen to collect his £6,000. He phoned Keith when he arrived, on a Monday morning. "Okay, man, said Keith, barely concealing his fury. "We'll give you the money on Thursday. I'll get someone to meet you at the Dorchester Hotel with it."

As the conversation finished Keith smashed the telephone down. He was angrier than I had ever seen him. We talked wildly of all the dreadful things we would like to do to this evil man.

At first Keith told me he wanted him executed and, for a moment, he seemed deadly serious. We tossed around the sums of money a hit-man would want to take the man out.

Then Keith ruled that idea out and we talked of having the character beaten to a pulp. This was an idea I was keen on. It was the least the guy deserved for the inhuman nightmare he had cold-bloodedly inflicted on Anita.

Finally, though, Keith just wanted to put the whole business behind him. I met the guy, paid over the cash, and that was the end of it.

The whole miserable incident served to increase Keith and Anita's mistrust of the world, and they both started to take more heroin to block out reality.

At this time most of their drugs were being supplied by Michael and John, two guys who started pushing in order to assure their welcome at Keith's house. Previously, they'd had a fashionable boutique in Kings Road, Chelsea.

Michael worshiped the ground Keith and Anita walked on, and he would always wash his long blonde hair and put on his very best clothes before coming to Cheyne Walk with his daily consignment of dope. Keith preferred to buy his dope daily, if possible, because it minimised the quantity of drugs lying around the house. Michael didn't see it quite like that, though. He was so eager for Anita to like him that he would feed her titbits of gossip to titillate her. Even so, she would usually brusquely take his drugs, pay him his money and get rid of him as quickly as possible.

There was always this slight tension between the two of them — Anita trying to get some peace and Michael trying to get into the kitchen for some coffee and gossip. In desperation one day Michael turned around as he was being eased out of the door and said, "I'll bet you'd love to know what Keith was up to while you were in Jamaica, wouldn't you?"

"Yes," purred Anita. "I really would. Come into the kitchen and have some coffee."

"You must promise that you won't tell Keith I told you," began Michael. "But while you were away, he fell for a German model who was staying at Ronnie Wood's house..."

"Of course, I won't tell Keith," vowed Anita. But the second Michael left she charged into the bedroom, grabbed Keith by the hair and screamed, "You fucking bastard. You've been messing about with this bird. I know all about you. Michael told me what's been going on. But I'll make damn sure you don't take the kid. You see if I don't."

"Just wait till I get my hands on that grass Michael," Keith muttered to me when the storm abated. "I'll teach him to go carrying tales to Anita."

It was arranged that I should 'phone Michael. "Hi, man," I said. "Keith has just been saying that he hasn't seen you for ages, so why don't you come over for the evening and bring a little coke with you?"

Keith was giggling insanely to himself now. "Just you wait and see what I've got planned for Mr. Mikey," he spluttered.

Michael arrived a couple of hours later, reeking of expensive after-shave and wearing glamorous clothes. "Come up to Keith's room," I said. "He's dying to see you again."

It was all I could do to keep myself from cracking up as Michael preened himself and assumed the expression of a lapdog about to be reunited with his master after a long absence.

Michael's little friend John had come, too; it was his job to carry the drugs. I told him to wait downstairs while Michael and I went up to see Keith. Keith welcomed the pusher effusively as I settled down in front of the TV in the corner of the bedroom, to watch some video tapes.

"Got the dope, have you?" Keith asked pleasantly.

"No," replied Michael. "John's got it. I'll run downstairs and get it from him."

He came back and handed over a few grammes of smack. Keith thanked him and took a snort while Michael sat on an antique chest at the foot of Keith's four-poster bed and gazed lovingly at him.

Keith unhooked a German sword from the wall and started to swagger around the room, slicing savagely at the air with it. Michael was talking to me, but I was looking at the television and pinching my nose to stop myself laughing. The tension in the air was impossible to ignore now, and even Michael was beginning to sense that something wasn't quite right.

Keith strolled casually toward him, and I knew that the action was about to start. He crashed the flat of the blade down on Michael's shoulder. Hard. I saw Michael wince with pain as he tried to feign an amused smile. Then Keith jabbed him in the chest with enough pressure to hurt, though not wound. "What's up, man?" pleaded Michael, though I could see from his eyes that he had a pretty good idea exactly what was up.

"You've been talking too much, Michael, haven't you?" growled Keith.

"What? What? How do you mean?" pleaded Michael.

"Yes, you know what I'm talking about," said Keith, jabbing harder and harder with the sword. "What have you been telling my old woman? You've been telling her all about me and Ushi, haven't you? Do you know what I'm going to do with you, Michael? I'm going to chop all your lovely hair off."

He grabbed hold of Michael's mane and took a swipe at it with the razor-sharp sword. At the last second Michael managed to deflect the blade with his hand. In the confusion which followed, Michael, who had turned white with fear, slithered across the parquet floor and under the bed. Keith started taking wild swings at him. I was afraid he would accidentally kill or blind him, so I started to play my part in the charade

270

by grabbing Keith and holding his arms behind his back.

"Let me go," screamed Keith, performing to perfection. "I'll get that little grass. Let me go, let me go."

"Quick, Michael," I called. "Get out of here. I can't hold him much longer."

Michael bolted from under the bed like a greyhound out of a trap. "Quick, John, quick," he screamed. "Keith's gone berserk. He's going to kill us."

After they'd fled, Keith and I rolled around on the bed laughing until tears came.

"Oh, man," roared Keith. "I've never seen anything so funny in all my life. I felt like Sylvester chasing Tweety Pie."

27

THOUGH THE WORLD OF ROCK MUSICIANS APPEARS ENLIGHTENED AND liberal, it is in fact one of the last bastions of total male chauvinism. Almost without exception women are bandied about, dropped, swapped and laid in a fashion that is little short of primaeval. Keith was unsurprised therefore when Joe Monk — the fuzzy-wuzzy poacher from Redlands — calmly offered him his girl friend one day. Joe was a guest at Cheyne Walk, Anita was away at a chalet she and Keith had bought in Switzerland and Joe considerately felt that Keith might be in need of a woman. "Thanks a lot," said Keith. "But no. You keep her, Joe, I can see you're fond of her."

The whole exchange was accomplished with about as much passion as declining the offer of a cigarette. Yet the idea seemed to play on Keith's subconscious, and some time later, when Joe was out auditioning for a new play, he leaped into his Bentley with the girl, and they raced off to the Lake District together, for all the world like a pair of eloping young lovers

The first anyone knew of the romance was when Keith 'phoned Mick from a remote mountain farm to say he wouldn't be able to make a photo session that day with David Bailey for the cover of *Goat's Head Soup*. Three days later he came sheepishly back to London and immediately phoned me. "Have you seen Joe Monk around?" he asked nervously. "I've heard he's telling people he's going to shoot me."

"Why should he kill you?" I asked innocently. "He hasn't got the guts to do that. I wouldn't worry about it."

"I don't know," replied Keith. "But that Joe is a madman. You never know what he is going to do next."

That night we went to see the Faces in concert at the Sundown, Edmonton. Afterwards there was to be a party, and Keith told Woodie,

"There's a guy called Joe Monk, a spade. Have one of your bodyguards stand by the door, and if he tries to gate crash the party, don't let him in."

In all the excitement of the show, Woodie forgot, and afterwards, as we sat chatting in the dressing room while the Faces changed, Joe Monk burst in through the door. In his turban and flowing Moroccan cape, he looked like a Mongol warrior.

"See, there," jabbered Keith. "I told you he was after me, Tony."

"Well, he hasn't made a move towards you yet," I told him. "So cool it."

"Yes, okay, but keep an eye on him. I think he's got a gun underneath his coat."

Suddenly the girl who was the cause of the altercation slipped into the dressing room and wrapped her arms around Keith, kissing him gently on the lips. I went up to Joe. "You've really got Keith worried," I said. "He thinks you're going to do something to him."

"Don't worry," he said. "I won't."

"Well, Keith doesn't know that. So won't you come over to him with me and show him you haven't got a gun or a dagger or something hidden under that cloak of yours? Just tell him there are no hard feelings."

Joe complied, saying to Keith, "Don't worry, man, you're welcome to her."

Keith's bravado came back in an instant. He turned to Rod Stewart and boasted, "Yeah, well, I've got a knife on me, and I'd have killed that fuckin' spade if he'd tried anything." But Joe seemed more genuinely hurt at Keith's betrayal of friendship than angry. I felt sorry for him.

Keith arranged for me to give Joe his things from Cheyne Walk, and then Keith and the girl settled down together to a life of cosy domestic bliss. Later a long, gentle, poetic letter arrived from Joe mildly reproaching Keith for stealing his girl and throwing him out on the street. "We're all brothers and I thought you were a good friend of mine," Joe wrote.

Prostration was not a pose Keith cared to understand — to him it was just a good chance to kick a rival in the head. He dashed off a hasty reply to Joe. "Don't ever come to my house again. If I see you in the street, I'll spit on you, you fucking spade," ran the message, which Keith asked me to deliver to Joe.

"I can't do that," I protested. "You've already completely demoralised the guy — you've taken his girl away from him. Why dig the knife in even deeper?"

"Just do it, Tony," Keith said icily. I took the letter from him without further argument and tore it up in secret. Later, when Anita 'phoned to say she would be home from Switzerland with Marlon and Dandelion the next day, Keith promptly turned around and threw the girl out. "Sorry, darling," he said. "But my family is very important to me."

With Anita back, life carried on much as before with everybody flying alternately up on coke and down on smack. The intimidation Keith had felt from Joe rankled, and he determined to arm himself. A chauffeur was despatched to Switzerland to bring in a .38 snub-nosed Smith & Wesson revolver that Leroy, one of the security men on the American tour, had given to Keith as a souvenir. Unfortunately there was no ammunition for the gun, so Keith asked me if I could buy some for him from my contacts in Soho.

A week later I picked up a box of .38 bullets for £30 from a contact in a pub on Wardour Street.

Keith pushed one of the heavy bullets into the chamber, but it slid straight through and fell to the ground. Each time he tried, the same thing happened. "I don't understand it," I said. "They're definitely the same size — thirty-eights."

"Yeah, well,' said Keith. "I understand it. The bullets for this gun should have a kind of rim around the back. You've got me thirty-eight sten gun bullets."

We laughed it off, but three days later, on June 26, 1973, we weren't laughing at all. There was a ring on the bell at Cheyne Walk. Luigi, the caretaker, opened the door, and ten cops led by Detective Inspector Charles O'Hanlon burst in. They charged straight into the master bedroom where Keith and Anita were sleeping and zeroed in on the gun and ammo with uncanny speed. They found a tiny scrap of hash, a few Mandrax sleeping tablets, and they took away Keith's water pipes and his beautiful brass pharmaceutical scales. They also managed to find an antique shotgun that had been left in the house by the late Johnny Braces. They appeared delighted with their haul, and after the customary cautions to Keith, Anita and a friend, Prince Stanislaus, who had the misfortune to be staying at the house that night, they were on their way.

"*Phewee,*" breathed Keith. "Thank Christ they didn't really start taking the place apart. God knows what they would have found."

Keith and Anita had cocaine and heroin stashed in all sorts of imaginative places about the big old house. One stash was hidden deep inside an old-fashioned washing machine in the basement. Another was inside a secret compartment that an American film special-effects man had built into their antique four-poster. The American had also built other devices which Keith used to carry dope around; there was an expensive pen which wrote but also contained a secret compartment large enough to hold four grammes of dope. Think of the customs men who've missed that one.

"The only thing I'm really worried about," Keith said that evening, "is the scales." He said that the police had sent them away to the laboratory; because he hadn't cleaned them since he'd weighed out an ounce of smack on them a week ago, he thought the police might use the size of the residue to allege that he had recently had an ounce of heroin in his possession.

Keith, Anita and Prince Stanislaus were freed on £500 bail. Prince Stanislaus was subsequently found not guilty, Anita was given a conditional discharge for possession of twenty-five Mandrax tablets and Keith was fined £250 at Marlborough Street court in October for having cannabis, a tiny quantity of Chinese heroin, Mandrax tablets, a revolver, a shotgun and 110 rounds of ammunition. In 1967 he would probably have got life.

Anita became obsessed with the idea that Joe Monk had tipped the police off to get even with Keith. "I'll get my own back on that black bastard," she snarled demonically. "I'll curse him."

A short while later Joe Monk was driving along a lonely cliff-top road in Majorca when his car crashed and he was killed. Nobody saw it; no other vehicle was involved. The police said it was the strangest accident they'd ever heard of. One can only assume it was a coincidence, of course.

Obtaining a steady supply of heroin remained a problem for Keith and Anita, mere wealth being no guarantee of a regular delivery. Pushers get arrested with monotonous regularity, and once a few big ones go, a drought can hit London for a week or more. Anita arranged for Mario, an Italian dealer she'd met in Switzerland, to smuggle in eight-and-a-half ounces of smack, enough to last for months. He called from Italy to say he was on his way, and I went to the airport to meet him in the Bentley. He had the drug hidden partly inside a hollowed-out photographer's tripod and partly inside secret compartments in his suitcase.

After he exchanged pleasantries with Keith and Anita at Cheyne Walk, he wanted to talk money. "It's worth a good eight thousand pounds," he said.

Keith appeared unshaken. "Exactly what sort of stuff is it?" he asked.

"Diamorphine," said Mario. "Your chemist can turn it into thirty or forty ounces of pure heroin with no trouble at all."

Keith was taken aback. Diamorphine is a crude form of heroin produced by heating morphine with acetic acid. We had no tame pharmacist on tap, so the stuff was of no use to us. Mario had genuinely believed he was doing us a big favour by giving us the base for a huge quantity of smack.

"Look," said Keith, 'you need a laboratory for all that. And I can't just go round advertising for a chemist to refine me some heroin. Besides, even if I was going to buy your stuff, I wouldn't give you more than £7,000 for it".

"Look, man," said Mario, glowering. "If you don't take this stuff, I'm going to make trouble for you. Your bird ordered it. Here it is. Now just pay me, and I'll clear off out of the country."

Keith insisted that if he agreed to the deal, it would be several days before he could rake up the necessary cash, and Mario decided to retire to one of the guest rooms. Keith asked me to try to find some way out of the problem. I went upstairs to sound Mario out.

"I'm absolutely disgusted at the way he is behaving," the Italian exploded. "He's got all the money in the world, and he won't pay me after I risked being arrested to bring dope here for his bird. I've never dealt with such cheapskates in my whole life."

I reported this to Anita, who was sufficiently moved to pay him from her own Swiss bank account. "No, don't do that, Anita," protested Keith. "I'll pay him, I'll pay him."

Keith promised to give me two ounces of the diamorphine if I would help him knock down Mario's price. Eventually the pusher was forced to settle for £3,500. With much cursing he stormed out of the house to the airport and Italy.

Keith and I tried to snort the stuff and quickly realised that it had only about one-tenth the strength of normal heroin. We snorted whole handfuls until it lay on our throats and made us sick. Like all junkies, we tried to convince ourselves that it was wonderful. "Not bad at all really once you get used to it, is it?", queried Keith hopefully.

"To be honest, it's about as exciting as snorting Home Pride flour," I was forced to admit at length. "I think you'd better just stash it away, Keith, and hope that one day we bump into a chemist who can turn it into proper dope."

"Perhaps you're right," said Keith lugubriously.

276

A week later Keith was peering out of the window of the house at a team of telephone engineers who were hard at work in a hole a few yards down the road from the house. "They're at it again," he moaned. "The cops are getting ready to tap my 'phone, and they're gonna bust us again. We'll have to get rid of all that diamorphine, or they'll have me in jail for certain."

He dashed up the ornate staircase and ripped away the carpet. "I've hidden it round about here somewhere," he said. "Inside one of these steps." But he couldn't remember which step he had hidden it in. We had to rip up half the carpet before we could find the loose board. There was more of the drug hidden in the attic, a little more in the basement and still more in the secret compartment in the bed.

"You've got to get rid of all this, Keith," I warned him. "If they come in and catch you with this lot, it won't be just a little fine. They're going to charge you with being a dope pusher, and you'll go to jail for certain."

"Yeah," said Keith. "I know. Let's go and stash it all at Woodie's."

I thought that was a little mean. I decided to check first whether the telephone was, in fact, being tapped. This entailed dialing 159, followed by the last four figures of Keith's number. A recorded voice said simply, "Start test." I replaced the receiver, and the 'phone rang automatically a few seconds later. Had the 'phone been tapped the interception on the line would have made it impossible for the exchange to ring back automatically.

Keith remained unconvinced. "They're getting nearer and nearer to me, he said. "I've got to find somewhere to hide."

He discussed the crisis with Woodie in Tramp that night, and Woodie had the perfect solution. "Look," he said, "I've got a little staff cottage at the end of my garden which isn't used. If you want to get it cleaned up a bit, you're welcome to stay there." It was agreed. Painters, builders and a custom kitchen firm were called in to make the place habitable while Keith fretted over his sack of diamorphine.

After a week he could stand the strain no more, and he suddenly turned to me and exclaimed, "Right, tonight we make the switch."

"Do what?" I queried.

You move the gear to Woodie's tonight."

I protested that I was not prepared to risk carrying that much dope on my own. Keith decreed that I take the drugs in his new Rolls-Royce Silver Shadow while he followed in the Ferrari. The night was dark, and the drive to Richmond went without a hitch.

When we arrived at the Wick, I protested to Keith that it wouldn't be fair to hide the diamorphine inside the little cottage in case the police found it there and charged Woodie with being responsible for it. Instead, we decided to hide it in a derelict stable in the grounds.

"Look," I said, "you go and hide it on your own. I don't want to see where you put it. It's best that you are the only person who knows where it is."

Ten minutes later he came out of the stable, beaming, and we drove back to Cheyne Walk. After that he started to buy regular dope supplies from a pusher named David, who lived in Abbey Road, St. John's Wood. By then Keith had succumbed to the meanness of all junkies. Once he would have offered me a snort every now and again, but he now lied to me, swearing that David had given him only a little. The third time we visited the pusher I was turning from Abbey Road to Hamilton Terrace in the Bentley when I heard a dozen police sirens. "Oh, my God," I yelled. "They've been watching the house. We're getting busted. Give me the stuff quick."

Keith tore the dope from its hiding place behind the sun visor and handed it to me. I was preparing to throw it out of the window when the first car shot past us with its blue light flashing. Mercifully they were after somebody else.

"Here, give me that dope back," said Keith greedily.

"Thanks very much," I said. "If we'd been stopped, it's me they'd have nicked — not you."

"Thanks," he said, and grudgingly gave me one of his seven little packets of heroin.

By the next morning he and Anita had taken it all. He phoned David, but David had no more left. He and Anita began to panic.

"Come on," he said. "Let's go to Woodie's and get that stuff out of the stables."

I waited outside while he went into the building, but after ten minutes there was such banging and crashing that I went in to see what he was doing. Keith had ripped down half the old ceiling, and he was about to begin demolishing the walls.

"What's up?" I asked.

He'd apparently hidden the dope inside the hollow angled ceiling, but it had somehow slipped down inside one of the walls. Which one was anybody's guess. "Come on," I said. "We're never going to find it in here."

"We've got to," Keith screamed. "I'm going to start withdrawals if

278

I don't get a fix soon." We spent an hour tearing the old building apart, but the diamorphine was firmly hidden, and to the best of my knowledge, it remains there to this day.

Keith was really panicking now. His hands were shaking, and he had broken out in a cold sweat. "I'm sick, Tony," he moaned. "I've got to get some stuff right away." I rang all my contacts. Dealers somehow sense when addicts are desperate, and Keith was forced to pay an extortionate £500 for a mere quarter-ounce of heavily cut, very low-grade heroin. He was so grateful he didn't quibble. "Thank Christ for that," was all he said as the colourless liquid pumped into his arm from the syringe.

While Keith and Anita were waiting for the cottage at the Wick to be made ready, they decided to stay at Redlands for a few weeks. But even there there was to be no peace. On July 31 they were in the main house while I was living in an adjoining property called the Fifth, which Keith had bought. Suddenly I saw smoke billowing into the air from the thatched roof of Redlands and heard the clamour of fire engines as they sped up the narrow country lane to the house. I ran over and saw Keith and Anita frantically dragging their possessions out of the blazing house. I dived into the garage to drive Keith's Ferrari and my Alfa out of danger, then helped Keith carry out his six-hundred-year-old refectory table and his set of Charles II chairs. When it was over, Keith and Anita moved into the Fifth, filled in their insurance claim and engaged an architect to rebuild the house so that it would be even bigger and better than before.

In the midst of this chaos it was time for the Stones to finalise plans for their seven-week tour of Britain and Europe. Keith knew that he was in no condition to go on the road, but there was no time for a cure. Withdrawing would have meant being laid up for weeks and that was out of the question.

Marshall Chess, however, had a solution. "There's a doctor from Florida who can get you off dope in a few days by changing your blood," he told Keith. "He did it for me in Mexico a while back, and it worked perfectly."

The Florida doctor would carry out the blood change for Keith in a villa called Le Pec Varp, in Villars-sur-Ollon, Switzerland. Keith would fly directly to Switzerland after the Stones' concert in Birmingham on September 19. He would then be cured in time to play with the Stones again in Berne, Switzerland, on September 26. Marshall was going to Switzerland with Keith to have his blood changed at the same time.

There was still the early part of the tour to stagger through plus promotion for the Stones' new album, *Goat's Head Soup*. Being strung-out on smack has never particularly impaired Keith's playing, and he somehow went on stage each night without playing a note wrong. One evening, however, came close to ending in disaster. On September 6 Mick hired Blenheim Palace, Winston Churchill's birthplace and one of the most magnificent of England's stately homes. There was to be a lavish promotion party for the album, and all his favourite young lords and ladies, influential disc jockeys and journalists had been invited. Anita didn't want to go; she rarely left the house now and loathed the very idea of parties. But Mick was putting on the pressure. "You've got to come, Keith," he commanded. "The whole band must be there. It's important."

Finally, Anita capitulated. She pulled on her old jeans, slipped on a sweat shirt and climbed into the back of the limo with Keith, Marlon and me. On the way to Blenheim Anita took a couple of snorts of smack. By the time we arrived she was asleep. Keith shook her, and she gazed out of the window in horror at all the beautiful girls climbing out of their Rolls Royces in exotic gowns of chiffon and satin. "That's it," she exploded. "I'm not going in there in jeans with everybody else dressed up like that."

Keith, irritated, said, "You've got loads of jewellery and expensive clothes at home, and you've had all day to get ready."

"Fuck off," she hissed. "I'm not coming in. I'll wait for you here in the car — but don't you dare stay in there for more than an hour."

Keith and I set off with Marlon. As soon as we arrived, we bumped into Bobby Keyes, saxophonist and junkie. I was still only snorting smack then, but Keith and Bobby both fixed. They went into a back room that had been set aside for the Stones, to shoot one another up. I was left outside on sentry duty. Ten minutes later Mick skipped past me, and I could hear him pleading with Keith, "Come on, man, you've got to just show your face."

Downstairs the party was in full swing with magicians, fire-eaters and mime artists performing around the fountains on the patio while the Stones mingled with the guests, making polite conversation.

Keith and I sat down quietly at a table, sipping champagne. Bianca came over to us, chatting merrily, obviously delighted that Anita hadn't shown up. A short while later some primitive instinct made me glance towards the door, where Anita was storming in like a harridan. "Look who's coming," I whispered to Keith.

His face turned white. "Hello, darling," He smiled at her.

"Don't you fucking darling me," she screeched. "You're supposed to be back in the fucking car."

Bianca, bewildered, could only stutter, "What's the matter, Anita? Where have you been?"

"Where have I been?" Anita screamed so that all heads turned. "It's nothing to do with you where I've been, you stupid bitch. Come on, Keith, we're going."

Mick heard the commotion and hurried over to Keith to whisper, "Hey, man, cool it. Just grab her and get out of here or this ruck is going to be on the front page of every newspaper in the country tomorrow."

"Okay, okay," said Keith, furious. He grabbed Anita roughly by the sleeve and hauled her out of the party by a side door.

I grabbed Marlon and ran after them. I climbed into the back of the car. Both of them glared at me so fiercely I figured I'd be better off in the front seat, beside the chauffeur.

As we drove onto the main road, all hell broke loose in the back seat. Anita leaped across the seat, grabbed Keith by his hair and jerked him down to the floor.

"What shall I do?" yelled the driver.

"Just drive," I told him. I had seen such displays before.

Every time I glanced in their direction Anita screamed and lunged at me. "You Spanish bastard. It's your fault as well. You're fired."

Little Marlon was peering intently out the car window, pretending not to notice what was going on. Every ten minutes or so, throughout the two-hour drive, Keith and Anita would attack each other again. She'd sit there sobbing. Then she'd work up the courage to scratch at his eyes. "Look what you're doing to Marlon," Keith exploded at one point.

"Fuck Marlon," she screeched. "Fuck you, fuck Tony and fuck the driver. Just get me home."

An hour later things were somewhat calmer, but then Anita started demanding heroin. Keith told her he didn't have any. I knew, in fact, that Bobby had given him some at the party. "I'm sure Tony can get you some, though," he said. "Thanks a lot," I thought.

When we arrived at Cheyne Walk, she bolted straight up to her room, and I could hear her tearing everything apart in case there were any crumbs of heroin there that she had forgotten about. "You'll have to go up and calm her down," I told Keith.

As soon as Anita heard him coming, she opened the door and threw a boot at him, screaming, "Get out of here. I can't get through the night without some drugs. I can't make it without anything."

"You'll have to get hold of something for her," Keith pleaded. I hustled around for a couple of hours, finally managing to buy a couple of grammes of low-grade smack at an exorbitant price.

I 'phoned Keith immediately. "Thank God," he said. "Come back right away and give it to her."

"I can't give it all to Anita," I explained. "I need some myself to stop me getting withdrawal symptoms in the morning."

I had expected Anita to be apologetic when I returned, but if anything, she was angrier than before. When I went into her room, she simply snatched the heroin from my hand and told me to get out of her house.

"But I need some..." I began.

"Get the hell out of here!" she screamed.

Keith suggested I hide in the kitchen until Anita fell asleep, and then he would give me some of my heroin back and I could be on my way. But minutes later Anita swept into the kitchen and ordered me out of the house.

"I must have the money for that dope I got you now," I pleaded. "Otherwise, I'm not going to be able to get any dope for myself."

"That's your hard luck," she hissed. "Now just get out."

Keith wandered in and whispered to me that he would give me some smack if I'd come back an hour later. So I hung around for a while, but still Anita's bedroom light was on. Early in the morning, though, I could feel cold turkey creeping up on me, so I rang the bell in desperation. I had no money; though I rang for twenty minutes, Keith refused to open the door, and I was forced to stagger home to begin the agonies of withdrawals. The next morning they were apologetic, and they gave me some heroin, but I never quite forgave them for that little piece of ruthlessness.

I flew out to Switzerland to arrange the final details of the blood change. The Florida doctor was to be paid £2,500 plus all expenses to supervise the course, and I booked him into the Le Renard Hotel for a week. I paid 1,000 Swiss francs (£80) for the rental on the villa and collected £1,000 from Keith's accountant, Norman Myers, in Regent Street, for my own expenses.

I flew to Geneva on September 17. By a stroke of luck the taxi I hailed had a Spanish driver. Since my French is poor, I hired the driver to work for me for the week as translator and chauffeur. I hired two nurses and a maid for the villa. These arrangements completed, I returned to Geneva to meet Keith, Anita and the kids at the airport.

On the way back to the villa the driver casually mentioned that he was taking a little shortcut through France. "Stop him, Tony," whispered Keith. "They've still got warrants out for Anita and me in France, so once we cross the border we're done for."

"I think we'd better go the long way round, thanks all the same," I told the driver, in Spanish.

We settled in at the villa, and shortly thereafter Dr. Denber drove up with a nurse. A while later Marshall arrived. You can have a cure as well if you like, Tony," offered Keith. "I'll pay for it."

I was frightened of the radical sounding blood change cure, and anyway, I had some methadone that had been prescribed by my doctor, so at least I was in no danger of suffering immediate withdrawal symptoms. I decided to return to England and leave them to their cure.

Eight days later the Stones performed at the Olympiahalle in Munich. I flew over to meet them and was astonished to find Keith and Marshall both looking as fresh-faced and healthy as schoolboys. "How the hell did that doctor do it?" I asked Keith.

"It's quite simple really," Keith explained. "He just changed our blood little by little so that there was no heroin in our bodies after forty-eight hours. There was no pain at all, and we spent the rest of the week just resting and building our strength up."

Later that night I saw him accept a snort of coke from Bobby Keyes and reproached him for his foolishness. "Yeah, well," said Keith. "It doesn't matter if I get hooked again now. I can give it up any time I like without any bother."

I couldn't help wondering where all this blood was coming from or resenting the decadence of debauched millionaires regaining their health, vampire like, from the fresh, clean blood of innocents.

While Keith was undergoing the blood changes, one of his closest friends, Gram Parsons, was at the centre of an even more macabre drama on the other side of the world. Though he is not well known, Parsons, a lanky dark-haired American, has been an important musical influence. Parsons, of the mellow voice and acoustic guitar, started the country rock sound that flowered with the Eagles and Crosby, Stills, Nash and Young. His seminal influence among musicians, through albums like *Safe at Home*, approached that of Chuck Berry and Jimi Hendrix. He helped form the Byrds and the Flying Burrito Brothers.

Gram's career was soaring like one of his songs when he came under Keith's influence and moved to Europe to play with him — and to be like him. Like most people who are sucked into the Jagger-Richard vortex, Gram became fascinated by dope and black magic. Some people are strong enough to dabble in such things, and others aren't. Gram wasn't.

On September 19, 1973, he was rehearsing in the desert near Los Angeles — the scene of Altamont and Charles Manson's odious Family — when suddenly, inexplicably, he died. A week later, while a pathologist prepared to determine the cause of death, Gram's body was snatched by his road manager and long-time friend Phil Kaufman. Kaufman carried the corpse to the Joshua Tree National Monument and burned it. Gram, it was said, had expressed a wish for his body to be cremated in this bizarre manner. Whatever motivated Kaufman's actions, the net result was that it was impossible to determine the cause of Gram's death, which, to this day, remains a mystery. Many Stones watchers observed that Satan's wings were flapping awfully close to the Rolling Stones again.

Keith had seen so much of death and violence that he took this latest blow in his stride. The boy from the suburbs who had made a million from playing a mean guitar was becoming the epitome of every black fantasy conjured up in the straight world by the mention of the Rolling Stones. He seemed to feel it incumbent on him to live out the legend in a way that Jagger, with his stronger will and superior intellect, had always just managed to resist.

The European tour ended at the Deutschlandhalle in Berlin on October 19. Riot police with guns, shields and water cannons sealed off surrounding streets and turned the gig into a siege against belligerent non-ticket holders. Afterwards a party was held at an hotel for the hundreds of people who had been with the band on the tour. It began in elegance — musicians playing waltzes, exquisite food piled high on antique tables — and ended in total decadence.

A senior executive with WEA Records waltzed around the crowded dance floor with a blonde Fraulein who was naked but for a pair of high-heeled shoes. There were four other completely nude girls calmly waltzing on the floor, for all the world as pert and confident as if they were wearing the latest Paris fashions.

Later, in a private suite, more girls demonstrated stunts with Beaujolais bottles — and one another.

28

MICK TAYLOR HAD BEEN YOUNG AND INNOCENT WHEN HE JOINED THE Stones — a wide-eyed boy who lived for his guitar, considered eating meat immoral and thought dope meant grass. Five years on the road had given him a crash course in world-weariness and a feeling of desperation had come over him — he had to get out now, while he was still young enough to make a new start, or go the perilous way of Brian, Keith and Mick. His relationship with Mick, particularly, was strange and strained.

At times the two Micks seemed to be the closest of friends. They would lock themselves up in Jagger's house in Cheyne Walk, talking together for hours. But then there would be rows and the two men would not speak to one another for days. It was a curious friendship.

I heard Taylor's girl friend, Rose Miller, having a screaming row with him one day about the closeness of his friendship with the head Stone.

After initial reluctance Taylor started to snort cocaine in ever-increasing quantities. Sometimes he would take so much that he would have to scrape the thick white residue out of his nose with a fingernail. I was not startled, therefore, when he told me he had burned away his nasal septum, the dividing membrane between the nostrils, with his excessive use of the drug. This is a common side effect among heavy coke users. "I've got to go into the London clinic to have a new plastic partition put in," Mick told me. And though, obviously, I didn't see the partition, I believed him implicitly.

On January 6, 1971, Rose gave birth to his daughter, Chloe, and his delight at the child's perfect miniature beauty was tinged with the fear that his life was more like Keith's every day.

"I'm getting tired of it," he confided in me. "I feel like I'm losing touch with reality."

Mick Taylor was quieter, less demonstrative than Brian Jones, but

I could see that he was beginning to slide into the same abyss. He was hurt when Jagger and Richard implemented his ideas for subtly changing the sound of the Rolling Stones — particularly on *Goat's Head Soup* and *It's Only Rock 'n' Roll* — but refused to acknowledge his contribution by granting a single song writing credit. He never confronted them, never had the strength to fight them, but he felt — just as Brian had — that he was being ill-used. Mick and Keith wanted the distinction and, to a lesser extent, the royalties that come from being the Stones' sole song writers. Yet one only has to listen to the complex musical tapestry that Taylor weaves on a track like "Time Waits for No One" to realize that this is quite outside the scope of the material that Mick and Keith have written. For a while Taylor was content in the knowledge that he was making beautiful music. Then he took to playing guitar on stage with friends like Mike Oldfield and Billy Preston. Finally, he knew that there was only one way to go. And that was out.

He talked with friends about his problem, and somehow word reached Jack Bruce, the former bass player with Cream. He asked Mick to join him in a new band. And that was that. Seeking a quiet, discreet departure, Taylor 'phoned the Stones' office and asked them to tell Jagger to find himself a new guitarist. Jagger was in Nicaragua with Bianca when he heard the news, and he was riled. "No doubt we can find another six-foot-three blonde guitarist who can do his own make-up," he told journalists, contemptuously, on his return.

In response to deeper questioning, Jagger revealed that Mick had said nothing about wishing to leave when the Stones had met three weeks previously. "He seemed okay then," said Jagger. "He obviously has a lot of troubles — personal problems — but they're nothing to do with us. I don't even know the true nature of them. I suppose it was a bit inconsiderate of him to inform us a day before we were about to enter the studios, but maybe he hadn't made up his mind till that point."

Jagger was quick to quash any suggestion that Taylor was quitting because he wasn't being paid his fair share of the band's income. "Oh, come on, I mean we'd all like more. Mick gets as much money as I do."

Taylor was determined to leave with a minimum of fuss. He told journalists, "There was no personal animosity in the split, nothing personal at all. I'm very disturbed by the stories going around that it was all to do with credits and royalties, things like that. It had nothing whatsoever to do with those things."

He added, "The last five-and-a-half years with the Stones have been

286

very exciting and proved to be a most inspiring period. And as far as my attitude to the other four members is concerned, it is one of respect for them, both as musicians and as people. I have nothing but admiration for the group, but I feel now is the time to move on and do something new."

He slid quietly away, married Rose, lived in a cottage with honey-suckle around the door near Rye in Sussex and rehearsed with Jack Bruce. Sadly, as Kipling once observed, he who rides the tiger finds it difficult to dismount. The last time I saw Mick he had split from Bruce, his marriage was in tatters, he was living with a lady who pushed cocaine for a living and he had been reduced to selling off his gold discs. He remains one of the most gentle, charming people I have ever known.

Mick's thirtieth birthday party was being thrown by his friend David Milinaric in Chelsea's Tite Street. Milinaric's exquisite house has a large, fairy tale garden with rare orchids and tropical trees.

I was living in Maida Vale with Madeleine then, and on the day of the party Anita 'phoned to ask for advice about what she should wear. It was to be her first big outing since the Blenheim Palace debacle, and she didn't want to make a fool of herself again. Madeleine agreed to go to Cheyne Walk that afternoon with some glamorous party clothes that Anita could borrow. We spent two hours at the house while Anita tried on all of Madeleine's clothes. We went back to Maida Vale, dressed for the party and returned to Cheyne Walk for Keith and Anita. Keith was taking the event extremely seriously; not only had he bought Mick an expensive piece of jewellery but he was even wearing a suit — the brown pin-striped one he'd bought at Granny Takes a Trip especially for appearing in magistrates courts. The suit was old, but it was well cut enough to make Keith still look almost elegant.

Anita, however, was still in her dressing gown, and she refused to even speak to us. "She's in one of her moods — can't find anything she wants to wear," said Keith. "I'll have to see you at the party later."

It was a splendid party. In every room there was a different atmos-phere. People danced to blasting rock 'n' roll in one area, feasted in another and then could fall out in quiet spots to smoke joints or enjoy conversation. In the garden gentle music played and candles flickered on the trees as the beautiful people wafted by — Bianca in a simple white gown; Rod Stewart busily chatting up Britt Ekland to the annoyance of his girl friend, Dee Harrington; Pete Townshend, Mama Cass and Paul Getty.

Keith strolled into the party with Anita stumbling along behind him.

The party had. been going several hours, and I had given up all hope of seeing them, but here they were. When I saw how Anita was dressed, I could hardly believe my eyes. Beneath a face caked with more make-up than a pierrot's she wore a billowing, scarlet, ballroom dancing dress with stilt-like red high-heeled shoes. She looked like a fortune-teller. All conversation ceased when she walked into the room. "It's such a shame," hissed Madeleine in my ear. "Anita is so beautiful, but she is making herself look like some mad, old tart."

Anita flounced over to us and at once asked Madeleine, "Go on, be honest, what do you think of my dress?"

"I'm not really completely crazy about it," said Madeleine with all the politeness she could muster.

"Huh," sniffed Anita. "Well, I don't think I'll be giving you any of my stash."

She and Keith stayed until their coke ran out — approximately an hour-and-a-half — then dashed home for more drugs lest reality should fall upon them. The incident was symptomatic of Anita's isolation from the real world. She was so spaced-out now that she had lost touch with how ordinary people dressed and spoke and related to one another. She was lost in fantasy.

In the newspapers the next day most of the photographs were of a beautiful, little-known model whom I will call Natasha. She stole the show with her caftan, turban and Oriental jewellery. Natasha was the ex-wife of Tony Secunda, one of the pop world's most competent wheeler-dealers. She drove a Bentley, lived in a mansion in Kensington, and always had more dope than she knew what to do with. This super-abundance of heroin and cocaine led to a close friendship with Anita, and several times Anita packed a suitcase and took the kids to stay with Natasha for days at a time. Keith became so upset over their friendship that he stormed into Natasha's house one day and told Anita, "Make your mind up. Either you live here or you stay at home."

"Well, I'm going to stay here," said Anita. Keith ended up sleeping there for the next two nights. Eventually there was a row over money. Natasha claimed Anita owed her £2,000, and the friendship broke up. It was the beginning of a series of traumas for Natasha. She went into hospital for many weeks to withdraw from heroin, she was forced to sell her Bentley and then a man died in her bathroom. This guy was an addict who owned a shop in Chelsea. Like many of Natasha's friends, he would sometimes get high in her big, thickly carpeted bathroom, but on this occasion something went wrong, and he died, sitting on the floor with a syringe hanging from his arm.

Keith shrugged his shoulders when he heard about it. He revelled now in the image the fans had of him as a debauched drug addict, and he carefully fostered it.

"I only ever get ill when I give up drugs," he said to one interviewer. And to another: "I gave up drugs when the doctor told me I had six months to live. I mean, if you're gonna get wasted, get wasted elegantly." And to another: "I find it a bit of a drag that certain people feel the need to project their death wishes on me. I've got no pre-occupation with death at all."

One day a reporter — I shall call him Peter — came to interview Keith. The interview lasted nearly four hours. As a girl photographer snapped away, Peter sought to clear up all the rumours about Keith.

"Is it true that you've had your blood changed in Switzerland? he asked.

"Oh, no," replied Keith, completely deadpan. "When I go to Switzerland I ski. I just don't know how these rumours start." It took all my self-control to avoid bursting out laughing at the preposterous notion of Keith attempting to slide down the Alps on a pair of skis.

He mixed in some of the truth to keep his story credible.

"Yes," he said, "I've smoked hash, I've taken acid and speed — but I've never touched heroin." The reporter nodded his head, obviously delighted at capturing so candid an interview.

The conversation turned to the Stones' new album, *It's Only Rock 'n' Roll*. Keith invited Peter to Cheyne Walk to hear a pre-release acetate. Peter was as excited as a little boy who's just been invited into the magic grotto by Santa. Keith showed him into the second-floor living room, switched on the record and hospitably passed a joint around. Keith left him with the joint and the music and disappeared for a quarter of an hour. Suddenly everyone in the house could hear that the record was stuck. When I went downstairs to fix it, I bumped into Keith, who had a little bag of cocaine in his hand. "Don't take that with you, man," I warned him. "You've just denied for a whole afternoon that you take hard drugs."

"Don't worry, Tony," he said. "I'm going to give him a little turn-on, that's all."

"Do you indulge?" Keith asked the boy, for all the world like Oscar Wilde offering a boy a glass of cognac.

"Thank you," said Peter, graciously assenting. From the way he fumbled, I could tell he'd never snorted cocaine before in his life. Keith showed him how to do it, and in seconds the reporter was high on coke, glowing with excitement. Keith wasn't content to leave it at that, and he kept pushing Peter to take another snort every five minutes. It was obvious that the reporter was thrilled at this sudden intimacy with a living legend. I'd seen this game before and knew what was coming. The cumulative effect of the coke hit Peter hard, and he started pacing up and down the room like a caged lion. His face, I knew, felt numb, and his mind was racing as fast as an LSD tripper's.

After Peter had politely endured this for a couple of hours, Keith padded downstairs again, grinning, and offered the young man a snort of heroin. As Peter passed out on the Moroccan floor cushions, Keith switched on a revolving mirrored globe which hung in place of a light in the centre of the room. Suddenly the whole room seemed to erupt into a flickering confusion of darting lights.

I could see Peter turning from green to yellow and back to green again, desperately trying not to vomit on the great man's carpet. At length he came to sufficiently for me to interpret that he wanted me to call a taxi for him. Keith grinned malevolently as Peter attempted to mouth out his apologies and thanks. I gently thrust the kid into the cab, and as he sank gratefully back into the seat, I heard him throwing up with convulsive force.

When the interview appeared, no mention was made of the evening's events, and Peter contented himself with faithfully reproducing all the denials and untruths Keith had spouted during the session at the office.

Six months later I met Peter again, and he begged me for heroin. He had been scoring, he said, from squatters in Pembridge Crescent, Notting Hill, and they had been selling him poison in order to make a little quick money. He had lost his job but seemed to imagine in some deranged way that to become a star, it was necessary first to be a junkie.

Corruption of innocents became one of Keith and Anita's favourite pastimes. Anita had a penchant for offering cocaine to the giggly, naïve maids and nannies who came and went in a never-ending stream. Coke users love company, it's a highly social drug, like alcohol and grass. Half the pleasure of taking it is the lucid, heady conversations that follow a couple of snorts. Invariably the girls would develop a taste for coke, and Anita would take to charging them for their supplies. "Don't worry," she'd say. "I'll just knock it off your wages at the end of the month." When the girls eventually realised that they were working for nothing more than board, lodging and dope, they tended to become disenchanted with the thrill of working for a Rolling Stone and leave. Word of what was happening eventually filtered back to the Chelsea agency that supplied Anita's staff, and they flatly refused to send her any more employees.

Occasionally Anita would even try to amuse herself with me. Though I was firmly addicted to heroin, I'd still never injected myself and vowed never to do so. When Anita could see that I was desperately in need of some smack, she would sometimes dangle a syringe full of the stuff in front of me. "Sorry, Tony," she'd say. "This is all I've got. But I'll do it all for you if you like. You won't feel a thing." I was still strong enough to say no. Given the choice between withdrawal symptoms and an injection, I'll take withdrawal symptoms any day.

Keith got a kick out of tape-recording telephone conversations. He'd lead people on, encouraging them, for instance, to criticise Mick, and then he would play the tape for Mick, and everyone would break up laughing. It became such a popular pastime that I took it up myself, recording my 'phone conversations with Keith. The dozens of cassettes I stored up have been an enormous help in writing this book.

My growing dis-affection for Keith and Anita crystallised at about the time of one particularly frightening incident. A record producer, I shall call Sebastian, and Keith were supposedly close friends, and since they were both addicts, they often bought supplies of dope together. One evening they split £500 worth of heroin at Cheyne Walk. They didn't use any of it during the evening, preferring to stick to cocaine. At about midnight Sebastian went back to his Knightsbridge hotel, and Keith went to bed. An hour later the 'phone rang for a few moments; then it stopped; I presumed Keith had answered it. A few minutes later it rang again, and once more Keith seemed to answer it. When it started to ring for the third time, I picked it up to hear Sebastian's distorted voice hissing at me, "I'm dying. Keith keeps slamming the 'phone down on me. Help me."

I guessed that he had probably taken an accidental overdose. I grabbed a bag of cocaine and a bottle of brandy, leaped into the Alfa and raced to Sebastian's hotel. Every second, I knew from experience, counted.

The door to Sebastian's room was unlocked, and I pushed it open to find him slumped in a chair with a syringe hanging from his arm. He was barely conscious. In front of him was a scrawled note explaining that he had taken some bad heroin and was paralysed down his left side. I plucked the syringe from his arm, shook him, forced him to snort some coke while I massaged his arm. "Don't call a doctor," Sebastian whispered at last. "I'll get deported." I poured huge shots of brandy into him and gave him more and more cocaine — anything to set his heart racing and overcome the poisonous, heart-stopping effect of the heroin. I walked him back and forth in the room until he seemed almost normal again. I was worried now about Keith. He had bought some of the same batch of smack as Sebastian I suspected it had been mixed with strychnine or some equally noxious substance. The effect of strychnine obtained from rat poison is not dissimilar to heroin, and consequently it is used as a cut by unscrupulous dealers.

"Keith," I screamed into the 'phone, "for Christ's sake, don't touch that smack. It very nearly killed Sebastian."

"Rubbish," said Keith. "Tell you what. If Sebastian doesn't want it, tell him I'll give him a hundred pounds for what's left. Don't let him throw it away whatever you do." I was flabbergasted. I came to realise later that when you are hooked, the risk of death is less important than the risk of not getting a fix. After a few thousand injections you start to believe that anything can be purified if you boil it up and filter it through a wad of cotton enough times.

The incident seemed to mark the end of Sebastian's friendship with Keith. "I really was dying, and he just left me to it rather than get involved," said Sebastian. "That wasn't the action of any kind of friend at all."

29

ALL THE ROLLING STONES WANTED RON WOOD TO REPLACE MICK TAYLOR, but he was committed to the Faces and felt a deep sense of obligation to Rod Stewart. In great secrecy Mick and Keith arranged to audition the cream of the world's guitarists in a remote studio in Rotterdam. Jeff Beck came over; so did Rory Gallagher and Robert Johnson. Although they were brilliant musicians, none of them had that indefinable funk that the Rolling Stones wanted. At last it was decided that the new man would be Wayne Perkins, but Mick hedged and held off announcing the appointment to the press. "Let's try just one more," Mick said. He arranged for Harvey Mandel to be given a try out. "He's more right for us," said Jagger, though Keith disagreed violently. Then Woodie jammed for fun with the Stones one night in Munich, and all other considerations flew straight out of the window. He looked skinny/ugly, beautiful, just the way a Rolling Stone should, and he played crude, vicious Stones-style guitar with none of the virtuoso fanciness that had eliminated the other musicians.

Woodie was totally committed to the Faces legally and morally. It was out of the question for him just to up and leave Rod. A compromise was evolved. Woodie would stay with the Faces, but he would help the Stones out by playing with them on their summer 1975 tour of the States. The announcement was made to the press on April 14, and one newspaper mentioned that Woodie was such a close friend of Keith's that Keith had been living in a cottage in Woodie's garden. A week later the cops, who had been wondering whatever happened to Mr. Richard, pounced at dawn on the Wick. Welcome to the Stones, Woodie!

At the time of the Wick bust, Keith and Ron were recording in Munich. All the cops found was an insignificant trace of cocaine and Chrissie Wood in bed with her friend, songwriter Audrey Burgon. Piqued at missing Keith, the thwarted cops decided to drag Chrissie and Audrey through the courts instead. Since they had only meagre evidence, they tried, disgracefully, to prejudice the jury by questioning the morality of two beautiful young women sleeping in the same bed.

The trial echoed the one Mick and Keith had undergone at Chichester nine years ago when the police had attempted to influence the jury by harping on the nude girl wrapped only in a fur rug. Thankfully for British justice, after a trial and a retrial, Chrissie and Audrey were acquitted at Kensington Crown Court twelve months later. Their legal bill for defending this farcical and malicious prosecution came to slightly over £20,000. Had they pleaded guilty in a magistrate's court, it is unlikely they would have been fined more than £50 each.

Keith had a conviction for heroin possession against him now, and that seemed to veto any chance of his being granted a visa to enter the United States for the tour that was scheduled to begin on June 3. But Mick is not one to concede defeat easily, and he went straight to his friend Walter Annenberg, the United States ambassador to Britain, to see if he could intercede.

Annenberg, obviously mindful of the enormous sway the Stones held over America's young voters, advised that Keith would be granted a visa — provided that a doctor certified there was no trace whatsoever of any drug in his bloodstream. Since Keith was by now heavily hooked on heroin once more, it was arranged that the Florida doctor should fly over to Switzerland to change his blood quickly As soon as the cure had been effected, Keith flew to London and presented himself at the American Embassy for examination. The doctor pronounced his blood as pure as spring water, his passport was stamped and he was back on the road again.

The band arrived in New York in late May to prepare for the tour, and Keith was taken aback when two heavy gentlemen banged at the door of his hotel suite on the evening of his arrival. Keith said they identified themselves as FBI agents and flashed their cards. Keith expected them to rip his belongings apart — "pray God they won't try to unscrew the shaving foam or the pen," he thought — but they settled down in easy chairs.

Keith said that the agents claimed that General Motors was sponsoring the tour, and millions of dollars were at stake. He said they knew he was addicted to heroin, and that there were people who'd like to see him busted and therefore they were going to supply him with enough dope so that he wouldn't have to take any drugs offered to him by anyone else.

Keith said the agents were as good as their word, supplying him with top-grade pharmaceuticals throughout the three months. He became so friendly with them that he subsequently hired one of their retiring colleagues to take charge of his security problems while he was in Canada and the States.

The only brush with the law during the tour came in Fordyce, Arkansas, where some hick cops decided to frisk Keith. They found his ubiquitous knife and gleefully charged him with carrying an offensive weapon. Keith was freed, unperturbed, on £100 bail and left the lawyers to sort it out.

This tour was different — nobody screamed; nobody rioted; nobody fought anymore. The Stones re-established themselves as the finest rock band on stage. Ronnie Wood flounced and postured and looked for all the world like Keith's little brother. Jagger took his own wrist-flapping, bum-wiggling, camp persona so far that he was now a parody of the threatening, sexually ambiguous guerrilla of yore. With his rhinestones and girl's blouses and make-up he was out of sync with the times, the price you pay for a rarefied life-style. He did his best to shock with a huge, inflatable phallus, but this was vaudeville, not the brash, uncompromising voice of youth. But not everyone saw through the charade.

Steve Dunleavy wrote in the *Star*:

"It's time we exorcised this demonic influence over our children!

Mick Jagger should come to America more often. I say that because it does us good, really good to look at ourselves squarely in the eye and see where we have failed.

Where have we failed that this pimple-faced disciple of dirt is a hero, a rootin', tootin' hero to our teenage kids?

We have this pale-faced foreigner, this Englishman, getting ten dollars a set from our kids to see him perform. And what do they see?

They are blitzkrieged by a tightly packaged excess of four-letter words and tacky smut.

Okay, squares like me can live without that outrage. But what I can't tolerate, and won't, damn it, tolerate, is

> seeing him come to our shores and bombard our kids with
> filth. No it's not our kids' faults. It's our fault. Somewhere
> between telling ourselves that we must "be modern," must
> "keep up with the changing world" — we forgot to tell them
> a few things — like the timeless values that have made us
> a great people. Things that have a lot to do with God, a flag
> and a country."

Jagger smiled when he read the piece. Thank God somebody still thought the Stones were a menace to society.

Bianca didn't come on the road with him on this tour. She was living her own life now, refusing to become like Chrissie Shrimpton and Marianne — a mere Jagger adjunct. Jagger revenged himself on her with gibes through the press. "There's really no reason to have women on the tour unless they've got a job to do," he told one reporter. "The only other reason is to screw. Otherwise, they get bored... they just sit around and moan."

The tour marked a watershed in Mick and Bianca's relationship. Previously they'd always been careful to preserve an image of perfect domestic bliss, but now the facade was cracking. In the beginning Mick loved Bianca passionately. At heart, too, he is a conventional product of London suburbia no matter how cleverly he tries to hide the fact. Marriage, in his view, should be as permanent and conventional as that of his parents. The man should go out and work, and the woman should look after him. You should never, ever, gossip about your partner or criticise him or her to outsiders.

Bianca broke all the rules. "I've never been Mrs. Jagger. Never. Always Bianca Jagger," she protested to a reporter. "We are two very strong-willed people," she stormed. "Maybe each of us should have married somebody different, somebody quiet and easy going. But maybe that would have been boring. I should tell you Mick is very critical of me. He is always watching me, saying if he thinks I look wrong or something. Still, it's not the same when he's away, and Jade misses him terribly. She says, 'Where is Daddy?' and he talks to her on the 'phone and explains that he is in America or wherever and he will see her soon. That consoles her a little. She is in love with her daddy."

"I think I was in love with my daddy for a while when I was little, and then my young brother came along and I felt he was transferring all his affection from me to the baby, and I was insanely jealous. Yes, yes, I am jealous now, but I try to control it. I am too sensitive in some ways, though in other ways I am very tough. Very tough."

Their mutual love of Jade had initially drawn Mick and Bianca close, but now the child became the focus of much of the friction between them. Mick was devoted to Jade, but he wanted her life to have an atmosphere of normality, privacy and wholesomeness — away from the drugs and excesses that were commonplace in the Rolling Stones' world. He hid her away in New York in his home on East Seventy-third Street. He refused to let photographers or journalists get near her, and as a result, she was able to attend a local kindergarten with other children without attracting undue attention. When he wasn't working, he spent almost all his time playing with his beautiful baby daughter, telling her stories and playing songs for her on his acoustic guitar.

Bianca appeared to be a loving mother. But sometimes she would leave Jade in the care of a nanny for days. Then, in the midst of a dinner party, she would jump up and insist that she had to read Jade her bedtime story. This, she said, came before everything. She would take Jade with her to dine in smart restaurants when Mick was away.

"I think it is bad for her to be with me as much as she is," she told one reporter. "She is too grown up. When she sees another little girl, she just goes mad; she wants to play, but she really doesn't know how to."

In fact, Jade seemed to me to be more and more on her own — living with nannies in palatial mansions all over the world while mummy and daddy were away being wonderful.

"It is hard being beautiful," said Bianca, intensely serious. "I don't like people who have this false modesty. I know that I am beautiful; I know that when I go out into the street or go to a party, people will take notice of me, but I don't expect to be the centre of attention all the time. I like best having no make-up and just wearing leotards."

She surrounded herself with powerful, sycophantic friends, who delighted in telling her again and again how beautiful, how wonderful she was. Mick, they told her, was very lucky to have her.

Her confidence carried her into the offer of a starring role in Ray Connolly's film *Trick or Treat* — even though she had never acted in her life. Equity was annoyed to see a plum role going to an amateur, but the magic Jagger name was sufficient to steamroller protest. She threw so many tantrums that her admirers affectionately dubbed her the new Judy Garland. Once, Bianca was reported to have stormed off the set in high dudgeon because the toilet in her mobile dressing room would not flush. Later the film — which was to have been a follow-up to Connolly's highly successful *That'll Be the Day* and *Stardust* — had to be abandoned. The bill for this disaster came to about £450,000. It seemed unlikely that she would ever be asked to act again. Yet somehow she managed to secure the starring role in another film, *Flesh Colour*, and this seemed to go more smoothly.

Similarly, her name was sufficient to intimidate magazines into paying her up to £1,000 a day to model. "Sure," she admitted. "I charge that for things I don't want to do. They say, 'Oh, we have to think about that.' OK, I don't want to do it anyway. Then they come back on the phone; yes, they will pay the money so I have to do the job."

Mick had never insisted on monogamy. When he was in faraway countries for long periods, he would sleep with girls occasionally, and he was prepared to tolerate Bianca having an occasional fling — so long as he didn't know about it. "What you don't know doesn't hurt," he explained.

Yet Bianca's all-consuming ego made her boast to friends, acquaintances, even newspapers, of her long-standing love affair with actor Ryan O'Neal — a love affair that was revived almost every time she and Ryan were in the same city at the same time. She relished being photographed with famous, sexually desirable men — it enhanced her exotic image. Yet, paradoxically, the men rarely came closer to Bianca than a hasty good-night kiss: Warren Beatty, President Ford's son Jack, David Bowie, Rod Stewart and Helmut Berger — labelled the most beautiful man in the world — all were twisted around her long fingers in this way.

She revelled, too, in her ability to use the press to enhance her mystique. "Mick will say go ahead if I want an affair, but he knows I won't do it," she said in one breath. Adding, ambiguously, in the next: "I have had very few affairs."

Mick was cut to the quick by her apparent desire to humiliate him. Not only was she exposing his marriage, the last vestige of normality in his life, to public ridicule, but she was seriously endangering his career: turning him from the world's number one sex symbol to a simpering cuckold in the mass imagination.

He started to take more and more lovers, as though desperate to regain his self-esteem. For a while friends whispered that he would leave Bianca for blonde Carintha West, the bubbly actress daughter of General Sir Michael West — but nothing came of it.

"He sleeps with many women," Bianca said contemptuously to the world's press, "but rarely has affairs with them. They are all trying to use him — they are all nobodies trying to become somebodies. But despite all this, Mick is a very conservative Englishman who thinks his wife should take care of the children."

Jagger was sufficiently perceptive to understand that Bianca needed to deride him publicly to prevent herself being swamped by his totally overwhelming personality — being sucked into the vortex as surely as Marianne and Chrissie had been. And that feeling of insecurity, of never quite having Bianca safely in his pocket, seemed to be necessary to Jagger if he was not to lose interest. And yet, it could never last. So I was not surprised when I heard that Bianca was attempting to divorce Mick.

It was 1976. The Stones were getting ready to hit the road again. I was losing interest in the band, losing interest in myself. Losing interest in life.

I had loved Madeleine for eight years. I had left my wife and our two children for her. When Madeleine was there, I wasn't interested in other women. My only infidelity had been with Marianne long ago. Madeleine knew that I would never have made love to Marianne if she had been around at that time. Anita had told her of the affair, and it seemed to fester in her mind. And then Madeleine and Marianne met, in my absence, at a party — and became close friends.

Soon after that Madeleine and I had a furious quarrel and she stormed out. We'd had break-ups before, and I was not unduly worried; she'd be back. I was peeved and concerned when I heard from a friend that she had moved into an flat with Marianne. I knew of Miss Faithfull's penchant for beautiful girls, and I suspected that she wanted to steal Madeleine from me. I started to hang out at their flat to see if I could draw Madeleine back to me. One evening things had gone particularly well. We'd killed half-a-bottle of brandy, smoked a few joints and taken a couple of snorts of heroin, and the girls had been teasing me and making risqué remarks about my performance in bed. I felt too tired to drive home and asked Madeleine if I could spend the night. "Well," she said, "we've only got a double bed. But I suppose Marianne could sleep on the couch for tonight."

"You must be joking." Marianne giggled. "I'm not missing out on all the fun."

I crawled naked into bed and left the girls laughing and plotting in the adjoining bathroom. Suddenly I felt the bed dip as a soft naked girl slid in behind me. I wrapped my arm around her, opened my eyes and saw Marianne's face beaming mischievously at me. "Hi," I said.

"Hi, yourself," she replied, stroking me seductively. "Why, Tony," she said, giggling, "you're harder than Japanese arithmetic." All I knew then was that I wanted her very badly.

But no sooner had I climbed between her silken thighs than Madeleine stormed into the room. "Aha," she shouted, in mock outrage. "I've caught you after all these years. I thought you said you didn't like her anymore."

She climbed into bed as well, and in the morning I felt in sore need of a good day's sleep. Marianne moved out soon after that, but Madeleine, for reasons of her own, wouldn't let me return to her flat in Maida Vale, though she knew that I was being eaten up with the misery of being apart from her.

Madeleine, Marianne and I all were junkies, though I still refused to use a syringe. I often spent evenings with one of them, taking dope or going out to a restaurant or a movie. One weekend I was staying with friends in Sussex when I began to feel a little depressed. I needed to hear the sound of Madeleine's voice. I 'phoned her flat, but 'phone was engaged and continued to be so for the next hour. Since Madeleine often slept during the day, I presumed she had left her 'phone off the hook in order to get some sleep. I rang again later, but still the line was engaged, and I began to worry. No matter how late Madeleine had been out she was always up and about by about six in the evening. At eleven I started to panic and called a mutual friend named Michel, who lived in a flat at Little Venice only a couple of doors away from Madeleine.

"Look," I said, "I know it sounds crazy, but I'm worried Madeleine might have accidentally overdosed or something. Could you just run around to her flat for me and check that she is okay."

"Sure," said Michel.

I was still worried, though, and I drove back to London soon after and went straight to Michel's flat. Marianne was staying there at the time, but Michel was out, and Marianne said she had no idea whether Michel had called on Madeleine. "Go round there yourself if you're so worried," said Marianne. "I don't know what you're making such a huge fuss about."

So I strolled to Madeleine's flat and rang the bell. There was no reply. But Madeleine's pet Shih Tzu dog was howling in an eerie and forlorn way that I had never heard before. I still had a key to the door of the flat, and I pulled it out in desperation. Though the key slid easily into the lock, it would not turn. The door had been double-locked from the inside. "Madeleine, Madeleine!" I called out through the letterbox. But there was no reply.

In a panic I ran back to Marianne to ask her what I should do. "Oh, you know Madeleine," she said casually. She's probably taken some sleeping tablets and gone to bed."

"No," I insisted. "I'm sure there's something wrong. I've been ringing her for twenty-four hours, and her dog is starting to go crazy in there."

We roused another of Michel's guests, Stefan Perrin, the burly nephew of Les Perrin, and set off to the flat, determined to break the door down if necessary. We rang the bell repeatedly, fiddled a little with the key, and finally, in desperation, Stefan charged at the door, smashing the lock asunder and bursting it open.

Inside the flat I knew at once that my worst fears were about to be realised. I could smell and taste and feel the presence of death. I paused, stunned, for a second. It was as though all eternity were momentarily halted. Then there were the voices of Marianne and Stefan, and we were running up to Madeleine's bedroom.

She was dead, hanging out of the bed with her golden hair brushing the floor. Her face was covered with blood, and it was dripping from her mouth. "Oh, God, no," I wept. "Some mad, crazy bastard has murdered her." After that came a blurred stream of policemen, reporters and photographers. I remember doctors shoving tranquilizers down my throat and waking up between crisp white cotton sheets at Stefan's apartment in the Water Gardens — crying softly to myself. I felt my life had ended along with Madeleine's.

The pathologist declared that Madeleine's death had been accidental. She had been taking methadone in an attempt to withdraw from heroin, and somehow the drug had driven her into an inexplicable frenzy. She'd banged her face again and again against a bedside cupboard until she was battered, bloody — and dead. Marianne shielded me from all the prying questions and even gave evidence at the inquest to spare me the ordeal. Subsequently she wrote and recorded the most beautiful song of her career, "Lady Madeleine."

Two weeks later a friend offered me a small amount of heroin, not enough, I knew, to produce the oblivion I craved. "Don't worry," said the girl. "I'll put it into a syringe for you, and you'll only need a tenth the amount you would have to take if you were snorting."

"Thank you ... thank you ... thank you," I breathed as she slid the ice-cold needle into my arm.

30

THE STONES WERE AT THEIR PEAK. THEIR WEALTH AND INFLUENCE PLACED them in the class of international corporations. Three months before their 1976 European tour, a team of one hundred sound and light engineers, lawyers, accountants and executives were working full time on the logistics of taking the band, thirteen trucks, fifteen tons of lights, a £150,000 stage — and Keith's eighteen guitars — around Europe for eight weeks.

The itinerary was complete, the crews hired and the halls booked. Peter Rudge, the twenty-nine-year-old Cambridge graduate master-minding the operation, informed Jagger the tour would cost a cool £1 million. Jagger skimmed through the books with the skill of the professional businessman, querying a detail here, suggesting an improve-ment there. The Stones would make a profit of £250,000 after taxes. Sales of their new album, *Black and Blue*, would be boosted by an estimated 400,000 copies, thanks to publicity stirred up by the tour.

They were the new royalty of the entertainment business. Keith and Mick were each spending about £200,000 a year now just in day-to-day living expenses.

Anita was pregnant again. She and Keith continued to shoot up. I was too absorbed in my own misery to see much of them anymore, but I was happy when I heard that their son Tara Richard, was born in a Swiss clinic on March 26, 1976. Tragically the child died when he was ten weeks old. The cause of his death was never publicly revealed.

Keith was on the road in Munich when Anita 'phoned with the news. He was anguished, of course, but there was a deeper desperation about him these days — a feeling that the drugs that had blackened and rotted his teeth were blackening and rotting his skeleton, burning him out inside as Brian had been burned out. Death seemed to be shuffling out of the mist toward Keith, coming into sharper perspective. He was passionate to spend every moment that was left to him with Marlon, his eldest son. Marlon, blonde haired, beautiful, very like Brian to look at, shared Keith's every hotel suite, bar stool and dressing room. There was something curiously knowing in the child's six-year-old eyes. He had seen too much of the groupies, the junkies, the drunks. At an early age he had to learn to recognise the false flatterers who tried to use him to charm their way into his father's life.

On the road he often lived Rolling Stones hours, crashing at dawn, waking bleary-eyed at sunset. It didn't matter; he had the most important thing of all — the constant reassurance of a father who loved him with a deep and unswerving fealty.

Keith seemed to neglect his second child, Dandelion. She became withdrawn — bullied by Marlon, the subject of fights between Keith and Anita. Eventually she was left more and more often with Keith's mother in Dartford. Later she let it be known that she wished to be called Angela.

Though Anita knew Keith no longer slept with other women, she became obsessed with the idea that he would have her committed to a psychiatric hospital and force her to give up drugs. Though she certainly needed to get out of the house and show her face to the world again, her paranoia was groundless. Her love held something strong and positive for Keith, and he still relied on her.

Woodie was a Rolling Stone on this tour. He was finally free to join full time when the Faces split up in a flurry of insults and bad feeling shortly before Christmas 1975. Woodie, enthralled by Keith, drank the same drink — Jack Daniel's — wore his hair in the same black-dyed mop and took cocaine with his new mentor. Together they openly teamed up against Mick.

"I mean there's always a split between a singer and a band," said Keith. "And Jagger certainly thinks there is. Maybe we do gang up on him. But I think of him as a musician — he plays good guitar and keyboards now."

Keith and Woodie dubbed themselves the Trampolini Twins. They'd jumped up and down on Jagger's hotel bed when he was in the midst of entertaining a lithe blonde lady.

It was strange for me to watch Woodie and Keith. I had seen it all before, though then Brian Jones had been the wild, big brother figure and Keith the awed, boyish initiate.

On stage the rapport of Keith and Woodie sparked a new tightness to the Stones, a bouncing of riffs from one to the other to create a smooth, powerful rock 'n' roll machine. Critics and press went overboard, and a million people tried to buy tickets for their London concerts at Earls Court in May. But fate was to remind them that they were not invincible. They were dreadful in London. The PA echoed and reverberated around the cavernous hall, and Mick, Keith and Woodie appeared thrown by the vastness and appalling acoustics of the place. They got rave reviews anyway.

Keith was flagrantly wearing the cocaine works I had given him, a snorting tube, a spoon and a tiny knife, around his neck so that all the hip world could see that he was using outlawed drugs with impunity. But there is a limit to how long you can stand in a bull-ring waving a red flag around. The night of Keith's come-uppance started normally enough with the Stones playing in Stafford. Backstage Jagger, Richard and Woodie smoked joints, then quickly hid the dope to shake hands with autograph seeking senior police officers who knocked on their dressing room door.

Far from remarking on the fact that Keith's Bentley had neither tax disc nor M.O.T. certificate, the police arranged for a motorcycle escort to guide Keith, who was both stoned and wearing sunglasses, from the hall to the start of the motorway. Keith's driving was erratic, but he managed to offer a regal wave to the cops on their bikes as they left him thundering onto the M1.

Keith began to nod off, and the big car careered across the road, across the hard shoulder and into a ploughed field. Neither Keith, Marlon nor any of the other three people in the car was hurt. The car, however, was stuck in the mud. A tractor would be needed to tow it back on the road again. All five tramped, dazed and weary, to an emergency telephone.

Minutes later a boyish police officer drew up beside them and offered a lift to the nearby Newport Pagnell service station. His friend-liness vanished when he recognised Keith, however, and he rapidly searched him. He pounced on Keith's coke-encrusted snorting tube and a solitary tab of acid. It was odd about the acid — Keith, like me, had given up LSD years ago. Eight months later, at Aylesbury Crown Court Keith was found not guilty of possessing LSD but guilty of possessing cocaine and was accordingly fined £500 with £200 costs.

The bust and the fear of imprisonment brought him briefly back to earth, and he gave up dope once more — and became friendly with Jagger again.

But the rift between the two was now virtually un-bridgeable. Jagger now was a conventional multi-millionaire show-business superstar. He had a diamond set into his front tooth which twinkled prettily. An emerald had to be removed because it looked like cabbage and a ruby because it looked like blood. He danced with Princess Margaret and became the darling of the rich and powerful everywhere. He still used cocaine but only because by now it was the official jet-set drug. He boasted that he used Elizabeth Arden beauty products for his face and perfume from Tangier "in my bottom, ears and on my wrists." When he said, "I'm, along with the Queen, one of the best things England's got," few disagreed. He was proposed for membership of the Marylebone Cricket Club. Truly he had arrived as a solid citizen.

Keith was unable to come to terms with his wealth as Jagger had. Like some thirty-three-year-old adolescent, he continued to carry knives, to brawl in the street with taxi drivers or anyone else who provoked him and to dabble ever more wildly with drugs. The authorities thundered down on him again after Anita was caught crazily trying to smuggle heroin and cannabis into Toronto. The police used this as an excuse to raid Keith's hotel room, where they found a huge stash of coke and smack and promptly charged him with possession of heroin for the purpose of trafficking and possession of cocaine. In an attempt to dodge a probable lengthy stint in prison, Keith was forced, reluctantly, to undergo a drug rehabilitation programme.

It took nearly two years for Keith's case to finally come to trial, two years during which he genuinely came to believe that he was facing lengthy incarceration in a Canadian prison cell. In court his defence counsel, Austin Cooper, pleading for probation, described Keith's nine years of heroin addiction and announced that Keith had promised to donate a million dollars to a drug rehabiliation clinic. Keith said he needed two-and-a-half grammes of smack a day simply to stay straight. He said he had gone through three unsuccessful rehabilitation programmes, but that the fourth one was now working.

When the judge asked Keith why so many Rolling Stones' songs glorified drugs Keith told him: "That's a misconception. I mean, about one per cent of our songs glorify the use of drugs, and Mick Jagger wrote them, not me." Amazingly Keith managed to escape with a one year suspended sentence and orders to play a special concert for the Canadian National Institute for the Blind. The Judge was not best pleased when fans in the packed public gallery cheered the sentence. It seemed Keith had escaped. Yet his life was never to be quite the same again...

31

A SOFT, WARM WIND BLEW THROUGH THE OPEN WINDOW, SLIGHTLY RUFFLING the curtains that night in July 1979. Inside the bedroom Anita Pallenberg poured herself yet another huge glass of Jack Daniels mixed with ginger ale. She was hideously fat now, a grotesque, inflated, Spitting Image caricature of the fawn-like, slender-thighed beauty of old.

Though the room was dim, close inspection would have shown that several of the expensive pieces of antique furniture lay smashed and sad on the floor. A chair propped up a corner of the exquisite, heavy oak bed. The room had the stale, mouse smell of drugs and alcohol squalor.

In the huge double bed, beneath grey, stained sheets, there slumped a slender, teenaged boy.

Anita swerved her way unsteadily to his side and they glassily watched a television programme about the tenth anniversary of man landing on the moon.

The flickering lunar landscape seemed as unreal to Anita as the heavy, black, .38 calibre Smith and Wesson revolver that the boy twirled endlessly around the forefinger of his right hand.

"Russian roulette," he slurred as a space man bounced his way across the dust. "Now there is an interesting game . . ."

His name was Scott Cantrell. He was seventeen-years-old, and he came from Norwalk, Connecticut.

In his own way Scott was as sad, washed-up and tragic as the lady whose bed he was sharing that night. His mother had killed herself on Christmas Day, he had dropped out of High School and he frequently complained that no one in the world cared if he lived or died. Anita had seen something in his haunted eyes that appealed and he had been staying with her for four weeks . . .

The house, where she lived now with her son Marlon, was a large,

307

detached place in Westchester County outside New York.

As far as the outside world was concerned she was still with Keith. But their relationship had begun to fall apart after the drugs bust in Canada.

Keith realised that he had to clean up for real this time or he would certainly go to jail and, far worse, his career with the Rolling Stones would probably be at end.

He went to Dr. Meg Patterson, the sharp-talking Scot who had helped Eric Clapton kick his two grammes a day smack habit with her revolutionary neuro-electronic acupuncture treatment.

Dr. Patterson arranged for Keith and Anita to stay at a special clinic in Pennsylvania. Wires from electronic black boxes were clipped to the lobes of their ears. When the pain of withdrawal became intense they could increase the electric current from the box to numb themselves. Keith took the cure intensely seriously, he was determined to really kick smack this time. Anita, however, used to creep down to the kitchen as soon as everyone had gone to bed. There she would gulp cooking sherry or any other form of alcohol she could lay her hands on.

Afterwards she staggered back to Westchester, back on drugs, drinking wine, vodka, tequila, anything to make life go away.

Yet still the dark forces seem to gather, like crows on a telegraph wire, around her. A young policeman claimed he had been set upon by a flock of black-hooded, caped devil worshippers only a quarter of a mile from Anita's house. Neighbours found the remains of cats and dogs, which appeared to have been sacrificed, nearby. Nuns at a local convent complained to police that they were frequently disturbed by the sound of strange chants, gun shots and loud music.

A fifteen-year-old neighbour, Steve Levoie, was reported as saying Anita had invited him to orgies. And he added: "She's a sick person, she should be put away. The house was filthy, really dirty, and Anita was dirty herself. She even asked my sister if she wanted some coke... She had a lot of young boys who would come to the house all the time. She would ask for sex and talk of sex quite often. She never asked me, but who'd want a dirty old woman like that?"

Anita knew she had lost Keith. Seemed to care little if she lived or died. Sought only oblivion.

It was 10.30 in the evening now, on that fateful night of July 20. Anita staggered from the bed, telling Scott she was going to clean up the room. As she turned her back there was an explosion, a flash of flame, then terrible silence. The silence of death. Cantrell had a small, neat bullet hole

308

through his skull.

The police came, then the reporters with their stories of Anita's wickedness and excess. The world looked on in astonishment, scarcely able to believe that this dead-eyed, thirteen-stone ghoul was the same Anita Pallenberg of the gossip columns and the glossy magazines.

At first the death was believed by police to be suicide. But then Anita said they had been talking of Russian roulette, and the wrath of straight society came down on her head once again. Four months later Anita was cleared by a Grand Jury of any involvement in the death. Then she was fined £500 for illegal possession of the gun and the file was closed.

"I didn't feel anything," Anita was to confide later to a journalist from the *Sunday Correspondent* newspaper. "That's one of the wonders of drugs and drink. You don't feel anything. I didn't even read the papers. Nothing."

Keith, meanwhile, was determined to stay clear of heroin. This time Anita would not again drag him back into the morass.

On December 18 he celebrated his thirty-sixth birthday and the end of the 1970's with a huge party at the Roxy Roller Disco, in New York. It was the first time since the 1960's that he had partied without the benefit of sundry chemicals pumping their way around his arteries. And he fell immediately, permanently, heart-stoppingly in love.

She was Patti Hansen, a clean-limbed, exhuberant, milky-toothed Vogue model. At twenty-two she knew who the Rolling Stones were, of course. But she had never bought any of their records, didn't know anything about the members of the band.

But she saw the way the courtiers swirled and danced in homage to Keith, liked his chuckle like the starter-motor of an old lorry. And she saw something else, the sadness and loneliness of a man who had come to a watershed in his life. He looked, she was astonished to realise, lost. As they talked Keith realised that she had no idea of his notoriety. She didn't even know which instrument he played.

So they talked about their lives and their dreams instead of the Stones.

"It's amazing," Keith thought. "This is the first girl I can remember meeting in years who doesn't want to talk about the band or the drugs. She really doesn't know anything about me. As far as she is concerned I could be a hairdresser."

Patti, too, was astonished at the impact the meeting had on her. She could see that he was rootless, lost. He needed to find a base before he could begin to sort his life out.

"And I want that base to be with me," she thought, to her surprise.

Suddenly, impulsively, she dived into her handbag and pulled out a spare front door key to her flat. "Here," she said. "You can stay with me whenever you like." He took the key and kissed her.

After that he tried to play it cool, he delayed 'phoning her for a few days. But soon he was spending every night with her, sharing a passion he had not felt since the early days with Anita.

At first the other Stones resented Patti's arrival in their midst.

"What's this Keith, another model you've dug up?" muttered Charlie Watts. "Who's this flighty piece? Oh dear, what have you done now?"

Similarly Patti's family — she's the youngest of eight children — were initially convinced that Keith was an evil seducer, hell-bent on destroying their baby sister.

But gradually both sides saw what Keith and Patti had known from the minute they met.

They married exactly four years to the day from their first meeting, on December 18 1983. It was Keith's fortieth birthday. The ceremony was staged ever so secretly at the Finisterra Hotel, in Cabo San Lucas, Mexico.

They settled down to a life producing beautiful babies and enjoying quiet evenings at home. Keith still had a tendency to walk about drinking Jack Daniels straight from the bottle, and he still enjoyed an occasional smoke, but he left heroin addiction behind. He seems to have cheated the grim reaper. I could not be more pleased for him.

Anita, too, achieved the amazing feat of ending her free fall into oblivion. In 1987 she went through a rigorous rehabilitation programme. She gave up alcohol and drugs even more completely than Keith had done, started to ride a bicycle, grew slim and attractive once again.

She studied fashion at St. Martin's School of Art with pupils half her age, became an administrator for Narcotics Anonymous. Last time I saw her I was astonished at the change that had come over her. She was unrecognisable as the great, bloated junkie I remembered. Truly, she was a great beauty once again, despite her age.

"I don't regret a single thing. Nothing," she says now. "I feel like I'm a child again."

With his Fine Arts degree, Anthony Price silk suits and flashing good looks Bryan Ferry was far and away the most elegant rock star of the 1970's. He lived in a palatial mansion in London's Holland Park with the most beauti-

ful model in the world. They surrounded themselves with glorious paintings, and made plans for their wedding. Truly he seemed to have it all.

Tonight, however, he was clearly rattled.

The evening had begun well enough. He had taken his fabulous
girl friend to see the Rolling Stones in concert. She had danced and
whooped along with the rest of the crowd, then she had seemed momentarily over-awed when Bryan took her backstage to meet with Mick Jagger.
Mick had been wearing a skimpy dressing gown which flattered his tight,
biscuit-brown body.

He had flirted outrageously with Bryan's girl friend and she had
gushed back. Bryan had smiled indulgently.

When Mick had dressed they went out for dinner in his limousine
and Bryan pretended not to notice when Mick used the squash of the car
as an excuse to rub his knees against the girl's knees. He had carried on
flirting with her throughout the meal.

But that was Mick, thought Bryan. Everyone knew what he was like
with women since it had all started to go wrong with Bianca.

They had gone back to Bryan's mansion with Peter Rudge, the
Stones' tour manager, and Bryan had challenged Mick to a game of pool.

Peter realised very quickly that Bryan was a gifted pool player and
that he was clearly determined to use the game as a means to humble Mick.
At first Mick was angry as his fluffed shots left him looking silly.

But then he began to flirt more and more wickedly with Bryan's
girl friend. He abandoned the game, ignored every attempt Bryan made at
conversation, treated him alternately as though he was a boring fan, then
as though he did not exist.

To make things worse, the girl was encouraging the attention, clearly
intrigued that her fiancé was being made to look ridiculous in his own
house.

When the girl went into the kitchen to make tea Mick abandoned the
pool game to follow her. Bryan tried to maintain his legendary cool but he
was so concerned by the distant giggles and shrieks that he could not stop
himself from sauntering off to investigate. In the kitchen Mick pointedly
ignored him. It was as though he was the outsider, he thought with anger
rising within him. Eventually he could take no more. "I'm going to bed,"
he told the room at large before stomping out, slamming the door behind
him. As Mick and Peter Rudge made to leave the house Mick lunged at the
girl, attempting to kiss her hard on the lips. But she was too fast for him
and ducked, laughing, to one side.

As Mick and Peter sped away in the back of the long black car Mick chuckled to himself.

"So that's Jerry Hall and she's going to marry Bryan is she?" he spluttered.

"I've got to save her Peter. I mean, how can I let anyone be lumbered with a name like Jerry Ferry?"

Bianca was still Mick's wife then. But their marriage had become a little like those favoured by the British royal family. Both led ful-filled, separate lives with a loving public image and little warmth. They were, after all, a perfect couple as far as the world was con-cerned. And, on the occasions when they were together, they genuinely seemed to enjoy one another's company. So, by 1976, Mick would sometimes go for weeks at a time without even seeing Bianca.

Yet Bianca was becoming increasingly weary of the whispers about Mick's other girls. "I feel that this is a man who has no respect whatsoever for women. He is a womaniser," she confided.

Mick had been busy touring the world with the Stones, working flat-out, since that first meeting with Jerry. Several times he snatched a moment to 'phone Bryan to invite the two of them to join him for dinner. But Bryan politely refused every invitation.

Then, suddenly, Bryan was off on tour and Mick was the one with time on his hands. In the Spring of 1977 he invited Jerry to join Warren Beatty and a few other friends for dinner at a restaurant in New York. Jerry found herself seated between Jagger and Beatty, with both men clearly vying for her favours.

When Warren, with his shimmering wit and charm, seemed to be gaining the upper hand Mick snarled at him then asked him for a quiet word.

"She's with me," snapped Mick as soon as they were away from the table.

But Beatty was not to be so easily dissuaded. In the end Jagger was reduced to going to a pay-phone with Beatty. There Mick started ringing around some of the most beautiful models in New York to see if any of them fancied a date with Warren Beatty. The quest took slightly less than a minute.

After dinner Mick's driver dropped the guests off one by one until only Mick and Jerry were left in the back of the limo.

"Come in and have a cup of tea?" he asked, as the car pulled up

312

outside his apartment.

Within minutes they were in bed.

Next day, and the day after that, and the day after that, he sent flowers, took her to dinner, sang songs to her, made love again.

Her father died then and Mick held her as she wept. Was there to comfort her while Bryan was away on tour.

Then, all too suddenly, Bryan was back. Jerry kissed Mick goodbye as tears ran down both their faces. The affair, it seemed, was over.

"I was so nervous and confused and desperate. I swear to you I loved them both," Jerry revealed in her autobiography, *Tall Tales*.

Bryan and Jerry moved to Los Angeles then and Jerry had to keep slipping out to the local supermarket in order to make clandestine telephone calls to Mick.

Finally she pretended she had a modelling assignment in Paris in order to escape her fiancé. Once there, she and Mick flew to Morocco and Jerry's engagement to Bryan was over.

On November 2 1979, after eight years of marriage, Bianca was granted a Decree Nisi and given custody of their nine-year-old daughter, Jade.

Exactly twelve months later a High Court judge awarded Bianca a confidential divorce settlement, widely reported to be in the region of one million pounds plus costs.

Many years later Bianca chatted with another exotic lady with whom she had much in common, Rod Stewart's ex-wife, Alana.

"We should write a book called How To Survive Marriage And Divorce To A Rock'n'roll Star," said Bianca.

"The most important quality needed to survive is submission. It's probably the most male chauvinistic society there is.

"A rock star is the worst husband a woman could have."

After the frippery and silliness of her marriage was at an end Bianca threw herself wholeheartedly into politics, becoming a powerful spokesman for the Sandinistas following the fall of Somoza in 1979. She entered her forties in 1985 as an elegant, formidable and forceful woman.

The black chicken was the first to be sacrificed. The flashing blade splashed crimson blood on to the floor of the small wood-carver's house in the thickly wooded Ubud district of Bali.

Then the white chicken was slaughtered and its sad little body placed to protect Mick and Jerry from evil from the East. A yellow chicken was killed to protect from the West. A black one offered protection from the North, a red fowl for the South and a multi-coloured chicken was killed for protection from the centre.

Mick and Jerry had come to Ubud with their two children and their friends Alan Dunn and author Lorne Blair to go through a glorious, six-hour long Hindu marriage ceremony.

Mick was 47 now, Jerry 34. She understood, loved and controlled him in a way neither Marianne, nor Bianca nor any of his other women had ever been able to.

When he had grown bored with her and began to make love with a string of nubile young women she ran off, began a very public affair with Robert Sangster, the multi-millionaire race horse owner. Robert, she was widely reported as saying, could buy and sell Mick many times over.

The Rolling Stone was brought rapidly, humiliatingly to heel.

So, though Mick had sworn he would never marry again after the Bianca debacle, he had finally given in to Jerry's gentle persuasion.

The first part of the ceremony consisted of Mick and Jerry changing their religion to Hinduism. Dressed in rainbow-coloured sarongs and yellow brocade tops, called kebayas, they vowed their belief in the Holy Soul, in reincarnation and the Supreme Being. They talked of Liberation, the tenet which says that all people are equal spiritual beings, and that their occupation and material situation are irrelevant.

Finally they explained their understanding of Karma, the belief that the good or bad things people do in their lives will always come back to them.

When the Holy Man, Ida Banjar, was satisfied with their conversion he invited the couple to bathe symbolically in a tub filled with scented water and flower petals.

"When they had bathed they changed into new sarongs for the ceremony of marriage," the Holy Man recalled later. "I cannot tell you in words how strong their presence was then. A special aura came out of them then and I could see they were greatly affected by the ceremony. There was a great spirituality around them that uplifted them." Jerry wore a head-dress of sweetly perfumed cempaka flowers for the second part of the ceremony. Candles shimmered and the air was filled with the bitter-sweet aroma of incense. Offerings of cake, fruit and flowers, representing the fruitfulness of this union, lay in front of Mick and Jerry.

314

Yellow marks were painted on to each of their foreheads and ancient Sanskrit prayers were recited by the priest. Then were given balls of coloured rice, which they touched to the sides of their heads and to their shoulders, in the shape of the cross. Jerry then lay a small, straw mat on the ground. Mick was handed a wicked looking sword, which he used to pierce the mat in symbolism of the union of a man with a woman.

Intriguingly, Mick and Jerry decided to ignore the legal, paperwork side of their most romantic marriage. But, from that day on, they told everyone they knew that they were husband and wife.

Jo Howard's first weekend with Ronnie Wood was a shade less romantic. Jo was in London and Woodie was in New York when he suggested she should meet him at L'Hotel, then the most sophisticated place to stay in all of Paris. She frantically scraped together every penny she could lay her hands on then jumped on the first flight from Heathrow to Charles De Gaulle. A cab found the quiet, back-street hotel easily enough but, though it was 8.30 in the evening, there was no sign of the spiky-haired guitarist — not even a message to say he had been delayed.

The receptionist was petulant. There was only one small room left, he said, and mademoiselle would have to pay cash in advance if she wished to take it.

Jo sat in the room, reading and watching television, until two o'clock the following morning. Finally she dozed off on the small, uncomfortable bed.

The screaming phone shook her to consciousness shortly before six o'clock the following morning. "There is a Mr. Wood here," said the receptionist. "He says he was delayed because of a problem on Concorde and he is asking permission to come up to your room."

Frantically Jo combed her hair and dabbed on a little make-up in the minutes before Woodie arrived at the door. He looked every bit as wonderful as she remembered him as he came into the room. But, behind him, shuffled a dark-eyed, gaunt, evil-looking man. Keith Richard came into the room, nodded at Jo, then quickly injected himself through his shirt before passing out at the end of their bed.

"What are we going to do with him?" asked the astonished and slightly indignant Jo.

"Sorry, he'll just have to stay there," Woodie murmured, as he stripped off and prepared to climb into the small double bed.

Keith snored so loudly that Jo was unable to sleep all night.

And so it continued for the next three days and nights, with Keith wandering around Paris with the happy couple by day and sleeping at the end of their bed by night. "Do you do everything with your friend?" Jo snapped at one point.

The couple's first meeting had been equally strange. Jo had no idea who Woodie was when they were introduced to one another at a party. Eventually he was driven to dig out a Stones' album in order to show her his photograph and convince her that he was who he said he was.

In return Jo reluctantly volunteered the information that she was a model but was currently working in the broken biscuits department of Woolworths, in London's Oxford Street, to subsidise her income. Woodie waited outside the shop in the back of his chauffeur-driven Mercedes for two hours the next evening before he realised Jo had been teasing him.

They moved in together a few months later.

Woodie started to spend huge sums of money on drugs — though he always shyed away from actually injecting himself. At one point he was paying out £1,400 a week to dealers. Eventually Jo decided she could stand no more and packed him off to a treatment centre at Plympton, in Devon.

Again and again Woodie wept during group therapy as he talked about his fears of becoming completely insane. The therapists tried to persuade him to give up alcohol as well as drugs.

"But you can forget that," Woodie told them. "I don't want to turn into one of those boring kind of re-born religious fanatics who can't even enjoy a few drinks." Like Keith, he emerged clear of drugs but with a deep fondness for booze of any kind.

Jo and Woodie married on January 2 1985. The wedding was blessed at a little church in Buckinghamshire. The best men were Keith Richard and Charlie Watts — "We're Siamese best men," Keith rasped at reporters. And there was much snuffling from private rooms later as guests like Rod Stewart, Ringo Starr, Eric Clapton and all the Stones except Mick partied the night away.

EPILOGUE

I HAD BEEN RUNNING FROM DEATH TOO LONG, KNEW THAT I COULD NOT LIVE this life much longer. But I wasn't ready to completely draw away. Keith called me occasionally, asking me to get drugs for him, and usually I would co-operate: it had become my way of life.

All the time, though, I could see my life as though I was a swimmer, deep under the sea, thinking only of where my next fix was coming from. Then the Stones were playing a huge outdoor concert and Keith and Mick called to ask me to bring some cocaine to their dressing room for them. I was given the wrong type of backstage pass, however, and in the midst of a wrangle with a security man I suddenly realised it was all over. I turned on my heel, walked away and the next day reserved a room at Bowden House for a cure.

I didn't see any of them for several years after that. Not until I was staying in New York, working hard on finalising this book.

I received a message from Keith saying he didn't want my story to be published, and asking me to meet him at the Mayfair Hotel, where he was staying. As soon as I arrived at the hotel four huge men pulled me roughly to the side of the lobby and frisked me from my shirt collar to my socks. Clearly Keith was taking no chances.

Then I was harshly shoved into a lift and hauled up to Keith's suite. Keith was sitting on a settee with his wife Patti beside him as I walked into the room. He unfolded himself to give me a huge bear-hug then rasped into my face: "You lousy bastard!"

I laughed, partly from nervousness and partly because I was genuinely pleased to see him.

"Lousy bastard yourself," I said. And this time he laughed with me.

We sat down then on a settee, chatted about old times for a few minutes, then Keith slipped his hand under a cushion, pulled out a small,

317

black gun and asked me: "Which do you want man, the .38 or the .45?"

I felt my stomach impersonating a tumble drier as I gently pushed the barrel of the gun away from my head and laughed. "Don't muck about Keith."

"I'm not mucking about, man," he snapped back. Then he chuckled.

"What do you think of the gun eh Tony? Good isn't it?" I took the .38 Smith and Wesson police special gently from him, told it was a splendid weapon and discreetly slipped the bullets out.

We downed a bottle of Jack Daniels whiskey between us and next day he 'phoned to ask me to join him on tour with the Stones.

I was sorely tempted but I knew that to go back on the road was to go back on to heroin. And if I went back again I did not believe I would be strong enough to survive a second time.

I refused and, to this day, I have not heard a single word from any of the Rolling Stones.

At last I was truly at peace...

Tony sanchez died peacefully on 14th June 2000